HURTIGRUTEN
120
THE COMPLETE STORY

John Bryant

Previous page: The *Lofoten* gliding through tranquil waters towards the Land of the Midnight Sun (Hurtigruten)

Right: After 56 years of service the *Nordstjernen* retired in late 2012; seen here on her 50th Anniversary Cruise in 2006 (Bryan Kennedy)

Ferry
Publications

First published in the
Isle of Man in 2012 by
Ferry Publications
PO Box 33
Ramsey
Isle of Man
IM99 4LP

ISBN 978-1-906608-68-2

Produced in the Isle of Man by Lily Publications Ltd. Ferry Publications is a trading name of Lily Publications Ltd.

Contents

Introduction

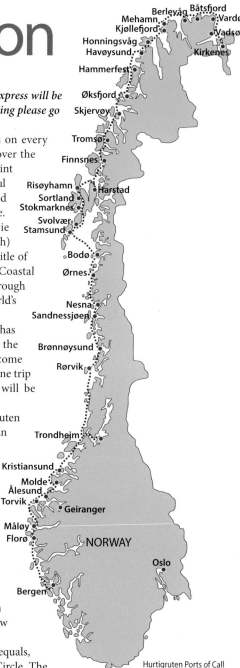

"Ladies and gentlemen, the northbound Coastal Express will be leaving in five minutes. Would all those not travelling please go ashore. Our next stop will be at ...."

This message will be repeated 66 more times on every classic round trip made by a Hurtigruten vessel over the course of the next eleven days. The somewhat quaint announcement will, after a while, burn into your soul with its intangible promise of something magical and mystical lying in wait for the traveller to experience.

'Hurtigruten' ('hurtigrute' in Norwegian, 'Die Hurtigrute' in German or l'Express Côtier' in French) literally means 'fast route', together with its other title of 'Coastal Express' or the more recent 'Norwegian Coastal Voyage', and evokes images of travelling serenely through fantastic vistas in what is rightly known as the 'world's most beautiful voyage'.

A fellow Hurtigruten enthusiast, David Parsons, has written 'that the sumptuous brochures about the Norwegian Coastal Voyage (Hurtigruten) should come with a "health warning" that it is more than likely one trip will lead to another ... and another, and each will be different, *very* different'.

He is absolutely right! A journey on the Hurtigruten from Bergen to Kirkenes and return is an unforgettable experience covering a distance of around 2,500 nautical miles (4,000km). That so many repeat this voyage several times in order to experience the moods of the differing seasons is a testament to its uniqueness. Depending on the time of year you can experience an endless summer's day, the uniqueness of a winter polar night and much in between, for whenever you travel it will be that indefinable quality of the natural light which dramatises the scenery and enhances the experience. Every day is different, with an ever changing backdrop, as the Hurtigruten ship glides serenely through open fjords and narrow sounds.

The voyage runs along a coastline which has no equals, with over half of the journey north of the Arctic Circle. The

Hurtigruten Ports of Call

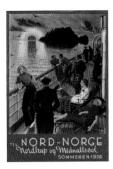

The delights of the Midnight Sun, VDS poster from 1938 (Bård Kolltveit Collection)

main attraction is the incredible natural environment, with its contrasts of massive snow capped mountain chains interspersed with lush green valleys; of tranquil islands and spectacular fjords with thundering waterfalls. The lush rich woodlands of the south gradually give way to the treeless (but not barren) ice and snow landscapes of Finnmark in the far north.

It is a journey of breathtaking sunrises and sunsets enhanced by the juxtaposition of your ship to the land where you could almost put your hand out and touch the overhanging rocks. It is also about the people you meet on the way, the small fishing communities, delightful rural settlements as well as modern bustling towns. Above all is the unmatched beauty of the landscape in which man's efforts to provide our energy and industrial needs somehow enable these edifices to appear in almost perfect harmony.

Whilst today cruise passengers make up the majority of those who travel on the Hurtigruten we must remember that this was not its original purpose and nor is it today. It is only as you actually make this trip that you begin to understand just how important the Coastal Express service was and still is to the communities who live along the 'long coast' of Northern Norway and to be able to appreciate the enterprise, experience and seamanship that was necessary to establish this link and maintain it. Why else would the current Norwegian Government contract with Hurtigruten ASA (which runs to 2020) continue to insist on and support a daily all year service involving 11 ships? Why else would Norway name this route as Riksvei No 1 – i.e. National Highway No 1?

The further north you go then the greater the importance of the Hurtigruten service to the lives of the local communities. It provides those of us who sail on the Coastal Express a unique insight into and closeness with the lives of the local communities it serves. The arrival of the ship is *the* event of the day and people come down to the quayside alerted by the ship's siren. Cora Sandel (1880-1974), a Norwegian writer and painter, movingly described the feeling of loneliness that would assail her as she watched the coastal steamer disappear down the fjord, with her fear of being left behind. People relied on it and missed it when it was not there, particularly in the difficult years of the Second World War.

On board the passengers constitute a community of their own, not just the cruise passengers, but from across all strata of Norwegian society. Many of the latter will board for just short periods of time; for business or meeting up with family and friends. Even romance blossoms on board, bonds of friendship are formed and babies have been known to come into this world en route. From its inception the Hurtigruten has been the undisputed means of communication between small and larger communities along Norway's 'long coast' for the past 120 years.

The experience, whether from the outside decks or panoramic saloons, is awe inspiring as the scene constantly changes; the thrill of expectation as the siren sounds and the beat of the engines change as the ship glides effortlessly through the water to the quayside; the rumble of the winches as the mooring ropes are run out, hooked over the bollards and tightened; the fascination of seeing the cargo doors and passenger walkway unravel almost before the vessel has kissed the quayside; fork lift trucks dizzily unloading and reloading cargo. The siren sounds again and everything is done in smooth reverse. The ship sails and the relative tranquillity of normal life resumes both ashore and on board.

The operating statistics of the Hurtigruten are quite remarkable. Each of the eleven vessels operating on the route averages just over 30 round trips per year, notwithstanding planned refit maintenance. This equates to over 75,000 nautical miles, so if multiplied by the eleven ships on the service to around 825,000 nautical miles per year, equivalent to 35 times around the equator. One still has to include the expedition ship *Fram* which travels to Greenland and Svalbard in the summer and Antarctica in the winter!

This book is not intended to be a comprehensive travel guide to the coastal voyage, as there are already several excellent publications, but seeks to chart the history of what is now known as Hurtigruten ASA from its beginnings towards the end of the 19th century to the present day now 120 years later.

I hope that you will find this book easy to read, stimulating and informative. Any omissions or errors will be entirely of my making. I trust that you will enjoy this as much as I have enjoyed writing it. Sadly, I too have not been able to heed the 'health warning' and yet another trip on the Hurtigruten has been booked!

John Bryant,
Crawley, West Sussex, England　　　　　　　　　　Autumn 2012

Another 1938 VDS poster with Sami (Lapp) family waving off the Vesteraalen (Bård Kolltveit Collection)

Double rainbow over Bergen's Bryggen (Isabel Daniel/ Hurtigruten ASA)

Sunset off Sognefjord
(John Bryant)

Bottom right: Looking down
over Bergen, note the
Hurtigruten ship berthed
centre left (Cornelius
Kok/Hurtigruten ASA)

The Classic Round Voyage

A classic round voyage on the Hurtigruten is a spectacular journey taking 12 days to complete with all the ports visited by night northbound being revisited by day southbound. The more you are able to put into the journey the more you will see which is why so many guests return and return again.

Day 1 Bergen, founded by Olaf Kyrre in 1070, is the bustling capital of Norway's fjord district, a beautiful city set between seven mountains. Stroll around the vibrant fishmarket and onwards to the old wooden buildings of the Bryggen (a UNESCO World Heritage site) with reminders of its Hanseatic past, enjoy the wonderful view from the top of the Fløibanen Funicular or even take the short bus ride to visit Gamle (Old) Bergen, the open air museum at Sandviken. For those with the afternoon free, then a walk along the attractive residential area of Nordnes will also afford a sight of your Hurtigruten ship arriving at the conclusion of her previous voyage.

After check in and embarkation guests have plenty of time to settle in and explore their ship before she leaves promptly at 20.00 (22.30 mid September to mid April) on its first leg of the journey northwards, gliding under the elegant bridge at Askøy, past Statoil's refinery at Mongstad, before rounding mainland Norway's most westerly point at Vardøtangen and sailing into the sunset off Sognefjord en route for a first call at Florø in the early hours of the following day.

Bergen - Florø

Måløy
Hornelen
Stabben Fyr
Florø
Askel
Sula
Steinsund
Ytre Sula
Sognefjord
Vardøtangen
Mongstad
Askøy
Bergen

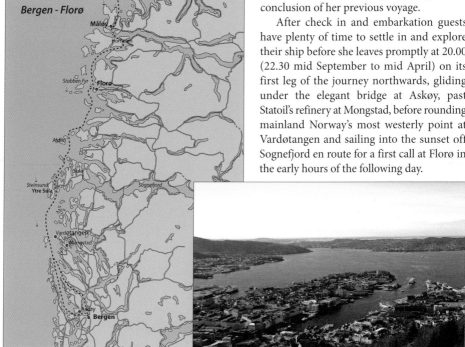

Day 2 Very early risers will wake up to the breathtaking beauty of Norway as the ship, having passed the 860 metre sea cliff of the Hornelen, the highest in Northern Europe, then drifts under the graceful 1,224 metre bridge at Måløy which, if the wind is in the right direction, will resonate to a high 'c'. Having left Måløy, at around 05.00 (06.30 in winter), as we begin to cross the open waters of the Stadhavet, the southbound Hurtigruten will pass by at close quarters. After a brief call at Torvik (opposite Ulsteinvik, where four of the current fleet were built) the ship brings travellers to Ålesund, a unique and fascinating art nouveau styled town, rebuilt after the disastrous fire of 1904. In winter, guests will have three hours to explore the town, including climbing the 418 steps to experience the fantastic view from the top of Mount Aksla. Summer visitors do not have this opportunity as the ship sails down Storfjord and on into the magnificent Geirangerfjord (another UNESCO World Heritage site) with its famous cascading waterfalls. Many passengers will opt for a spectacular drive back to Ålesund via the Eagle Road, a steep stretch of road up the mountain side from Geiranger through 11 hairpin bends. Others will prefer to stay on board to enjoy the return cruise.

With everyone meeting up again at Ålesund the ship sails for an early evening call at prosperous Molde, the 'Town of the Roses', situated in the heart of the 87 beautifully snow capped Alps of Romsdalen and host to an International Jazz Festival each year. In summer, there is the possibility of being able to greet another southbound Hurtigruten ship.

Florø – Kristiansund
165nm 306km

On board the *Nordkapp* cruising towards Geiranger (Inga Herman/ Hurtigruten ASA)

The jewel that is Ålesund as viewed from Mount Aksla (John Bryant)

Trondheim - Rørvik
125nm 232km

Day 3 It will be a breakfast time arrival at 'royal' Trondheim, the first capital city of Norway, with the ship berthing behind the southbound Hurtigruten, affording the chance to go on board and to have a look around a fleet mate. Trondheim is a jewel of a city, founded by Olaf Trygvasen in AD 1000 and the starting point for Leif Erikson's journeys to the New World. Many will want to visit the Nidaros Cathedral where the new kings of Norway once were crowned, the Ringve (Music) Museum or just take a casual stroll around its charming streets, crossing the Gamle Bybro (the old city bridge) to see the restored wooden buildings in Nygata and Bakklandet. The midday departure takes you past the small island of Munkholmen, its medieval monastery and 17th century fort, returning down the long Trondheims-fjorden, passing the Agdenes lighthouse and the NATO air base at Ørlandet. Once the attractive red painted Kjeungskjær Fyr (lighthouse and a family home until 1947) has been left behind, the ship navigates her way through numerous skerries and if the weather is kind, heads for the narrows of the Stokksundet, passing under the road bridge before making a spectacular and seemingly blind 90° turn to port in order to go out into the open sea of the Folda (or Folla). As you pass under the tall Nærøysund Bridge an evening call at Rørvik, capital of Vikna, beckons, as well as the opportunity to visit another southbound Hurtigruten ship.

Kjeungskjær Lighthouse guides the ship through the skerries of the Frohavet (John Bryant)

Trondheim's Nidaros Cathedral, with the famous Gamle Bybrua (old bridge) across the River Nid (John Bryant)

Day 4 This will be a busy day as you will need to be up around 07.00 to witness the crossing of the Arctic Circle at 66° 33' north; from now on in high summer you are in the 'Land of the Midnight Sun', passing the island of Vikingen with its illuminated globe on the port side and the tall mass of Hestmann Island in the background. Sometime after 08.00, the next southbound Hurtigruten will come past at speed and almost immediately afterwards our ship will stop to allow guests to board the tender to visit the famous Svartisen Glacier and later on experience the sight of the famous Saltstraumen tidal current which can flow at amazing speed (22 knots/40km per hour!). Ørnes is a pretty little settlement at which a brief call is made, surrounded by mountains, and then it is on to Bodø, a town well worth exploring with its modern cathedral and Nordland Museum. It also boasts one of Norway's largest airports, a combined civil and military base, which in the U2 Cold War days was of significant importance.

A mid afternoon departure takes the ship past the island of Landegøde, which probably has the most photographed lighthouse in the country, and across the Vestfjord to the Lofotens (see also Day 9 Map). The forbidding 100km Lofoten mountain wall can be seen from a long way out, as the ship calls first at Stamsund where, in summer, you can go off on a 'Viking Feast' experience. The ship continues its journey parallel to the 'wall', passing the southbound Hurtigruten somewhere off Henningsvær, its cliffs teeming with sea birds. An evening call at the artists' paradise of Svolvaer provides the opportunity to have a gentle stroll up to the local church, get close up views of the stock-fish drying racks and the traditional red painted fishermen's cabins known as rorbuer, as well as gazing from afar at the famous Svolvaergeita (Goat Mountain) with its twin peaks, which intrepid adventurers are dared to leap across.

Crossing the Arctic Circle with Hestmann Island in the background (John Bryant)

Inset map: The icy blue Svartisen Glacier south of Ørnes (Nick Widdows)

The day will end with the ship traversing the Raftsundet, a 20km channel which separates Lofoten from Vesterålen. If conditions are right, then towards midnight, the ship will sail into Trollfjord, the sight of the famous battle in 1880 between the traditional sailboat fishermen and the new steam powered trawlers. At the end of the narrow fjord, the ship will turn on its axis, with seemingly little room to spare, before continuing its journey.

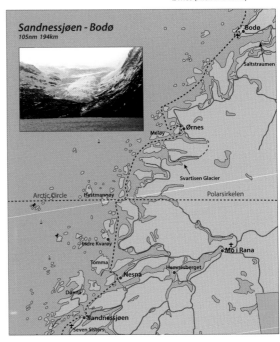

Sandnessjøen - Bodø
105nm 194km

Tromsø, the capital of arctic Norway, is in a wonderful setting (Mai Kisch Harald/Hurtigruten ASA)

Day 5 Guests will wake up to an early morning arrival at and departure from Harstad, the main town for Norway's largest island, Hinnøy. The southbound Hurtigruten will arrive just as our ship gets underway and after a few minutes Trondenes Church, the oldest stone church in Norway dating from 1250, will be passed. The ship sails across Vagsfjord, past the great island of Senja, with its diverse countryside of farmland, pine trees and plunging peaks, calling at Finnsnes, a busy settlement dominated by the magnificent 1,220 metre Gisund Bridge which links the island to the mainland. It is an afternoon arrival at Tromsø, the 'Gateway to the Arctic', known also as the 'Paris of the North'. Tromsø is a thriving town of 60,000 inhabitants with an excellent shopping centre, its harbour dominated by the bridge which takes you across to the Arctic Cathedral with its wonderful stained glass capturing the light. A number of excursions are on offer here including a tour around Tromsø, visiting Polaria and the Arctic Cathedral en route, to the Arctic Adventure Centre or the Wilderness Centre where, in winter, you can go dog sledging.

The ship then heads north for the old trading post of Skjervøy, founded in 1622, passing the soaring slopes of the daunting Lyngen Alps, a mountaineer's paradise. In the winter months if conditions are right from now on you have a good chance of observing the Northern Lights, as well as seeing a southbound Hurtigruten ship passing us mid evening.

Harstad - Skjervøy
134nm 248km

Map inset: A glorious rainbow arches over Tromsø's Arctic Cathedral (Joachim Pfeff/Hurtigruten ASA)

Lopphavet
Loppa
Skjervøy
Reinøy
Lyngen
Kvaløya
Tromsø
Lyngseidet
Senja
Andenes
Finnsnes
Vågsfjorden
Trondenes Kirk
Harstad
Foldvik
Grat
Narvik

Day 6 Whilst most people will still be asleep when the ship calls at Hammerfest early that morning, it is a day of expectant excitement as we head for Honningsvåg and Nordkapp (North Cape) passing the next southbound Hurtigruten, just prior to a call at Havøysund, dominated by its large wind farm, and look out for the painted stone troll opposite the ship's berth. Finnmark's landscape is austere in its beauty, teeming with wildlife; watch out for puffins and gannets along the cliffs. After an early lunch time arrival at Honningsvåg the ship will empty as nearly everyone takes the coach to Nordkapp, almost, but not quite (that's at Knivskjellodden just to the west), the most northerly point of mainland Europe at

71° 10' 21"N and just 2,000 km from the North Pole. It is *the* excursion of the voyage with an opportunity in summer to visit a Sami encampment on the way. Some will opt to visit the Gjesvaer Bird Sanctuary to witness the thousands of seabirds which nest there, including puffins, kittiwakes, guillemots and sea eagles. For those who like a quieter time, a stroll around Honningsvåg can be very rewarding, remembering that the only building left standing at the end of the Second World War was the local church.

Nordkapp, its globe, exhibition hall and monument to the 'Children of the world' (John Bryant)

The ship then heads eastwards to Kjøllefjord and home of the giant king crab, passing the strange rock formation known as the Finnkjerka (Cathedral) which once was a Sami sacrificial site. Calls at the pretty fishing ports of Mehamn (average summer temperatures are never higher than 10° C, so officially it doesn't qualify as having a summer) and Berlevåg help one to appreciate the isolation of this part of Northern Norway and of the importance of the Hurtigruten to the local communities. Late evening at Berlevåg there is usually a very loud and raucous exchange between the crews of the two passing Hurtigruten ships as they try to outdo each other, making it a great end to a long and exciting day.

The Nordkapp globe lights up the winter darkness (Thomas Haltner/Hurtigruten ASA)

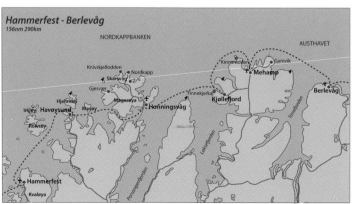

Hammerfest - Berlevåg
156nm 290km

Signpost at Kirkenes, it's a long way to anywhere! (Herbert Ware/ Hurtigruten ASA)

The Christmas Star on board ship (DDB/Hurtigruten ASA)

Day 7 By the time Vadsø (in Varangerfjord) is reached around 07.30 the next morning we are very much further south and east than yesterday, in fact as far east as St Petersburg and Istanbul. Vadsø has strong Finnish connections, with the language still taught in all the local schools, and was also once an important 'pomor' trading centre between Russia and Norway. Sea eagles and hooded crows are frequently sighted, but notice how stunted the vegetation has become. To the east of the Hurtigruten berth is the preserved mooring mast constructed for the airship 'Norge' flown by Roald Amundsen in 1926 and Umberto Nobile two years later. Kirkenes, an important fishing and ship repair port (and formerly with an extensive iron ore mining industry) is reached around 10.00, the end of the journey for some. Many will take advantage of the excellent excursions on offer, visiting a snow hotel, dog sledging or a riverboat safari. Others will take a tour to the Russian border just 10 kilometres away or just enjoy the 20-minute walk into town.

Three hours later and the ship begins to retrace her path to reach Vardø (note the NATO early warning installations) during the late afternoon. The old fort built in 1737 (a popular visit) is still part of the military, guarded by one officer and four men. It also has the most cared for tree in Norway, a rowan which is wrapped up by the soldiers in October and only unpacked in April. Alternatively, visit the distinctive contemporary church where you will get a warm welcome. Båtsfjord is the next port of call with a sheltered harbour, well used by both local and visiting fishing trawlers. Båtsfjord's remoteness ensured that it was the only large community not to be razed to the ground by the German retreat from Finnmark in 1944. In late evening, the ship sails on to meet the northbound Hurtigruten off Berlevåg for a noisy repeat performance from the rival crews. Until 1973 embarkation and disembarkation was always by tender until the two breakwaters were constructed with massive 15 tonne tetrapod blocks which finally made the harbour a safe haven.

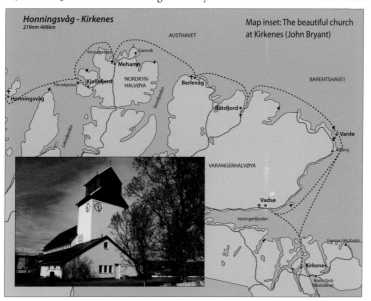

Honningsvåg - Kirkenes
219nm 406km

Map inset: The beautiful church at Kirkenes (John Bryant)

AUSTHAVET

Kinnarodden　　Gamvik
Mehamn
Finnekjerka　Kjøllefjord　NORDKYN-　Berlevåg
HALVØYA
Honningsvåg
NORDKYN-HALVØYA
BARENTSHAVET
Båtsfjord
Vardø
Kiberg
VARANGERHALVØYA
Vadsø
Varangerfjorden
Grense Jakobselv
Kirkenes
Boris Gleb
(Russland)

Day 8 Insomniacs may have risen early to take the excursion from Honningsvåg in order to have breakfast at Nordkapp. Having passed another northbound Hurtigruten around 09.00 near Havøysund, the day's highlights will include an extended stop at Hammerfest, officially the world's most northerly town (and the first Norwegian town to have electric street lighting and its own power station), with the opportunity to do some shopping, visit the Polar Bear Club or pause for thought in one or both of its lovely modern churches. In summer, those who take the zig zag path behind the town to the top will be rewarded with stunning views across the whole area. The gas flare from the giant Melkøy oil and gas terminal can be seen from miles around. Øksfjord is visited mid afternoon and is an isolated but thriving community with the Øksfjordjøkulen Glacier opposite. This calves into the sea at Jøkelfjorden, just around the corner. There is another brief evening stop at Skjervøy, the pretty little settlement with its church dating from 1728, surrounded by mountain peaks. Tromsø is reached very late in the evening (having passed the northbound Hurtigruten around 21.00); in summer you can experience a midnight concert at the Arctic Cathedral with its 140 m^2 glass mosaic, the largest in Europe or just stroll around the still busy city in the 24 hour daylight.

The Northern Lights flare over Tromsø as the Trollfjord arrives (Knut Jensen/ Hurtigruten ASA)

Havøysund - Tromsø
176nm 326km

TROMSØFLAKET

Map inset: Looking down over Hammerfest with the Finnmarken berthed at the port (John Bryant)

Ingøy · Havøysund
Rolvsøy

Hammerfest
Sørøya · Kvaløya
Seiland
Øksfjord
Øksfjordjøkelen
Jøkelfjorden

Lopphavet
Loppa

Skjervøy

Reinøy
Lyngen
Tromsø
Lyngseidet

The Troll at Havøysund, found opposite the Hurtigruten berth (John Bryant)

The *Trollfjord* negotiates the narrows of the Risøyrenna (Trym Ivar Bergsmo/ Hurtigruten ASA)

Day 9 So much is the pace of change, as early morning finds the ship back in beautiful Hinnøya arriving at Harstad just in time to see the northbound Hurtigruten depart at 08.00. This will be the day when the ship will carefully negotiate the shallow waters of the man made Risøyrenna Channel, with the sand banks visible through the clear green water, pausing for a brief stop at Risøyhamn, nestling in the shadow of the modern bridge which connects Hinnøya with Andøya. You will then pass through the stunning scenery of the islands of Vesterålen, berthing at Sortland, the home of Norway's North Atlantic Coastguard Patrol Fleet, noting just how many shades of blue have been used to paint the houses. Later on the ship will arrive at Stokmarknes, the spiritual home of the Hurtigruten, where Richard With, the founder, was based. Here is the Hurtigruten Museum, an integral part of which is the previous *Finnmarken* (1956–1993) preserved high and dry out of the water and Norway's largest museum exhibit. Mid afternoon sees the ship travelling along the spectacular Raftsundet to re-enter Trollfjord, (just as impressive in daylight as at night). Some guests will transfer to an excursion boat which precedes the Hurtigruten ship into the fjord and then stays on in order to witness the sea eagles feeding. After a return call at Svolvær and the opportunity to take a coach excursion around the Lofoten Islands, the ship will cruise along the Lofoten Wall, passing the northbound Hurtigruten before a last call of the day at Stamsund.

Harstad - Bodø
170nm 315km

The Aurora Borealis over Svolvær (Backpack Foto/Hurtigruten ASA)

The *Nordkapp* turns on its axis at the end of Trollfjord (Trym Ivar Bergsmo/ Hurtigruten ASA)

Day 10 Following a breakfast time stop at the attractive settlement of Ørnes (see map for Day 4), the ship will glide southwards in crystalline waters, past lush agricultural fields, through the islands and skerries, meeting up with the next northbound Hurtigruten vessel before re-crossing the Arctic Circle. Nesna, a very pretty village with a stunning mountain backdrop, is visited briefly during the late morning and has an important direct road link to the industrial town of Mo i Rana. The ship will berth for an hour at both Sandnessjøen and Brønnøysund, each framed by attractive bridges linking the islands, the former being an

important shipbuilding and repair centre serving the offshore oil and gas industry. Between the two ports are the famous Seven Sisters mountain peaks of Helgeland where, according to Norwegian folklore, trolls are turned into stone. Brønnøysund is a fine town, but for most travellers the real attraction is when the ship takes a wide westerly arc in order to get a good view of Torghatten Mountain with its hole (160m long x 30m high and 15m wide) right through the middle; a troll tale claims that it was caused when the local hero Hestmann fired his arrow through the Brønnøy king's hat, turning him to stone. Tonight is also the occasion when the evening meal is designated as the 'Captain's Dinner' and gives an opportunity for guests to thank the crew for their wonderful service. A late evening arrival at Rørvik offers the chance to visit a third member of the Hurtigruten fleet at the end of a busy day.

Preparing for tonight's Captain's Dinner (Andreas Mihatsch/Hurtigruten ASA)

The bridge at Brønnøysund with Torghatten in the background (John Bryant)

Soft serenity, the Romsdal
Mountains as seen from
Molde (John Bryant)

Day 11 Back in Trondheim again, a shorter stay southbound (until 10.00),
but still enough time to revisit the city or to have a look around the next
northbound Hurtigruten vessel. Some will take the Dovrebanen (train)
through the stunning Norwegian countryside to end their journey at Oslo.
The ship retraces her path along the fjord and then westwards through the
channel which separates the islands of Hitra (the island of deer) and Smøla
from the mainland. It will be over six hours before Kristiansund is reached,
an attractive town in a lovely setting with its three islands linked by bridges,

Gamle Bybrua (the old bridge)
at Trondheim (John Bryant)

famous as far back as 1691 as the 'klippfisk' (dried salted cod) capital of
Norway. It is a town made prosperous today by the offshore oil and gas
industry. It is also an opportunity to go on a sightseeing tour of Kristiansund
prior to experiencing the full length of the Atlanterhavsveien (Atlantic
Road), before rejoining the ship at Molde. Here, in summer, you will also
meet up with the northbound Hurtigruten.

Trondheim - Molde
139nm 258km

Map inset: Agdenes Fyr
(lighthouse) at the entrance
to Trondheimsfjorden
(John Bryant)

Day 12 All too quickly it is the final day of the voyage. Very early risers may see the northbound Hurtigruten as we approach Måløy. Florø, a large fishing town and oil industry supply base, is Norway's most westerly based town and the final stop before Bergen. Yet still ahead lies mile after mile of spectacular scenery, the extreme narrows to be negotiated at Steinsundet, crossing the mouth of Sognefjord before gliding serenely through the archipelago on the approaches to Bergen. Once Statoil's refinery at Mongstad is sighted, the journey is almost over. Whilst arrival at Bergen is around 14.30, many will be in no spiritual hurry to leave the ship which has been their home for the past eleven days. Some guests will stay on in Bergen for another day. For whatever reason people have travelled, whether it was for the scenery, the wildlife, the camaraderie or just relaxation, it will have been a truly memorable experience. For it is 'the world's most beautiful voyage'.

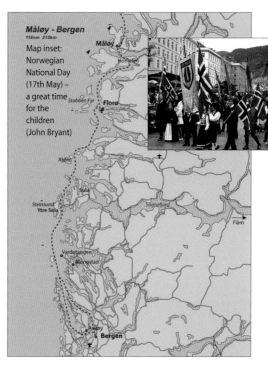

Måløy - Bergen
118nm 215km
Map inset: Norwegian National Day (17th May) – a great time for the children (John Bryant)

You may have time to take another casual stroll along Bergen's famous Bryggen (John Bryant)

Who's who?
AN OVERVIEW

Vesteraalens Dampskibsselskab AS (VDS) 1893 – 1987
The company was founded on the initiative of Richard With based at Stokmarnes, Vesterålen on 10th November 1881. That same year, the shipping company's first ship, *Vesteraalen* (*ex Arendal* 1865), was purchased from Arendals Dampskibsselskab and went into regular service between Senja, Vesterålen, Lofoten and Bergen. It was not until the establishment of the Coastal Express that VDS became one of the major players on the 'long coast' of Norway. In 1985 Ofotens Dampskibsselskab secured a majority stake in the company, and at the end of 1987/88 the company formally merged into Ofotens og Vesteraalens Dampskibsselskab (OVDS).

Det Bergenske Dampskibsselskab AS (BDS) 1894 – 1979
BDS was formed on 12th December 1851 to operate regular shipping services between Bergen and Hamburg. The company soon expanded with routes to England, France and Iceland and later ventured into cruise liners. The distinctive black company funnel with its three white rings became well known across the shipping world. From the 1920s to the late 1960s the company had 2,500 employees and a fleet of 30-40 ships; however, the 1970s were more difficult. In 1979 their four Hurtigruten ships were sold to TFDS (see below). In November 1984, the company was taken over by AS Kosmos in Sandefjord, later being sold on to RoNoTro AS in December 1988, at which point the company lost any individual identity and the white rings disappeared forever.

Det Nordenfjeldske Dampskibsselskab AS (NFDS) 1895 – 1989
NFDS came into being on 28th January 1857 to provide a regular shipping service from Trondheim to Hamburg and Newcastle. NFDS had a close association with BDS and in addition to the Coastal Express were involved in international routes to the Mediterranean as well as later on with tankers and cruise ships. In 1984 Norcem acquired a majority share and within a year the company had been sold on to AS Kosmos who had also acquired BDS. The same fate awaited NFDS when their Hurtigruten ships were transferred to TFDS in August 1989.

Det Stavangerske Dampskibsselskab (DSD) AS 1919 – 1979
Founded on 12th February 1855, DSD began to develop services from Stavanger to Bergen, Oslo, Kristiansand and Frederikshavn (Denmark). In 1919 they joined the Hurtigruten, extending the service to Stavanger, but this only lasted until 1936. Their vessels remained on the route and it was not until 1978 that they sold their last remaining ship ms *Kong Olav* to VDS

and as a result ceased to be part of the Hurtigruten. Today, the company is still very much in business being a major shareholder in both Tide A/S (operating bus, car ferry and fast craft services) and Nor Lines (coastal cargo).

Ofotens Dampskibsselskab (ODS) AS 1936 – 1987

Ofotens Dampskibsselskab AS was founded on 24th July 1912 to carry traffic in the Ofotfjorden (Narvik) area. The company later started an express Trondheim-Narvik service in 1924, whilst also extending local routes. From 1st November 1936, ODS became part of the Hurtigruten with Narvik having its own weekly calls. From the mid 1980s there was a rapid expansion of assets, culminating in the acquisition of Vesteraalens Dampskibsselskab (VDS). The new company was renamed Ofotens og Vesteraalens Dampskibsselskab (OVDS) but retained the ODS logo.

Det Nordlandske Dampskibsselskab (NDS) AS 1945 – 1958

The company came into being on 13th August 1927 when it introduced the *Skjerstad* from Salten Dampskibsselskab onto the Saltdal-Bodø-Trondheim service; a move which caused friction with both BDS and NFDS, a situation which wasn't resolved until 1936. After the Second World War in autumn 1945, the company became a member of the Hurtigruten using a replacement *Skjerstad* which underwent a major refit. However, in 1958 they forfeited their place on the Coastal Express as they were not able to provide more modern tonnage for the route.

Troms Fylkes Dampskibsselskab (TFDS) AS 1979 – 2006

TFDS's ancestry dates from 1866 with its involvement in the coastal trade around Troms. Over the years the company built up an extensive route network, the name became modernized into the present form in 1925. Through various mergers and acquisitions, particularly of the BDS and NFDS fleets in 1979 and 1989, TFDS became one of just two operators managing the Coastal Express. Based in Tromsø the company has also operated a number of car ferries and passenger ferries, primarily in the Troms area. Listed on the Oslo Stock Exchange until 2006 when it merged with Ofotens og Vesteraalens Dampskibsselskab to create the Hurtigruten Group.

Ofotens og Vesteraalens Dampskibsselskab (OVDS) AS 1987 – 2006

In 1985, after Ofotens took a majority stake in VDS, the two companies formally merged in January 1988 together with some of the regional ferry operators to become OVDS. The new company became a major force operating six Hurtigruten ships, as well as having interests in tourism and international cruising. OVDS's main office was in Narvik while the ferry section was located in Stokmarknes. The company merged with Troms Fylkes Dampskibsselskap in 2006 to form Hurtigruten ASA. At the time of the merger the company had about 1,500 employees and operated 14 ships, 18 car ferries and 14 fast passenger ferries.

Finnmark Fylkesrederi og Rutelskap (FFR) 1988 – 1996

Finmarkens Amtsrederi was founded in 1916 to take over local ferry routes that had previously been run under contract from the Government. The name was later changed to Finnmark Fylkesrederi og Rutelskap as the company extended its activities to bus services and in particular tourist traffic to North Cape. In the autumn of 1988 the company became part of the Hurtigruten set up but this ceased when the *Lofoten* was resold to OVDS in 1996. FFR's responsibilities for local bus routes and ferry routes in Finnmark are now under the management of Boreal Transport Norge AS.

Hurtigruten ASA 2006

Hurtigruten ASA was the result of the long-awaited merger on 1st March 2006 between Troms Fylkes Dampskibsselskap (TFDS) and Ofotens og Vesteraalens Dampskibsselskab (OVDS), although the name did not formally change until 26th April 2007. In 2013 the company moved its headquarters from Narvik to Tromsø.

HURTIGRUTEN

The *Børøysund* (1908), although not a Hurtigruten vessel, was in service with VDS from 1925 until 1968. In active preservation, based in Oslo, she is a reminder of past elegance (John Bryant)

In the Beginning

'Snapshot' histories of the Hurtigruten can rather give the impression that its advent in 1893 marked the beginning of trade along Norway's North Sea coastline. Whilst this date was indeed a major watershed, man has travelled and traded up and down the 'long coast' of Norway with wares of dried fish, cured meats and animal skins for well over a millennium.

Bergen, founded by Olaf Kyrre in 1070, had long been the commercial hub for the country. Whilst its development as a major player in the Hanseatic League brought great prosperity to those involved its protective practices rather prevented the development of the more local indigenous trade. It was not until the early 1600s when King Kristian IV finally removed the Hanseatic League's monopoly on trade that merchants from within Norway, as well as the Dutch and the British, could trade on more equal terms.

A traditional jekt seen off Munkholmen, Trondheim 1906 (Anders Beer Wilse/ Norsk Folkemuseum)

At that time the traditional form of trading ship was a 'jekt', a small vessel with one or two sails, about 100 feet in length and capable of carrying around 40 tons of cargo. A voyage south to Bergen was not easy as there were no navigational aids to guide them, therefore knowledge of the sea routes were those passed down from one generation to another. Sailing in darkness was extremely dangerous and so comparatively little business was done outside of the summer season. Trade from the north was basically in three tranches; firstly the 'spring meeting' (vårstevne) in late May, then the 'in-between meeting' (mellomstevne) in early July, with the 'autumn meeting' (høstverne) in late August, with upwards of 1,000 jekts visiting Bergen in each tranche. Strangely enough, traders from the north tended to bypass Trondheim preferring to make for Bergen.

Even though in 1647 the Norwegian Government's General Auditor, Henrik Moran, had begun to establish a national postal network, it was overland and journey times were to say the least, unpredictable. By the beginning of the eighteenth century there was a little more organisation as the Government, seeing the need to get important documents and mail to the regional administrations more efficiently, had built up a chain of designated villages roughly a day's sailing apart to act as refuges and trading posts. Each village was required to provide a least one inn (gjestgiveri) where travellers could stay overnight. A single journey from Tromsø to Bergen could vary from six days in perfect weather conditions to four or five weeks during the winter over the same distance.

Båtpost (Mike Bent)

At the turn of the nineteenth century a båtpost (postal boat) service was introduced from Trondheim to Bodø, Tromsø and Alta. These boats were in reality little more than large rowing boats with a small sail, crewed by teams of 4 rowers. Not surprisingly, post would still take an inordinate time to arrive, up to three weeks to reach Tromsø and anything up to five months if it were ever to reach Hammerfest! It was a perilous undertaking at times and the alternative fjellpost (mountain post) by foot or river boat in the summer or by horse or reindeer in winter was generally the more reliable.

The introduction of the steamship was to change everything when, in 1827, two wooden hulled paddle steamers were ordered by the Norwegian Government to carry mails from Christiania (Oslo) to Kristiansand, Gothenburg and Copenhagen. Despite being of only 100 feet in length and with a service speed of 7 knots both the *Constitutionen* (250 gross tons) and *Prinds Carl* (375 gross tons) were immediately successful. As steamship operations elsewhere demonstrated their worth it increased the pressure on the Storting (Norwegian Parliament) to provide a passenger and mail service between Trondheim and Hammerfest. In 1836 the Storting allocated 15,000 speciedalers (the currency at that time) annually for three years to cover the cost of setting up and maintaining this service.

The first organised coastal route to north Norway began on 14th March 1838 using the paddle steamship *Prinds Gustav* which was of 215 grt, 124 feet in length and had a service speed of 8 knots. She sailed between Trondheim and Tromsø during the summer months only and on her first voyage carried just 7 passengers. Her passenger accommodation was spartan with dormitory type cabins and she had almost nil space for cargo. By 1845 the Storting had expanded their coastal steamer service to link Christiania with Kristiansand (using the *Prinds Carl*), Kristiansand to Trondheim (*Nordcap*) and Trondheim to Hammerfest (*Prinds Gustav*).

The *Constitutionen* at Arendal 1848 - from an engraving by Christian Tønsberg (unknown)

Over the next two decades the demands grew and routes were expanded so that by 1865 the Norwegian Post Office had 11 vessels on its books of which 9 were needed at any one time. However, as these ships began to show their age, several private shipping companies introduced competing passenger and cargo services (albeit without mail) with far better appointed ships.

The *Prinds Carl* was normally used on the Christiania (Oslo) to Kristiansand service in the 1840s (unknown)

In 1857 the Storting, bowing to increasing pressure, agreed that private companies be allowed to carry mail and to receive a state subsidy for doing so. Two of these companies, Det Bergenske Dampskibsselskab (BDS) and Det Nordenfjeldske Dampskibsselskab (NFDS), became the major players in this 'kombinerte' (passenger/mail/cargo) enterprise and effectively creamed off the market before then entering into a joint tariff system.

As with all Government subsidised routes, there were the inevitable rumblings over the standards of service, especially when, in 1875, the two companies asked for and received an increase in subsidy to 90,000 speciedalers per annum. This currency was replaced at the end of 1875 by the krone (4 kroner = 1 speciedaler). In 1880, 260,000 kroner per annum had become available for mail services between Bergen, Trondheim, Hammerfest and Vadsø but only one NFDS shipmaster was prepared to venture beyond Hammerfest in the winter.

Other revenue earning developments came in the form of increased

Norwegian State Coastal Mail Steamer Services - 15th April - 6th October 1845								
Port	Time	Day	Ship		Port	Time	Day	Ship
NORTHBOUND					SOUTHBOUND			
Christiania (Oslo)	09.00	Wednesday	Prinds Carl		Hammerfest	08.00	Friday	Prinds Gustav
Kristiansand	19.00	Thursday			Tromsø	09.00	Saturday	
Kristiansand	07.00	Saturday	Nordcap		Tromsø	17.00	Monday	
Bergen	17.00	Monday			Trondheim	19.00	Thursday	
Bergen	10.00	Wednesday			Trondheim	06.00	Thursday	Nordcap
Trondheim	16.00	Saturday			Bergen	10.00	Sunday	
Trondheim	12.00	Thursday	Prinds Gustav		Bergen	06.00	Tuesday	
Tromsø	09.00	Monday			Kristiansand	15.00	Thursday	
Tromsø	15.00	Tuesday			Kristiansand	16.00	Friday	Prinds Carl
Hammerfest	16.00	Wednesday			Christiania (Oslo)	15.00	Sunday	

Mike Bent (James Pedersen – Den Aeldre Norsk Dampskibfart)

tourism particularly during the early 1880s, with both BDS and NFDS
promoting summer cruises from Trondheim to the Nordkapp via Molde
and the Lofotens; these were later extended to and from Bergen. A number
of these steamers led dual roles which continued right up to the onset of the
First World War, whereby each spring, having spent the winter primarily as
black hulled cargo carriers, they were transformed into cruise ships with
white hulls and superstructure, canvas dodgers along the deck rails and large
awnings to protect passengers from the weather. Skylights replaced cargo
hatch covers and portable cabins were erected in the holds. By the 1880s it
was estimated that around 14,000 foreign tourists would visit Norway each
year, the majority arriving through Bergen.

The rich herring fisheries industry of the Vesterålen and Lofoten Islands
had, as early as the 1860s, highlighted the need for better transport services
in order to distribute their catch more efficiently. Growing pressure
eventually led on 10th November 1881 to the formation by Captain Richard
With of Det Vesteraalens Dampskibsselskab (Steamship Company) based
at Stokmarknes, the municipal capital of the area.

Det Vesteraalens Dampskibsselskab (VDS) raised 4,000 kroner to
purchase the steamship *Arendal* which they renamed *Vesteraalen*. Built in
Gothenburg in 1865, the vessel had berths for 18 passengers, a speed of 10
knots and was reinforced for service in ice conditions, in which sailing
ships could not easily operate. She was a modern vessel for her time and
became a successful investment for the company, in particular during the
winter season. By the end of 1892 she had earned an operating profit of
5,000 kroner.

The *Vesteraalen*, with Richard With as master, went into direct
competition with Det Bergenske Dampskibsselskab (BDS) and Det
Nordenfjeldske Dampskibsselskab (NFDS) on the route between Bergen
and Vesteraalen. Her main cargo was transporting the local herring
southwards to Bergen. Around this time the world's largest ever herring

catch was landed; it was said to be so great that the entire Eidsfjord was blocked until the herring could be landed. Over 40,000 barrels of herring were salted, but much was left to rot as they didn't have the capacity to process all the fish.

Lofoten (1884)

The *Vesteraalen's* success resulted in the construction in 1884 of the *Lofoten* for the fledgling company. Delivered from the Aker Mek Shipyard, Christiania (Oslo) she was luxuriously fitted out, even boasting a piano in the ladies' lounge. It was not all plain sailing for VDS as on 9th September 1885, having just departed Haugnes, Vesterålen, the *Lofoten* ran aground and sank. There was an exceptionally low tide and the ship appeared to have struck an unmarked reef. The *Lofoten* did not return to service until the following April. After this the two ships settled down to provide a weekly service to Bergen carrying both passengers and cargo. When the new *Vesteraalen* (see below) was out of service for scheduled maintenance work the *Lofoten* acted as a relief ship from 1893 until 1903. Sadly, the ship was destroyed by fire in August 1912.

By 1890 the *Vesteraalen* was becoming a victim of her own success as she was now far too small for the traffic on offer. Finding nothing suitable in the second hand tonnage market VDS ordered the construction of a new and larger triple expansion engined vessel from the Aker Mek, Oslo. Costing 235,000 kroner, the ship was delivered in January 1891, a combined passenger and cargo vessel with an insulated cold room for the carriage of fish, her staple trade. As built, she had a greater cargo capacity in comparison to other ships plying the same trade, being designed specifically for VDS's regular services between Tromsø and Bergen, where freight was of greater importance than passengers or mail.

Measuring 540 gross tons, she had an overall length of 173 feet, a beam of 27.1 feet and a service speed of 10 knots. As new, the ship had a passenger certificate for 200 in three classes, with sleeping accommodation for 25 passengers in 1st class and for 15 passengers in 2nd class, boasting electric lighting throughout. She too was named *Vesteraalen*.

The first *Vesteraalen*, which did not see Hurtigruten service, was then sold to Erik Rusten (Bergen), who renamed her *Nordfjord* prior to selling her on to Vestenfjeldske Dampskibsselskab in Bergen in 1891. She had a long career under several more owners, and was even converted into a diesel powered coaster in 1947, before finally being scrapped at Stavanger in 1971 at the grand old age of 106!

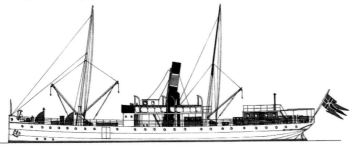

Vesteraalen (I)

The Hurtigruten Takes Shape

VDS ship *Vesteraalen* off Bodø in 1893 embarking passengers by tender in the first year of Hurtigruten operation (VDS/ Hurtigrutemuseet)

Below: Postcard of *Vesteraalen*, location and photographer unknown (VDS/ Hurtigrutemuseet)

August Kreigsman Gran, National Steamship Advisor for Norway in 1891 (DSD)

In 1891, August Kreigsman Gran, national steamship advisor for Norway, began to actively promote the idea of an express boat service between Trondheim and Hammerfest. There were a number of factors behind this submission. The growth of the 'kombinerte' (cargo/passenger/mail) services meant that there were now 58 ports between Bergen and Hammerfest (48 of which were north of Trondheim) and as a consequence travel was very slow as operators wanted to call at as many ports as possible in order to maximise their profits. Government administrators, merchants and travellers needed something quicker and began to vent their frustration. The opening of the Christiania (Oslo) to Trondheim Railway in 1880 meant that the two cities were now only 12 hours apart and travellers wanted to see this improvement translated further north. For freight businesses the protracted sailing times also tended to reduce the value of perishable goods, particularly fish. By limiting the calls to 9 intermediate ports it was felt that a 'coastal express' service could succeed.

Det Nordenfjeldske Dampskibsselskab (NFDS) and Det Bergenske Dampskibsselskab (BDS) were offered the route by Gran, but turned it down as sailing safely during darkness in stormy waters was still considered impossible. At that time only two marine charts existed and there were only 28 lighthouses north of Trondheim.

It was left to Det Vesteraalens Dampskibsselskab, still a small shipping company, to take up the challenge. Captain Richard With had, with his pilot, Anders Holte, kept accurate records of courses, speeds and times taken to sail the route and was confident that such a service was viable. Their application to run the service dated 15th November 1892 was immediately accepted. When it became clear that the *Vesteraalen* was going to serve on the extended route, she was sent to Bergen for a hasty rebuild with additional cabins and a spacious mailroom, raising her tonnage to 623 gross tons.

On May 18th 1893, the Government signed a four-year contract with the company to support a weekly sailing between Trondheim and Tromsø all year extended to Hammerfest during the summer. For this VDS would receive an annual state aid of 70,000 kroner. Under the terms of the contract the company were obliged to provide at least 40 first class sleeping berths (30 in winter) together with 16 second class and 50 third class berths on each service, as well as having a second steamer ready in reserve at all times.

On 2nd July 1893 the new *Vesteraalen* , with Captain Richard With as master and Hans Hveding Berg Jensen as pilot, left just after 08.00 on her first round-trip journey from the Brattøra Quay, Trondheim for Hammerfest, with intermediate calls at Rørvik, Brønnøysund, Sandnessjøen, Bodø, Svolvær, Lødingen, Harstad, Tromsø and Skjervøy. On board were some 60 passengers, mainly guests invited by the company. The ship arrived at Svolvær (Lofotens) on Monday 3rd July just before 20.00 (after 35½ hours), reaching its northbound destination of Hammerfest on Wednesday 5th July at 03.30 amid much excitement, some thirty minutes ahead of

The beautiful lines of the *Vesteraalen* (Hurtigrutemuseet)

The *Vesteraalen's* crew on the occasion of the very first Hurtigruten sailing (Mike Bent Collection)

Commemorative stamp (1977) depicting the *Vesteraalen* at Bodø on her inaugural voyage

schedule. The vessel had completed the northbound leg between Trondheim and Hammerfest in a total of 67 hours. Today, the journey between Trondheim and Svolvær is covered in 33 hours, only marginally quicker than in 1893.

The 'express' had been born! It transformed expectations and communications completely. Mail could now be received within a few days. Route plans were printed as colourful brochures, one for summer routes and one for winter routes. Admittedly, it was still not always easy to keep time and delays were frequently recorded.

Initially, they sailed at night only during the summer, when it stays light for most of the time. Soon, with his accurate notes on courses, speeds and times, Captain Richard With began sailing in the dark throughout the year.

The *Vesteraalen's* long career was not without its share of incident. On 19th December 1913 she went aground and sank off Valdersund, near Ålesund. She was raised and towed to the Aker Mek Shipyard (Oslo) for a complete refit, sporting a black hull on her return to Hurtigruten service. Replaced by the new *Lofoten* in 1932 she acted in a relief capacity before being leased to Narvik Dampskibsselskap for their services between Narvik and Trondheim. She remained active until 1941 when on 17th October she was torpedoed and sunk off Øksfjord by the Russian Submarine SHCH-402 with the loss of 60 lives. Only 7 survived. *(see also War – For a Second Time)*

This modest beginning heralded a new era for the remote coastal communities, providing business and inhabitants with a ready means of transport between the cities and ultimately to the outside world. During the first few years of operation mail and passengers provided the main income on the Coastal Express, but slowly the cargo element was to become more and more prominent as the original 'kombinerte' (passenger/mail/cargo) coastal services began to suffer a long slow demise.

Hurtigruten Timetable - Summer 1893

NORTHBOUND		SOUTHBOUND
08.00 Sunday	Trondheim	04.00 Saturday
19.00 Sunday	Rørvik	17.00 Friday
23.30 Sunday	Brønnøysund	13.00 Friday
03.00 Monday	Sandnessjøen	09.00 Friday
12.00 Monday	Bodø	00.00 Friday
14.00 Monday	Bodø	22.00 Thursday
20.00 Monday	Svolvær	16.00 Thursday
00.00 Tuesday	Lødingen	11.30 Thursday
04.00 Tuesday	Harstad	08.00 Thursday
12.00 Tuesday	Tromsø	00.00 Thursday
16.00 Tuesday	Tromsø	20.00 Wednesday
21.00 Tuesday	Skjervøy	15.00 Wednesday
04.00 Wednesday	Hammerfest	08.00 Wednesday

Richard With

THE MAN (1846–1930)

Richard Bernhard With was born in Tromsø on 18th September 1846, the son of shipmaster Sivert Regnor With and wife Anne Bergitte Dahl who was of Dutch descent. His father moved to Tromsø in 1832, where he became skipper of the schooner *Alexandra* for the trading firm of Mack and Aagard. In the school holidays he would accompany his father on voyages as far as Vadsø and Bremen. On leaving school he signed on as a deckhand on the trading brig *Julia* bound for the Mediterranean. Over the next two years he saved enough money to attend the officers' training college in Trondheim.

Richard With – founder of the Hurtigruten (VDS/Hurtigruten ASA)

In 1864, successfully passing his exams he signed on as second officer on the schooner '*Tromsø*' spending the next eight years at sea visiting both North and South America, Africa and most of the Mediterranean coast. A family illness brought him back home to Northern Norway in 1873 and settling in Risøyhamn, he purchased a ship's chandlery business in partnership with Theodor Kill of Skjervøy. In the September of that year he married Oline Sophie Wennberg from nearby Andenes. They had a daughter, Nanna, but sadly his wife died in November 1878. In 1879 he married her sister Augusta Septimia Wennberg.

Richard With recognised the need to improve the inadequacy of transportation in the region, particularly with regard to the distribution of the herring. He became the driving force leading to the creation of Det Vesteraalens Dampskibsselskab in 1881. Over the next decade the company went from strength to strength so when the opportunity came in 1891 to start a Coastal Express service between Trondheim and Hammerfest, Richard With grasped it with both hands. He was very much a 'hands on' person and sailed as the captain of the *Vesteraalen* for the first two years.

A later 1939 VDS poster – little did Richard With know how his dream was to develop (Bård Kolltveit Collection)

In 1894 he stepped down as the ship's master to become CEO of VDS. In the following year he was made Knight First Class of the Royal Norwegian Order of St. Olav. After almost 20 years as company president, he stepped down in 1908, citing health problems as his main reason. However, in the same year he became active in the setting up of Norwegian America Line and in 1910 served as deputy chairman of the board.

Involved in local politics, he served as a Member of the Storting (Norwegian Parliament) for the Vesterålen constituency from 1910 to 1912. Probably his biggest achievement was in persuading the Storting to finance the dredging of the Risøyrenna, the narrow channel at the northern end of the Risøysundet, between Andøya and Hinnøya. Over the centuries silting had made this stretch of water impassable to all but very shallow draught vessels. The project finally got under way in 1911 and was not completed until 1922 at a cost of 3,000,000 kroner (*see Risøyrenna article*).

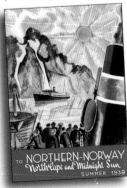

By then he had moved to Christiania (Oslo) where he lived until his death in February 1930. Known as the 'Father of the Hurtigruten' his name has been used for two Hurtigruten ships: the ss *Richard With* (1909) and current ms *Richard With* (1993). A bronze bust of him is prominently placed outside of the Hurtigruten Museum in Stokmarknes. In Tromsø there is a square named Richard Withs Plass and several roads are named after him; Richard Withs Gate or Richard Withs Vei are to be found in Andenes, Trondheim, Bodø, Sandnessjøen and Vardø. He died in Oslo on 9th February 1930 at the age of 84. His widow survived him by a further eight years.

The modern day Hurtigruten as the *Richard With* serenely traverses the Raftsundet (Trym Ivar Bergsmo/ Hurtigruten ASA)

Doubling Up

The original proposals were for a twice-weekly Hurtigruten and in 1894 both NFDS and BDS were again approached to see if they might now participate. Their positive response was met with some alarm by VDS who felt that this would be a competing service and not a complementary one. However, common sense prevailed, firstly by writing in a clause preventing unfair competition and secondly by extending the contract until 30th June 1898. BDS and NFDS agreed to share their part of the contract by alternating their ships on the route each year. Det Bergenske Dampskibsselkab introduced the nine year old *Sirius* on July 3rd 1894 and in the following year it was the turn of the *Olaf Kyrre* to come onto the service for Det Nordenfjeldske Dampskibsselskab. Departures from the Brattøra Quay, Trondheim, were every Thursday at 08.00, timed to link up with the overnight train from Christiania (Oslo) whilst the *Vesteraalen* had the departure on Sundays.

The *Sirius* was slightly larger than the *Vesteraalen* at 877 gross tons, delivered in April 1885 from Flensburger Schiffbau Gesellschaft in Flensburg. Her passenger interior was divided into three classes, with cabins for 24 first class passengers, 22 in second and 24 in third. Most of the cabins and saloons were on the main deck, with cargo both fore and aft of the engine room. The machinery was a 2-cylinder compound steam engine of 700 ihp with coal-fired boilers giving a service speed of around 10 knots. In 1896 electric light was installed and in 1908 she was lengthened to 207 feet and fitted with a new triple expansion engine of 950 ihp. The ship was to sail on a variety of routes, including to Iceland. In 1927, she lost her passenger cabins and was then used purely as a freight ship between Hamburg, Oslo and Finnmark. She was 55 years old when her long career came to an end, being sunk by German aircraft in May 1940.

One of NFDS's newest ships, the *Olav Kyrre* was a large combined cargo and passenger ship of 927 gross tons and 195 feet in length, with berths for

The *Sirius* at Molde in 1890 (photographed by Axel Lindahl/Norsk Folkemuseum)

NORTHBOUND				SOUTHBOUND		
BDS	NFDS	VDS		BDS	NFDS	VDS
00.30	00.30	00.30	Trondheim	19.00	00.00	19.00
03.00		03.00	Beian	16.00		16.00
12.00	12.00	12.00	Rørvik	08.00	12.00	08.00
16.00	16.00	16.00	Brønnøysund	04.00	08.00	04.00
20.00	20.00	20.00	Sandnessjøen	00.00	04.00	00.00
	22.00		Vikholmen		02.00	
04.00	06.00	04.00	Bodø	15.00	18.00	15.00
06.00	08.00	06.00	Bodø	14.00	16.00	14.00
	14.00		Kabelvåg		10.00	
13.00	15.00	13.00	Svolvær	09.00	09.00	09.00
17.00		17.00	Lødingen	03.00		03.00
	21.00		Evenskjær		03.00	
20.00	23.00	20.00	Harstad	00.00	01.00	00.00
	01.00		Havnvik		22.00	
	06.00		Gibostad		17.00	
05.00	09.00	05.00	Tromsø	15.00	14.00	15.00

Departures from Trondheim   Thursdays (BDS), Saturdays (NFDS) and Sundays (VDS).
Departures from Tromsø   Saturdays (BDS), Mondays (NFDS) and Tuesdays (VDS).

Steamers – *Jupiter, Erling Jarl* and *Vesteraalen*.

Hurtigruten Timetable, autumn/winter 1896

Above (left) an early 1890s picture of the *Olaf Kyrre* at Bergen's Festningskaien and (right) the ship in white summer livery acting as the Royal Yacht in 1908 (Mike Bent Collection/ Sogn og Fjordane Archives)

Erling Jarl (I)

Right: An inter war view of the *Erling Jarl* at Risøyhamn in 1935 (Enerst Benjaminsen/ Vesterålen Info)

Below: The *Erling Jarl*, NFDS' first purpose built ship for the Coastal Express seen here in her original white livery (Bjørn Andersen Collection)

85 passengers. The ship had been built in 1886 by Martens, Olsen & Co. at Laksevåg in Bergen at a cost of 360,000 kroner, specifically designed for the Hamburg service. The ship had a triple-expansion steam engine and was also the first built to have electric lighting, albeit only for those in first class. It remained on the Hurtigruten until 1896 when replaced by the *Erling Jarl* but returned again in 1899 before spending the next four years on the Trondheim – Tromsø service. The *Olav Kyrre* was to only have a short career as on 10th July 1909 whilst crossing the Hustadvika in dense fog en route from Molde to Kristiansund it became stranded on rocks and sank. Fortunately the steamship *Mercur* was able to rescue all the passengers and crew.

Up to now none of the three ships on the route had been purpose built but this changed with the arrival of the *Erling Jarl* delivered from Trondheim Mek to NFDS on 9th December 1895. The *Erling Jarl* measured 677 gross tons and had an overall length of 189.6 feet. Unlike the usual coastal steamer ships of the time the cargo holds were set forward in front of the boiler room, with the lounges and cabins on the main deck and a continuous promenade deck above. The accommodation was divided into three classes, with 1st class aft, 2nd class amidships and 3rd class towards the bow. As the

holds were forward the ship had a tendency to dip its bow deep into the water when running at full speed. The ship's engine was of the usual triple-expansion type developing 810 ihp, giving an 11-12 knots service speed. As new she was painted with a grey hull, which was later painted black, in line with all the other ships in the company.

The sharing arrangement between NFDS and BDS meant that ships would only normally serve on the Coastal Express for one year at a time. Thus whilst the *Erling Jarl* was the first purpose built ship for the route for NFDS, she needed to find other employment after 1st July 1896 as the *Jupiter* from BDS would take over for the next 12 months. The ship was then put on the weekly Trondheim – Bergen tourist service. In the summer of 1897 the ship returned for another 12 month spell on the Hurtigruten.

In February 1909 the *Erling Jarl* was rebuilt at Trondheim, receiving a new boiler and funnel as well as being lengthened to 196 feet (736 gross tons), improving load capacity as well. The ship was in regular service for many more years and it wasn't until June 1937 that retirement came, although remaining in reserve. The ship did return to service in the Second World War but did not survive, grounding and sinking off Brønnøysund twice. The first incident happened on 29th January 1941, with the loss of one life. Raised, sold and repaired by Erling Sannes of Bodø, the ship was renamed *Bodø* and in April 1942 leased to Det Ofotens Dampskibsselskab for their coastal service between Trondheim and Narvik. The second grounding and sinking proved fatal; this time it was in strong winds off Bogskjærene just north of Brønnøysund, the *Bodø* hit rocks, fortunately not sinking until everyone had been saved. It was another 17 years before the wreck was finally broken up.

From NFDS having the newest ship on the route BDS chose their oldest ship *Jupiter* as their replacement vessel. It had been delivered to them in May 1856 from Caird & Co. in Greenock for service between Hamburg and Tromsø. As new she had an elegant cut bow and three masts, schooner rigged. Her overall length was 160 feet, with two continuous decks with a small lounge on the top deck. Her original steam engine was primitive; of the direct-acting vertical type, both difficult and unreliable, the boilers which used sea water as feed water had to be replaced every 4-5 years. Worse still was her very high coal consumption, 10 barrels an hour at 12 knots!

The BDS ship *Jupiter* (1856) had a long career of 57 years before being sold for scrap in 1913 (Hurtigrutemuseet)

Jupiter (I) 1856

Modernised several times in the intervening years including improvements to the accommodation, the *Jupiter* must have been a sturdy ship, for in 1905 when now almost 50 years old she was given another costly refit including the installation of electric lighting. Autumn 1907 saw her on the route between Bergen and Vadsø and, together with the *Lyra*, also undertook summer cruises to London on Saturdays. Her demise came on 4th December 1912 when southbound she went aground at Rautingkalven, Fensfjorden, close to Bergen. She was at that time Norway's oldest passenger ship. Her wreck was sold at auction on 15th April 1913 for just 5,000 kroner.

1898 saw a third weekly steamer contract awarded to BDS and NFDS, with again the former being responsible for the first year. They introduced their comparatively 'new' 24 year old *Orion* to the Hurtigruten. Like the *Jupiter*, built in Scotland at H Murray and Co., Port Glasgow (681 gross tons; 180.5 feet registered length) she had the reputation of being accident prone, sinking off Meløyvaer in 1874 and then having her engine explode during testing after a refit in 1889. From July 1898 she sailed opposite the *Vesteraalen* until the October, Bergen by then having become the southernmost port on the route. Increasing pressure from the important fishing ports of Kristiansund and Molde had resulted in a new weekly round trip between Bergen and Tromsø. NFDS's *Erling Jarl* returned to the route yet again and this time was joined by the BDS ship *Capella*.

The *Orion* alternated with the *Kong Halfdan* on the route around Finnmark to Vardø from July 1901 to July 1902 and then again from mid-July 1903. In Autumn 1902 the ship had another extensive refit at the Laksevåg Shipyard in Bergen, including the installation of a new 750 ihp triple-expansion engine.

However, accidents did not go away for the *Orion* as

The *Orion* (BDS), which was broken up after a fire in 1903; however, her engines lived on in the new *Lyra* of 1905 (unknown)

The perils of ice and probably no steam heat! The *Kong Halfdan* will need some attention before sailing again (unknown)

A rather grainy picture of the 1874 built *Kong Halfdan* which saw most of her Coastal Express service between Tromsø and Vardø (Hurtigrutemuseet)

on 12th December 1903 when eastbound off Båtsfjord, fire broke out on board when an oil lamp tipped over in the 2nd class accommodation amidships. The fire spread rapidly and seven of the crew perished in the flames, while the others abandoned ship. The burnt-out wreck was then towed to Vardø. Meling's bought the wreck at auction for 9,000 kroner and had it towed to Stavanger for breaking up. Her almost new triple expansion machinery and boilers were bought back by BDS and in 1905 installed in the new coastal steamer ship *Lyra*.

The October 1898 contract also expanded the Coastal Express route with a separate connection between Tromsø and Vardø. With the contract being jointly held by BDS and NFDS, the latter sent their *Kong Halfdan* north for the first year. The ship dated from 1874, built by W Lindberg's Warf & Werkstads in Stockholm as the *Sirius* for Rederibolaget Svea. In 1878 NFDS bought the vessel for 200,000 kroner renaming it *Kong Halfdan*. Two decades later in 1896, the ship received another major rebuild including a new compound engine and boilers at the Trondheim Mek Shipyard. With a length of 171.1 feet and now 574 gross tons, the vessel had a capacity for 300 passengers.

The route along the exposed coast of Finnmark with its unprotected ports made for greater demands on both ships and seamanship. In the winter it was a weekly round trip service from Tromsø to Vardø but in the summer it became twice weekly from Vardø to Hammerfest. In July 1899, as per the contract agreement the *Kong Halfdan* was replaced by *Orion*, but sailed again in 12-month periods from July 1900, 1902 and 1904.

At the end of 1917/18 the *Kong Halfdan* made a brief comeback on the Coastal Express, but in a heavy snow storm on 19th January 1918, northbound with 70 passengers on board, the ship grounded at Ruselv, Lenangen, north of Tromsø. All passengers and crew got ashore safely but the ship became a total wreck.

As we have seen the 1898 contract led to the introduction of further

The BDS ship *Capella*
photographed at Hammerfest
by the well known
photographer Axel Lindahl

services from Bergen. BDS proposed that in order to save time, instead of calling at Trondheim, their recently introduced *Capella* should call at Beian, at the mouth of Trondheimsfjorden, where a local steamer service would provide a connection. It prompted a great deal of protest, in particular from NFDS as they thought the proposal might marginalise Trondheim. They threatened to break off cooperation if BDS did not include Trondheim in their timetable. Common sense prevailed, so that from 5th April 1899 Trondheim was to have three weekly Coastal Express departures to Hammerfest every Wednesday, Friday and Sunday. The *Vesteraalen* had the Sunday departure, while *Erling Jarl*, *Orion* and *Capella* retained the other round trips.

The *Capella* had been built by Martens, Olsen & Co. at Laksevåg, Bergen in December 1885 and was the first BDS ship where particular attention was paid to the tourist needs in the summer. She was 873 gross tons, had a registered length of 191.9 feet with cabins and lounges below deck in three classes. Her machinery was of the compound type developing 800 ihp with a service speed of 11 knots. The *Capella* continued to sail on the route until 1900 when she was replaced by the BDS new build *Astraea*.

The First World War caused tourists to stay away and as the priority had to be for cargo during 1915/16, the *Capella* was converted into a freighter. Saloons and staterooms gave space for hatches and cargo and with a loading capacity of 790 deadweight tonnes (dwt) the ship returned to serve on the company's long freight route between Oslo and Finnmark.

In 1924, in an effort to improve her operating economy, she was given a replacement triple expansion engine and boiler, originally installed in a British trawler dating from 1919. Unfortunately this only gave her a service speed of 8.5 knots, which rather slowed up the timetable. By the time 1939 came she had been earmarked for retirement.

She survived the Second World War, including a sinking on 28th April 1940 by German aircraft in Tingvollfjorden near Molde, being raised and sold in 1943 to Anders and Gabriel Andersen of Stavanger for further service. Renamed *Hillevåg*, in early 1950 the ship was chartered for an expedition to western Greenland, which sailed with 35 passengers on board.

Left: Pictures of the *Røst*
(1898) are hard to come by.
Seen here departing Svolvær
with the Hadsel (1892) to the
right (unknown)

Above: The *Røst* high and dry
under repair possibly after
one of her several groundings
(unknown)

However, the ship suffered propeller damage and had to be towed back to
Norway. The *Hillevåg* was then sold on to Thv Schjølberg-Knudsen
(Kristiansand) and then on to Johan Gerrard (Kristiansand), who sent the
ship, now 67 years old, to Belgium for scrapping in January 1952.

VDS regularly drafted the tiny *Røst* on the Coastal Express in a relief
capacity between 1899 and 1905. A product of the famous Trondheim Mek
Shipyard, the ship was built for Det Vesteraalens Dampskibsselskab and
delivered in April 1898. Of only 290 gross tons (100 dwt) with an overall
length of 139 feet, she was powered by a TMV triple expansion engine
developing 364 ihp. She had an eventful career, grounding and sinking on
13th January 1912 off Mortsund (Lofotens), but was later raised and
rebuilt at Mjellem & Karlsen, Bergen increasing her tonnage to 379 gross
tons and her length to 155 feet. The ship was then used sporadically as
relief on the Hurtigruten between June 1916 and October 1920. Involved
in the civilian evacuation of Finnmark in 1944, her long career came to
an end on 15th May 1952 when, under the ownership of Høvding
Skipsopphugging of Sandnessjøen, working on the site of the sunken
Tirpitz, she too sank with 100 tonnes of munitions on board. The *Røst* was
raised and immediately scrapped.

The *Astraea* (1900) was designed to be an auxiliary cruiser, complete with 120mm cannon. Very popular though somewhat heavy on fuel, she had a short life, being scrapped after grounding near Florø in 1910 (Hurtigrutemuseet)

In 1899, BDS ordered another Coastal Express steamer from Aker Mek in Oslo for delivery in 1900. Costing some 458,000 kroner and registered as being 193.0 feet in length and 765 gross tons, the *Astraea* was slightly larger than the *Erling Jarl* but had the more conventional arrangement of cargo space both fore and aft of the engine room. With razor sharp lines and her BDS black hull, the tall, dominant funnel with its three white rings on a black background gave the impression of both speed and strength. Indeed this was true as her large and fuel thirsty triple expansion engine could help her to achieve 14.25 knots. She was really a wolf in sheep's clothing being designed to double up as an auxiliary cruiser in the event of mobilisation. This was a very real scenario as tensions between Norway and Sweden over sovereignty were beginning to get rather heated. On board she had a 120 mm cannon on the foredeck, with six 76 mm guns and six 47 mm placed elsewhere on board.

A popular vessel on the coastal route thanks to her excellent speed, however, her large machinery and consequent high fuel requirements meant that her load capacity was rather limited. The *Astraea* was to have a short life and became the first ship to be lost whilst on Coastal Express duties. Northbound on 5th January 1910 she grounded on Gesskjærene, just northeast of the Stabben Lighthouse, near Florø. Fortunately all the passengers and mail were saved, but the ship sank in shallow water. The *Astraea* was later raised and towed to Bergen but following an inspection she was condemned and sold for scrapping. Some of her machinery was saved and stored and saw the light of day again in the 1921 built BDS Bergen – Newcastle ship *Mercur*. After the loss of the *Astraea*, the *Capella* came back into Hurtigruten service until the delivery of the new *Polarlys* in 1912.

Rather strangely in 1902 NFDS decided to replace the *Erling Jarl* and *Olaf Kyrre* with one of its oldest ships, the *Haakon Adalstein*, originally delivered to them in September 1873 by C Mitchell & Co., Walker on Tyne. As new the ship measured 679 gross tons and was 185.5 feet in length, but had been extensively rebuilt in 1901 at Trondheim with new cabins and lounges for 213 passengers as well as having its engine and boilers replaced, increasing the service speed to 12.5 knots and being more economical in coal consumption.

Left: The *Haakon Adalstein* (1873) had a long and distinguished career spanning 63 years; her last Hurtigruten service was in 1945. Above: she is depicted in her pre 1914 summer livery (Bjørn Andersen Collection)

In the spring of 1905 and 1907 the *Haakon Adalstein* replaced the *Kong Halfdan* on the Finnmark leg of the Coastal Express and from 1909 served in various roles, destined to have a surprisingly long life on the Hurtigruten. Withdrawn in 1932 and transferred to the Salten-Bodø-Trondheim service, in 1936 the *Haakon Adalstein's* cabins and saloons were stripped out in order to turn it into a cargo only vessel. The vessel was to do valuable supply work during the Second World War and indeed in November 1945 actually returned to Hurtigruten service between Tromsø and Kirkenes.

In March 1946, the *Haakon Adalstein* was laid up and in the October sold for 50,000 kroner to Ole T. Flakk of Kristiansund and renamed *Goma*. On 10th September 1947, somewhere off Tylö on Sweden's Halland coastline, during a journey from Aalborg to Gdansk with 271 horses on board the ship capsized and sank in 70 feet of water. The crew escaped, but the horses were drowned. It was a sad end to of one of the most long lived ships from the Coastal Express.

Left: The *Andenæs* (1903) was mainly used on the Hurtigruten by VDS in a relief capacity. Here she is photographed at Narvik (Anders Beer Wilse)

Below: Seen off Andøya in 1930 (unknown/Norsk Folkemuseum)

In addition to the *Røst,* VDS used a number of other casual relief ships intermittently on the Coastal Express including the *Andenæs,* which had been built by Fredrikstad M/V, Fredrikstad in 1903. The ship is recorded as having served as a relief steamer on the Hurtigruten for the *Vesteraalen* between 1903 and 1909, then again in 1915, and more occasionally until the arrival of the new *Lofoten* in February 1932. Of 813 gross tons, the ship had a registered length of 186.1 feet, and her FMV triple expansion engine developed 550 ihp, giving a service speed of 10 knots. For the summer of 1907, the *Andenæs* undertook a series of cruises for VDS to Nordkapp from Trondheim via Narvik and Tromsø, the ship being given a white hull. In 1911 VDS successfully re-launched their Svalbard cruise programme from Trondheim, the *Andenæs* visiting Nordkapp and Bjørnøya and sometimes venturing into the ice cap well beyond 80°N.

After a long career, spanning thirty five years, on 20th May 1938, whilst alongside at Stavanger, the *Andenæs* was rammed by the BDS steamer *Leda,* sinking the following day. The ship was sold to Eilert Østbø of Stavanger who scrapped her on the spot.

With the loss of the *Orion* off the coast of Finnmark in December 1903, BDS ordered a new ship for the Hurtigruten from the Bergens Mek Shipyard. Ready in January 1905, she was named *Lyra* (784 gross tons, 185 feet in length, 11.5 knots). With her machinery and boilers having been recycled from the condemned *Orion* this enabled the construction costs to be kept down to 310,000 kroner.

Her accommodation differed in that instead of the first class dining room being farthest aft it was now located amidships on the main deck, just ahead of the boiler room. This gave greater comfort and would eventually become the common practice for future new builds. She continued to be a three class ship with 42 first class berths aft, 20 second class berths midships (which were marketed as first class in the tourist season) and 42 forward in third class.

With both the *Lyra* and *Astraea* in service BDS now had two modern purpose-built vessels serving the Coastal Express route. From July 1905 the *Lyra* operated on the Tromso/Hammerfest and Vardø route until the *Kong Halfdan* again took over in July 1906. The *Lyra* continued on the

A BDS postcard of *Lyra* (Bjørn Andersen Collection)

Above: A 1930s view, now sporting a black hull (Norsk Folkemuseum/unknown)

Left: The *Sigurd Jarl* (1884) was introduced to the Hurtigruten in 1907. Photographed in Hardangerfjord on a 1905 summer cruise (Anders Beer Wilse)

Hurtigruten routes until December 1913 when she was sold to Turkish interests (Vapeur Ottomane) and renamed *Biga*. Caught up in the First World War the *Biga* was torpedoed and sunk on 10th July 1916 by the British submarine E-7, near Mudanya in the Marmara Sea.

In 1907, the Norwegian Government allocated monies to BDS and NFDS for a fourth weekly round trip on the Hurtigruten, of which two services wereextended from Bergen to Vadsø and subsequently to Kirkenes from 1st October 1908. The NFDS vessel, *Sigurd Jarl*, dating from 1884 was no stranger to the area having been transferred from its normal Hamburg – Vadsø route. Another product of Aker Mek Shipyard, Oslo the ship was 208.1 feet in length, fast at 12 knots and of 884 gross tons, with berths for 78 passengers in three classes with a certificate for up to 506 passengers for coastal work. Initially, the ship was painted white for the summer tourist season. From the autumn of 1907 the *Sigurd Jarl* took up the long Bergen-Vadsø service under the command of Captain Axel Aarøe, the start of a long and distinguished 33 year career on the Hurtigruten.

In 1920 she had a major refurbishment at the Trondheim Mek Shipyard, where the interior was modernized, boilers replaced and a new taller and fuller funnel erected. Further alterations were made in 1931 to the third class accommodation including a new dining saloon and promenade deck. In 1933 the *Sigurd Jarl* became one of the first Coastal Express vessels to be equipped with a radio telephone.

The ship's career came to an abrupt end early in the Second World War, on 23rd April 1940, when it was attacked by German planes and sank in shallow water in Vågseterbukta near Molde, fortunately without loss of life. It was not until November 1942 that the ship was raised. NFDS considered putting her back in service and even bought the wreck back from the insurance company. Towed to Fredrikstad for inspection, the estimate of 1.7m kroner made it an uneconomic repair. It was not until 1947 the ship was towed away for scrapping at Stavanger.

New Builds
1909–1912

Surprisingly, there were few new purpose built ships in the first two decades of Hurtigruten operation, the shipping companies preferring to cascade older vessels onto the route. The Coastal Express with its all year round service was still quite understandably viewed as a high risk operation. It was not for another decade after suffering war losses between 1914 and 1918 that ship owners actually started to insure their vessels. Older ships were obviously more expendable than younger ones.

The awarding of a contract to BDS and NFDS to provide a fourth weekly round trip in 1907 had not gone down well with VDS who had proposed to transfer their *Andenæs* (1903) from other duties but it was rejected. In the event VDS decided to order a new ship to join the *Vesteraalen*. Built at the Trondheim Mek Shipyard the ship was named *Richard With,* after the founder of VDS, on 24th June 1909. For the first year the *Richard With* was under the command of Captain Frederik Hegge. It was the largest ship yet to be built for the Hurtigruten and was of 905 gross tons with a length of 193 feet. The ship's triple expansion engine developed 1,150 ihp, which gave it a 12 knots service speed. The ship was said to be designed for rough weather and had beautiful sharp lines complemented by a slightly sloping funnel which gave an impression of great speed. The design also called for both holds to be situated forward which meant that when fully laden the ship would bury its bow rather deep in the water and as a consequence affect manoeuvrability. As new, the hull of the *Richard With* was painted white

Right: A fine study of the *Richard With* at Svolvær in 1910 with a traditional jekt passing in the foreground (Anders Beer Wilse)

Below: a day of celebration as the *Richard With* glides towards her next port of call (Norsk Folkemuseum/ unknown)

A Mittet postcard of the
Midnatsol at full speed,
possibly on her maiden
voyage (Bjørn Andersen
Collection)

with brown painted upperworks and teak panelled deckhouses but after the
1914-1918 war the hull was painted black in line with other vessels on the
Hurtigruten.

The *Richard With* had a full promenade deck, the amidships deckhouse
contained the mail room and captain's cabin as well as the first class smoking
lounge. The passenger certificate was for 300 persons and cabins were
provided for 101 in three classes.

The *Richard With* was to have a long life on the Hurtigruten before being
torpedoed and sunk off Rolvsøya, north of Hammerfest with much loss of
life in September 1941. *(see also War – For a Second Time).*

The opening of the Bergen to Oslo railway in 1909 offered new
opportunities for the city of Bergen. Having been awarded the contract in
1907 for a fourth weekly service on the Coastal Express BDS seized the
moment to introduce a larger ship as a statement to further strengthen their
grip on Bergen as a hub for both the Coastal Express and North Sea routes
to Britain. Expensive to build at 504,000 kroner, in June 1910 the new ship
entered service as the *Midnatsol* (a name still happily perpetuated in today's
fleet). She had been built at the local Bergens Mek Shipyard and was of 978
gross tons (510 dwt) with a registered length of 202.8 feet. The *Midnatsol*
had an elegant profile with fine lines to the bow and stern and was the first
coastal steamer to have the bridge placed above all the other decks which,
with the dining room immediately below on the shelter deck, gave the ship
a majesterial look. Her BMV triple-expansion engine generated 1,508 ihp
to give a service speed of 13 knots. There was cabin accommodation for 132
passengers in three classes.

In line with the rest of the fleet she had a significant refurbishment in
1930, transforming her into a two class ship with berths for 35 first class
passengers and for 46 in third class.

The *Midnatsol* safely negotiated the 1939–45 war, though whilst nearing
Øksfjord on 30th August 1941 on passage from Hammerfest to Tromsø she
had to witness two German supply ships being torpedoed within half a mile

of her. The ship picked up around 200 survivors though unconfirmed reports suggested that between 1,000 and 2,000 others were killed or drowned. It had been the intention to withdraw her in 1942, but at the end of hostilities she was made ready for the first Hurtigruten service from Bergen. She was by then the oldest BDS ship on the Coastal Express. *(see also War – For a Second Time)*

In 1949, with a new *Midnatsol* being constructed at Ancona, Italy her name was changed to *Sylvia*. She finished service on 10th October 1950 and by the end of the month she had been sold and towed away for scrapping by SA Elba of Antwerp. It was the end of a long and illustrious career.

BDS immediately commissioned a second new ship to replace the *Astraea* which had sunk off Florø in January 1910 and this was delivered as the *Polarlys* in April 1912. Instead of using a Trondheim or Bergen shipyard, the contract went to the Burmeister and Wain Shipyard in Copenhagen. Having her named in Christiania, the Norwegian capital, was an advertising masterstroke as it brought together all the various parliamentary, local government and transport authorities.

The *Polarlys* was an impressive ship, similar to the *Midnatsol*, of 1,069 grt (536 dwt), with a length of 208 feet, some six feet longer than her consort. There were cabins for 141 passengers spread over three classes. Part of the hold was insulated and had cooling systems. Her B&W triple expansion engine developed 1,473 ihp, giving a service speed of 13 knots. She was said to look 'superb' in her BDS black and white livery and separate bridge deck, underneath which was a much appreciated observation shelter.

A popular and reliable vessel she served the route well, though in mid career in February 1930 she was very much in the news. Caught late one evening in a storm south of Rørvik en route to Trondheim, Captain Norli prudently elected to ride it out in more open water. However, in those days the equipment to communicate with anyone ashore wasn't available on the Coastal Express steamers. It wasn't until 32 hours later (to the relief of many) that the *Polarlys* slipped into her berth at Brattøra, Trondheim. This incident began to raise a number of awkward questions with regard to operational safety issues in the running of the service.

Later on that same year, the *Polarlys*, in similar fashion to the *Midnatsol* was further modernised into a two class ship with improved cabin facilities,

The *Polarlys* was a sister ship to the *Midnatsol*; looking (right) at the flags this could be her inaugural voyage, with (left) another A B Wilse picture believed to have been taken at Oslo (unknown)

bringing her into line with the rest of her fleetmates.

World War Two saw the *Polarlys* being requisitioned on 9th April 1940 for use as an accommodation ship at the Navy Island, Bergen. Her name was insensitively changed to *Satan* before being renamed and shortened to *Tan*. By Christmas 1940, she had reverted to her original name and was back in limited service on the Hurtigruten. She was requisitioned again to serve in the evacuation of Northern Norway for the retreating German army during October and November 1944. Finally in March 1945, she was laid up in Østerfjord (near Bergen) and stayed there until peace was declared.

That summer the *Polarlys* was one of the few Coastal Express ships available. After a somewhat basic 'essentials only' overhaul, on 7th July 1945 she was ready for her first peacetime Hurtigruten sailing in six years albeit only as far as Tromsø. There was to be a more extensive renovation, at the BMV Laksevåg Shipyard, Bergen in the spring of 1948, but the ship remained coal-fired to the end.

With Captain Frithjof Quigstad in command, she finished her last journey on the Hurtigruten on 11th October 1951. With an overdue passenger certificate she was laid up in Bergen, and as from April 1952, in deference to a new *Polarlys* taking shape on the stocks at Aarhus, as with the *Midnatsol* before her, she was temporarily renamed *Sylvia*.

A new career awaited as the Royal Norwegian Navy bought her to act as a 'mother ship' to their motor torpedo boat (MTB) fleet. In July 1952 she returned again to the BMV Laksevåg Shipyard for a further rebuild, emerging eleven months later as KNM *Valkyrie*. She was to serve the Navy for another ten years before being finally scrapped in 1963.

The camera of Anders Beer Wilse captures the *Polarlys* arriving at Molde in February 1927 (Norsk Folkemuseum)

A 1950s postcard depicting the busy scene at Finsnes (now spelt Finnsnes) with the arrival of the *Polarlys* (Bård Kolltveit collection)

As we have noted, Det Vesteraalens Dampskibsselskab had felt rather marginalised as to the way the Hurtigruten was developing, for having been the initiators to make the route possible, the next three contracts had all gone to their competitors. However, the contract awarded in 1911 for a fifth weekly service did at last go to VDS. This was for a weekly sailing between Bergen and Vadsø, which initially was covered by the *Richard With*, while the older *Vesteraalen* took over the Trondheim-Tromsø sailings. It was only intended to be a temporary deployment, for in August 1911 VDS ordered a new and larger vessel from the Trondheim Mek Shipyard. The *Finmarken*, as she was named (note the spelling), entered service on 7th September 1912 and was to serve the Hurtigruten for 44 years, only being scrapped in 1960 just two years short of her 50th birthday.

She was the largest ship on the route, 1,119 grt (589 dwt) with a registered length of 214 feet. Building on previous experience Richard With had created an extra hold aft of the engine room. The interior decoration was of the highest order, the passenger accommodation keeping to the traditional layout of first class amidships and aft, second class forward of this with third class towards the bow. There was also a first class dining room for 70 people as well as a smoking and music lounge at the stern. As on the *Polarlys* the ship had an observation shelter on the boat deck underneath the bridge. Her machinery was again of the triple-expansion type developing 1,550 ihp giving an impressive service speed of 14.5 knots.

The Finmarken was to become a legend in her time, a greyhound with a sleek white painted hull and large funnel complemented by the VDS blue boot topping. Captain Hegge transferred his command to her, later to be succeeded by Captain Ragnar Falck. Her entry into service marked the end of any more new builds on the Coastal Express for another 13 years until in 1925 the *Dronning Maud* was delivered from the Fredrikstad Mek Shipyard for NFDS.

Appropriately, it was the *Finmarken* which had the honour of being the ship that opened the Risøyrenna Channel between Andøya and Hinnøya in June 1922. Richard With had been the driving force behind this project and had used all his influence as a Member of Parliament to get it realised taking nearly 11 years to complete (*see Risøyrenna article*).

Captain Fredrik Ottar Hegge and the *Finmarken* were by all accounts inseparable right up to his retirement in 1929. He earned the reputation of being able to find his way around even in the most difficult weather conditions. A well known tale records the time when in thick fog approaching Svolvaer in the Lofotens, he asked the lookout if he could see anything. 'No', was the reply. 'Put your hand out, can you feel anything?' 'Yes, wood' was the reply. They were safely berthed.

During the Second World War under Captain Falck, the *Finmarken* was involved with troop transports to Nordfjord (Bodø). On 9th April 1940, painted in wartime grey she made an audacious attempt under cover of fog to escape to the Shetlands with just a crew of seven, but her fuel reserves were too low and she only made it as far as Stokmarknes. With the fall of Norway, overnight on 7th/8th June various ships slipped out of their hiding places and steamed westwards to Britain, including the *Finmarken*. She was

A VDS postcard of the *Finmarken* departing Stokmarknes (VDS/ Hurtigrutemuseet)

somewhere between 100 and 150 miles from the Norwegian coast when she was spotted by a German bomber which managed to score a hit on one of her lifeboats. Such was the force of the explosion that it sprang a leak in her hull. Making water, she was forced to turn back. A radio message was sent to Tromsø Skipsverft to be ready to receive her; they managed to cope but the repair took some considerable time. *(see also War – For a Second Time)*

When things had settled down again a basic Coastal Express service was restarted and the *Finmarken* was on this almost continuously throughout the hostilities. In the autumn of 1944 the ship was requisitioned by the Germans for the evacuation of northern Norway.

At the end of the war in May 1945 the *Finmarken* was one of only three Coastal Express ships that were remotely serviceable for the reintroduction of Hurtigruten between Trondheim and Tromsø. Getting increasingly run down the ship was eventually was sent to Gøtaverken AB, Gothenburg for a thorough refit and refurbishment. It wasn't until 15th November 1946 that she was ready to return to service with new lounges and cabins and her boilers converted to oil firing.

The ship continued in service for a further 10 years until in 1956 with a new *Finmarken* (note the new spelling) on the stocks at Blohm & Voss, Hamburg, her name was changed to *Vågan*. At the beginning of June 1956, the ship was laid up in Bergen until the following year when she was sold to Sjøguttskole Rogaland, Stavanger, for 600,000 kroner. Renamed *Gann* the ship was repainted with a light grey hull to be used as a youth training ship whilst also offering summer cruises to the general public. After an incident at Moss on 22nd September 1960, where she suffered damage to her bow, the *Gann* was withdrawn and later sold for scrapping in the Netherlands. Before she left Norway her first class smokeroom was dismantled and presented to Bergens Sjøfartsmuseum. Most of her interior was sold to a local Dutch entrepreneur who intended to reuse some of it in a new motel. In the end the cabins, saloons and deckhouses were resold to become part of 'Villa Finmarken' in Beekbergen, near Apeldoorn in the Netherlands. In 2003 some of these furnishings and rooms were returned to Norway and now form part of the excellent exhibition at the Hurtigruten Museum in Stokmarknes. The *Finmarken* of 1912 still lives on!

A pre WW1 picture of the *Finmarken* laying down a thick black trail of smoke (Olaf Andreas Knutsen Storegjerde - Sogn og Fjordane Fylkesarkiv)

To the Land of the Midnight Sun

PART 1 TO 1914

The *Mira* and *Kong Harald* on a cruise around the Romsdalen fjords near Molde (unknown)

The seeds for today's tourist industry along Norway's 'long coast' began to germinate in the middle part of the 19th century when regular steamship sailings between Britain and Norway became established. Those who did visit Norway, other than for trade or affairs of government, were in the main adventurers or involved in academic or scientific research. Once accessibility to Norway from Britain had been established some of the more intrepid visitors began to use the government mail steamer services to venture further afield. Encouragingly for them, on 9th July 1845, the *Prinds Gustav* sailed from Hammerfest on a special excursion to Nordkapp which was repeated the following year to Tanafjorden to the east of Nordkapp.

It was not until the 1870s that interest in the west and north of the country began to gain any momentum. The Coronation of King Oscar II at the Nidaros Cathedral in Trondheim on 18th July 1873 and the monarch's subsequent travels along the coast to Nordkapp changed perceptions completely, especially as the journey was followed by a host of journalists from all over Europe reporting back their experiences. Paul du Chaillu, a Frenchman, who made visits to northern Norway in 1871 and 1878, published his experiences in a two volume book entitled 'The Land of the Midnight Sun'. This title caught the public's imagination and is still used profusely today. The publication also aroused the interest of Thomas Cook & Sons, the London travel agency, which in 1875 organised the first ever escorted excursion to Nordkapp.

Both BDS and NFDS would use their newest ships with their higher standards of accommodation to exploit this new business opportunity. From 1878, steamers on their Hamburg to Vadsø service were diverted round the northern side of Magerøy during the summer months so that passengers could visit Nordkapp. They were put ashore either at Gjesvær or Kjelvik and then taken by rowing boat to the foot of cliffs, some three hundred metres in height.

Nordkapp as seen in 1906 (unknown)

In 1883, BDS and NFDS decided to offer their own series of weekly cruises from Trondheim via Molde ('the town of the roses') to Nordkapp, expanding to twice weekly in 1884. By 1889 the cruise programme had expanded so much that four ships were needed for the cruises, the *Capella*, *Sirius*, *Olaf Kyrre* and *Sverre Sigurdssøn*. Publicity became more elaborate, evolving from simple newspaper advertisements in 1883 to a 72 page, full colour, multi-lingual brochure by the early 1900s.

Cruising also created new demands on the ships' masters as in addition to having to command the ship, they also had to be able to speak several foreign languages. Not only that, they had to arrange shore excursions and the on-board entertainment!

The ships too, had dual rôles. In winter it was freight, fish being the main source of revenue as passengers were relatively few during the dark months. Every spring, those vessels to be used for cruises were overhauled and repainted; black hulls became white, awnings were rigged, hatch covers replaced by skylights, the cargo handling equipment removed, canvas screens tied to deck rails, and even the hold spaces were converted into temporary cabins with furnishings not dissimilar to those in first class.

It was not until 1907 that VDS started cruises to Nordkapp from Trondheim, using their *Andenæs*. This steamer also served as a relief vessel on the Hurtigruten. For her popular cruising rôle in the summer she was given a

Above: A pre 1900 joint BDS/NFDS poster for the French market advertising the delights of cruising the Norwegian coast (Bård Kolltveit Collection)

Left: A well known colour postcard depicting BDS ship *Neptun* rounding Nordkapp (author's collection)

Above left and right: Two 1906 views of *Kong Harald,* one taken in Trollfjord (both Anders Beer Wilse/ Norsk Folkemuseum)

white hull. These cruises continued until 1913, with the *Andenæs* sailing from Trondheim to Narvik and then on to Tromsø and Nordkapp where a stay of several hours gave passengers ample time to ascend to the high plateau. On the southbound run, visits were made to Trollfjorden and Torghatten (near Brønnøysund).

The tourism boom, which continued right up to the summer of 1914, was remarkable when set against the general economic recessions of that period.

Trondheim – Nordkapp Cruises – Summer 1910

Trondheim	22.00 Tuesday, Thursday
Svartisen	
Tromsø	
Hammerfest	
Nordkapp	pm Friday. Sunday
Nordkapp	am Saturday, Monday
Lyngenfjorden	
Tromsø	
Raftsundet	
Torghatten	
Trondheim	08.00 Tuesday, Thursday

Steamers – *Neptun* every Tuesday from 14 June to 19 July, *Kong Harald* every Thursday from 16 June to 21 July.

Above and right: Two posters from the Bård Kolltveit collection

Svalbard Adventures

TO 1914

A 1913 joint BDS/ NFDS poster produced for the French market 1913 (Bård Kolltveit collection)

Around 400 nautical miles to the northwest of Nordkapp is the Svalbard archipelago. For four months in the winter there is no sunlight and the islands are in the grip of the Arctic pack ice. From late April, however, the ice retreats sometimes beyond the 80° North mark. On shore, rare and colourful Arctic flowers blossom and temperatures can become quite comfortable.

Whilst the Dutch had exploited the natural resources of Svalbard during the late sixteenth and early seventeenth centuries, by 1645 the archipelago was left to the explorers, scientists, mineral prospectors and wandering polar bears until the late 1800s.

BDS's *Pallas* was the first steamer to make a cruise to Svalbard in 1881, chartered by Henry Clodius of Tromsø. Around 60 people (zoologists, botanists and hunters for the most part) made bookings. The voyage was plagued by drift ice and bad weather, which meant that the time spent on Svalbard was shorter than planned. Complaints later appeared in several newspapers with the excursion being dubbed (possibly unfairly) as 'The Spitsbergen Swindle'.

Fridtjof Nansen's explorations on board the *Fram* between 1893 and 1896 attracted worldwide interest in the polar regions. The more adventurous tourists wanted to follow in his footsteps, at least for part of the way.

It was Richard With (who else!) who took up the challenge. He proposed a series of weekly cruises from Hammerfest to Adventfjorden, on the west coast. His fellow VDS directors were, not surprisingly, cautious. In mid June 1896, Captain With took the *Raftsund* (built 1873, 689 gross tons) north to Adventfjorden with a team of builders and a cargo of timber. They arrived there on 17th June, precisely 300 years to the day since the archipelago had been discovered by William Barents. The building materials were used for the construction of a small hotel, which featured a balcony, a heated lounge and beds for up to 30 guests.

DSD's *Irma* in the Svalbard pack ice 1924 (Oscar Holte)

Above/below: Two Mittet postcards of the *Kong Harald* cruising off Green Harbour, Spitsbergen (Eric Hagger Collection)

The *Lofoten*, commanded by Captain Hegge, sailed from Hammerfest on the morning of 8th July for the first cruise, calling at Adventfjorden, before returning south via Nordkapp and the whaling factory on Rolvsøy. Eight cruises were made that summer and a total of 40 passengers carried.

Promoted as 'The Sportsman's Route', the VDS Svalbard cruise itinerary involved a departure from Hammerfest at midnight every Tuesday (connecting with the Hurtigruten) and an arrival at Adventfjorden on the Friday morning. The return trip, via Nordkapp and Rolvsøy, started the same evening, with Hammerfest being reached late on Monday morning. Eight cruises were offered in both 1897 and 1898 with around 60 passengers were carried. However, with increasing competition from the larger cruise liners, coupled with finding it difficult to make a profit, VDS pulled out.

The hotel was closed but remained on the company's books until it was sold to John M. Longyear, who later acquired coal mining concessions on the shores of Adventfjorden in 1904. The building was converted into the mining company's office, and the small town of Longyearbyen grew up around it. Although seemingly abandoning their cruising activities, VDS continued to engage in lucrative private charters using the *Lofoten* to Svalbard and to the ice cap until 1910.

In 1911 VDS re-launched the Svalbard cruise programme, using the *Andenæs*, incorporating Nordkapp, Bjørnøya and the ice cap into the itinerary (sometimes venturing well beyond 80°N) with Trondheim as the departure point. Not to be outdone, BDS and NFDS followed suit with their *Erling Jarl* and *Kong Harald* with cruises starting from Hamburg and Antwerp.

Below: The *Kong Harald* and *Neptun* at Gudvangen (Sognefjord) en route to Spitsbergen 1911 (Mike Bent Collection)

Growth

1913–1914

Between 1892 and 1914 there was a steady expansion of services, both in frequency and length as passengers and forwarders of perishable goods transferred their allegiances from the slower 'kombinerte' services. Tourism was also booming. However, operating results were prone to fluctuation, as were profit levels between the three companies and between the individual steamers. In both 1903 and 1905 VDS, with only the one steamer, recorded profits of 60,000 kroner on their Hurtigruten sailings. Early records indicate that their passenger numbers had shown a rapid increase from just over 6,000 in 1893 to over 70,000 in 1916.

The steady expansion of services also came with increasing costs both in fuel and labour and as a result profit margins became tighter. Additionally, whilst some new and faster vessels had come onto the route, the number of intermediate ports of call had increased (Beian, Indre Kvarøy, Grønøy and Finnsnes had been added to the timetable) so that the service from Trondheim now took longer than it did in 1894, with schedules being based on the speed of the slowest vessels on the route. In addition, the larger a ship's cargo capacity then the longer it took to handle it.

In 1913 BDS introduced the *Hera* as a running mate for their *Midnatsol* and *Polarlys* replacing the rather slow *Lyra*. The *Hera* was not new and dated from 1899, built as the *Juno* at Earle's Shipbuilding & Engineering Co. Ltd, Hull, for Thos. Wilson, Sons & Co. Ltd, designed as a combined cargo and passenger ship for service between Hull and Scandinavia. Rebuilt in 1906 and again in 1912/3 she was a large and spacious vessel of 1,097 gross tons (900 dwt) and some 215 feet in length. The *Hera* had a certificate for 600 passengers but cabins for only 58 in three classes. The ship's powerful triple expansion engine developed 1,200 ihp which gave a good 12 knots of speed,

In 1913 BDS introduced the *Hera* (1899) to be a running mate to the *Lyra*, originally being designed as a North Sea cargo/passenger ship for Wilson, Sons and Co Ltd. (Hurtigrutemuseet)

ideal for the Coastal Express. In addition, she boasted a large refrigerated hold for fresh fish. Further rebuilding in 1920 made her into a two class ship. On the night of 17th/18th March 1931 with the *Hera* southbound from Honningsvåg to Hammerfest, battling against a head wind in heavy seas and adverse currents, she grounded on the unlit headland of Havøygavlen. The sea was too rough for *Hera*'s crew to attempt to launch the lifeboats so the second officer, Einar Ramm, tied a rope around his waist, leaped overboard and swam ashore. A breeches buoy was rigged up, using two lifebelts tied together, and whilst six people were swept away and drowned a total of 56 managed to scramble to safety. Einar Ramm subsequently received a medal for his bravery.

With five weekly sailings from Bergen to Kirkenes from 1st July 1914, logistically this meant that ten ships were needed to run the service. NFDS were forced to introduce the *Haakon Jarl* which dated from 1874 to the route. Originally constructed for their Hamburg–Finnmark route the ship was built at the Motala Mek–Lindholmens Verksted Shipyard, Gothenburg. Lavishly furnished with comfortable accommodation including adjustable cabin heating, the *Haakon Jarl* had in 1887 played host to Prince Gustav and Princess Victoria on their voyage to the North Cape. Lengthened in 1891 at Aker Mek, Oslo, and further rebuilt in 1906, the ship now had a registered length of 197 feet, displaced 873 grt and had a service speed of 11 knots.

The *Haakon Jarl* sailed for ten years on the Coastal Express, but in thick fog on the night of 17th June 1924 some six nautical miles off the island of Landegøde, just north of Bodø, the ship collided with the southbound ship, *Kong Harald,* sinking in eight short minutes with the loss of 17 lives. Both captains were acquitted of any blame at the subsequent inquest into the collision, blame being laid solely on the poor visibility prevailing at the time. The tragedy shook the nation, a reminder of the constant challenge between nature's capricious whims and human vigilance.

The *Haakon Jarl* (1874) was already 40 years old when NFDS introduced the ship onto the Hurtigruten in 1914. Photographed here near Tromsø (Axel Lindahl - Norsk Folkemuseum)

Retrenchment

WORLD WAR ONE

Even though not directly involved in the First World War, Norwegian commerce was affected as fearing that the North Sea would become a battleground, effectively blockading Norway, there was a rush on the banks, coupled with panic buying and foreign tourists deserting the country. When the realisation came that the battle was going to be centred on Belgium and Northern France, some degree of normality returned. Being a neutral country opened up all kinds of opportunities for Norway and the economy began to flourish. As a precaution, ships painted neutrality markings on their hull sides which were illuminated at night. On the down side, coal supplies were becoming very scarce as in 1915 Britain had placed an embargo on foreign exports. Schedules were slowed down in order to save coal consumption. It was welcome news in 1916 that the Arctic Coal Company (USA) based at Longyearbyen (Svalbard) had been persuaded to sell off their coal mines to a Norwegian consortium which included some of the coastal steamer operators.

Two well known views of BDS' *Capella* before she was converted into a freighter (Erik Hagger Collection/Trondheim Byarkiv)

On the Hurtigruten itself, 1917 saw the service reduced to only three sailings a week between Bergen and Hammerfest together with two from Trondheim to Kirkenes.

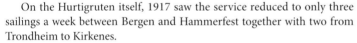

Hurtigruten Timetable

Northbound	Monday	Tuesday	Wednesday	Thursday	Friday		
Bergen	22.00				22.00	1	
Florø	08.00				08.00	2	
Måløy	11.30				11.30	2	
Ålesund	19.30				19.30	2	
Molde	00.00				00.00	3	
Kristiansund	06.30				06.30	3	
Trondheim	16.30	16.30		16.30	16.30	3	1
Trondheim	00.00	00.00		00.00	00.00	4	2
Rørvik	13.00	13.00		13.00	13.00	4	2
Brønnøysund	19.00	19.00		19.00	19.00	4	2
Sandnessjøen	01.00	01.00		01.00	01.00	5	3
Indre Kvarøy	04.30	04.30		04.30	04.30	5	3
Grønøy	07.00	07.00		07.00	07.00	5	3
Bodø	12.00	12.00		12.00	12.00	5	3
Bodø	14.00	14.00		14.00	14.00	5	3
Svolvær	21.00	21.00		21.00	21.00	5	3
Svolvær	01.00	01.00		01.00	01.00	6	4
Lødingen	05.30	05.30		05.30	05.30	6	4
Harstad	09.30	09.30		09.30	09.30	6	4
Harstad	11.30	11.30		11.30	11.30	6	4
Finnsnes	16.00	16.00		16.00	16.00	6	4
Tromsø	20.00	20.00		20.00	20.00	6	4
Tromsø	00.00	00.00		00.00	00.00	7	5
Skjervøy	05.30	05.30		05.30	05.30	7	5
Hammerfest	14.00	14.00		14.00	14.00	7	5
Hammerfest		19.00		19.00		5	
Honningsvåg		03.00		03.00		6	
Kjøllefjord		07.30		07.30		6	
Mehamn		11.30		11.30		6	
Berlevåg		16.00		16.00		6	
Vardø		21.00		21.00		6	
Vardø		00.00		00.00		7	
Vadsø		04.30		04.30		7	
Vadsø		06.00		06.00		7	
Kirkenes		09.00		09.00		7	

24 June 1917 to 30 June 1918

Southbound	Sunday	Monday	Tuesday	Wednesday	Thursday		
Kirkenes		21.00		21.00		1	
Vadsø		00.00		00.00		2	
Vadsø		01.00		01.00		2	
Vardø		05.30		05.30		2	
Vardø		08.00		08.00		2	
Berlevåg		13.30		13.30		2	
Mehamn		18.30		18.30		2	
Kjøllefjord		22.30		22.30		2	
Honningsvåg		03.30		03.30		3	
Hammerfest		09.30		09.30		3	
Hammerfest	21.00	21.00	21.00	21.00	21.00	3	1
Skjervøy	05.00	05.00	05.00	05.00	05.00	4	2
Tromsø	11.00	11.00	11.00	11.00	11.00	4	2
Tromsø	14.00	14.00	14.00	14.00	14.00	4	2
Finnsnes	18.00	18.00	18.00	18.00	18.00	4	2
Harstad	22.30	22.30	22.30	22.30	22.30	4	2
Harstad	01.00	01.00	01.00	01.00	01.00	5	3
Lødingen	05.30	05.30	05.30	05.30	05.30	5	3
Svolvær	10.00	10.00	10.00	10.00	10.00	5	3
Svolvær	14.00	14.00	14.00	14.00	14.00	5	3
Bodø	21.00	21.00	21.00	21.00	21.00	5	3
Bodø	23.00	23.00	23.00	23.00	23.00	5	3
Grønøy	04.30	04.30	04.30	04.30	04.30	6	4
Indre Kvarøy	07.00	07.00	07.00	07.00	07.00	6	4
Sandnessjøen	12.00	12.00	12.00	12.00	12.00	6	4
Brønnøysund	17.00	17.00	17.00	17.00	17.00	6	4
Rørvik	23.00	23.00	23.00	23.00	23.00	6	4
Trondheim	11.00	11.00		11.00	11.00	7	5
Trondheim	21.00		21.00		21.00	5	
Kristiansund	08.00		08.00		08.00	6	
Molde	14.00		14.00		14.00	6	
Ålesund	19.00		19.00		19.00	6	
Måløy	02.00		02.00		02.00	7	
Florø	05.30		05.30		05.30	7	
Bergen	15.00		15.00		15.00	7	

Post War Blues
1918–1923

NFDS' *Olaf Trygvesøn* (1876) saw intermittent Hurtigruten service for NFDS between 1916 and 1921. She was photographed (below) in earlier days by Jørgen Wikstrøm at Trondheim in 1893 (Trondheim Byarchiv/unknown)

In 1916, NFDS's *Olav Trygvesøn* (named after the King of Norway from 995 to 1000) was one of the steamers to be drafted in as a temporary replacement on the Coastal Express, though was seen more regularly on the route between 1919 and 1921. Already 40 years old, dating from 1876, the ship had been built at the Newcastle shipyard of J. Wigham Richardson & Co. at a cost of £70,000. An iron hulled vessel measuring 593 gross tons and 176 feet in length it was successively rebuilt, refurbished and modernised in both 1899 and 1902, eventually measuring 663 gross tons (398 dwt) with an overall length of 192 feet. The *Olaf Trygvesøn* had a crew of 26 and could carry up to 199 passengers on the coastal route. After 1921 the *Olaf Trygvesøn* was mostly used on freight services along the Norwegian coast until the spring of 1934 when the ship was sold to Anda Brothers, Stavanger for scrapping.

With normality returning after the end of the First World War the Coastal Express was enhanced from July 1919 with a sixth weekly round trip. The upshot of this was that older tonnage had to be drafted onto the Hurtigruten in order to fulfil the requirements. With this expansion came a new company to the route, Det Stavangerske Dampskibsselskab

(DSD). Over the following six decades the company's three red rings around the funnel would become a familiar sight along the coastline. Indeed this company is still very much in evidence today along the Norwegian coastline with interests in sea freight services through Nor Lines A/S and in transport and tourism through Tide ASA. DSD's involvement meant a further extension of the route to Stavanger and although this ceased in 1936 the company remained as part of the Hurtigruten organisation until 1979.

In 1919 the *Kong Haakon* became the first DSD ship to serve the Hurtigruten and remained there until 1927 when it returned to its original Oslo – Bergen route run jointly with Det Arendals Dampskibsselskab. The ship dated from 1904, having been built by Schömer & Jensen at Tönning, in northern Germany and measured 874 gross tons with a length of 196 feet and cargo holds fore and aft of the engine room. The machinery, typically a triple expansion engine, produced 1,200 ihp giving the ship a service speed of 12.5 knots. The ship had a passenger certificate for 400 persons.

Formerly DSD's flagship, the *Kong Haakon* (1904) is photographed by Anders Beer Wilse (above left) at Bergen in 1925 and (above) arriving at Ålesund (Norsk Folkemuseum)

The ship was to have a long career, including a return to the Coastal Express in 1942, which entailed a change of name to *Kong Sverre* by order of Quisling's Nasjonal Samling (National Government). Despite being attacked by a submarine in March 1944 and avoiding three torpedoes the ship's luck ran out as when in Bergen a month later, it was badly damaged after a cargo of dynamite exploded on board the nearby *Voorbode*. Repaired at the SDS shipyard in Stavanger during 1945 and reverting to its original name, the *Kong Haakon* was back on the Coastal Express in January 1946, initially between Trondheim and Hammerfest. Four years later came the final withdrawal from service and the ship was laid up in Stavanger. It was not until January 1953 that *Kong Haakon* was sold for scrapping to Eisen & Metall AG of Hamburg for 230,000 kroner, being towed there at the end of the following month.

Three views of the Kong Harald of 1890, (top) off Torghatten, Brønnøysund in 1906 by Anders Beer Wilse, (above right) in the Raftsundet en route to Svolvær and (above) in her rebuilt 1948 guise off Trondheim (Norsk Folkemuseum/ Erik Hagger Collection/STFM)

No less than 13 vessels were now required for the Hurtigruten to maintain a sixth weekly round trip. Fortunately for NFDS, the restructuring of activities on the Hamburg route meant that they now had ships to spare, one of which was the *Kong Harald*. Indeed, the ship had been on the Coastal Express route in a relief capacity since the spring of 1919 and had gained the reputation of being a sturdy and comfortable ship. By then the *Kong Harald* was already 29 years old, having been built in 1890 at the John C Tecklenborg shipyard in Geestemünde, Germany. The main deck accommodation was in the usual three classes with berths for 70 persons and a summer certificate for 502 passengers. By 1909, successive rebuilds had increased the ship's length to 220.6 feet and her gross tonnage to 1,110, her new triple expansion engine developed 1,100 ihp giving a service speed of 12 knots.

As has already been noted, in the summer of 1924 the ship was involved in the tragic accident which resulted in the loss of 17 lives and that of the *Haakon Jarl*, off Landegøde north of Bodø. Then, on 17th February 1929, fire broke out aft in the first class lounge shortly after departing from Kirkenes. Whilst the blaze was extinguished quite quickly it meant a visit to the Trondheim Mek Shipyard where it underwent yet another major refit. A new bridge was constructed and the passenger accommodation reconfigured so that the ship became a two class operation, second class being phased out.

The *Kong Harald* was to have a long career in Hurtigruten service, only being finally retired in 1950 after running aground near Florø. She was finally scrapped at Bruges in 1954 at the age of 64 years.

The *Neptun* was another ship which came to the Hurtigruten in 1919 as a result of the increase to six weekly round trips. However, her career on the route was to only last a couple of years, as in October 1921 the post war depression forced the Coastal Express to be once more reduced by one weekly round trip, the *Neptun* becoming surplus to requirements.

The *Neptun* was, in essence, a sister ship to the *Kong Harald*, delivered

The NFDS steamer *Neptun* photographed in 1906 traversing the Raftsundet (Anders Beer Wilse - Norsk Folkemuseum)

to BDS in June 1890 from same John C Tecklenborg shipyard in Geestemünde, Germany at a cost of 400,000 kroner. Built for the Hamburg – Finnmark route she originally measured 970 gross tons and 198 feet long, with a service speed of 12 knots. Prior to each summer season the ship would undergo a thorough clean and repaint to make her suitable to accommodate the tourist passengers on their travels to the Norwegian fjords, Nordkapp and occasionally to Svalbard.

Following her withdrawal from the Hurtigruten in 1921, the *Neptun* returned to the Hamburg route only to be sold by BDS in April 1926 to the Stavanger Skiba Ophugnings Co. for scrapping. Compared to her sister, it was a very short career indeed.

The post war boom was not to last long and came to an end in 1920. Inflation was rife as Norway, along with the rest of Europe, suffered an economic recession. Output was down, unemployment was up and there was industrial unrest. For the Hurtigruten companies a number of their vessels had to be laid up in May 1921 when stokers, seamen and engineers walked out on strike. It was to be six weeks before they returned.

One of the ships NFDS were forced to withdraw from traffic was their *Haakon VII* which they laid up at Trondheim in 1921. When delivered from the Trondheim Mek Shipyard in May 1907, the *Haakon VII* was Norway's largest ever passenger ship and built specifically for their Trondheim – Bergen – Newcastle service to run in tandem with BDS's *Irma*, *Vega* and *Venus*. Of 1,347 gross tons and 259 feet in length, her triple expansion engine developed 1,850 ihp, giving a service speed of 14.5 knots. As new, the ship had a white hull with teak or dark brown painted deck housing. Expensive to build at 700,000 kroner with staterooms for 144 passengers, this three class vessel set a new trend in design with the lounges stretching across the full width of the main deck.

In a bold move the *Haakon VII* was reactivated and placed in service on the Coastal Express for the summer of 1922. She became an immediate success and a much sought after ship on which to travel. The loss of the

The *Haakon VII* was built in 1907 for NFDS and is seen photographed that same year at Trondheim by Anders Beer Wilse (Norsk Folkemuseum)

Haakon Jarl saw the *Haakon VII* on the route permanently from 1924. In keeping with the changing needs the ship was converted into a two class vessel in 1926.

The ship's new Hurtigruten career was to be rather short lived, as at around 22.30 on 6th October 1929 during a heavy rain storm coupled with gale force winds, the *Haakon VII* deviated from the normal course off Melshølmen, just south of Florø, hit rocks, rolled over on its starboard side, and sank by the stern. Nine passengers and nine crew members were lost, many of them trapped in the stern. *Haakon VII*'s Boatswain Anders Andersen from Brønnøysund, in an act of heroism, managed to transfer 55 people from the bow onto land, where they found shelter. They were rescued three hours later by the Spanish vessel *Elin Jens San Lucar* and brought safely to Florø.

The ship remained where it lay all winter until March 1930, when it was patched up and towed to the Laksevåg dry dock at Bergen. The damage was too great and the *Haakon VII* was then sent to Stavanger to be scrapped.

A Mittet postcard of the *Haakon VII* at Øye on one of her summer cruises. In a touch of déjà vu Hurtigruten ships visited this area in September 2012 as part of the 'Autumn Gold' experience (Bjørn Andersen Collection)

Design Parameters & Propulsion Units

The fuel shortages of the 1914 – 1918 war had thrown open the question as to the size of ship, service speed, preferred propulsion method and fuel to be used on future Coastal Express vessels. It was a debate which continued throughout the 1920s.

Prior to 1914 the general consensus was that for practical purposes, the upper gross tonnage limit for Hurtigruten ships should be no more than 1,000 grt with a hull length of 200 feet. This rather inward thinking slowed down the design development for a number of years. The *Skibsbygning* debate between engineer E. Mowinckel-Larsen and Nordenfjeldske Captain Andreas Aarøe during 1920 and 1922 was the first occasion in which Hurtigruten steamer design came up for open debate and although in the end it bore no immediate fruit, it offered some intriguing alternative ways forward. Both favoured a vessel with a registered length of at least 250 feet, in other words, considerably longer than any ship that had yet appeared on the Hurtigruten. It would not be until after the Second World War that their foresight would become a reality.

Speed too was a contentious issue. The Finnmark Regional Government which was anxious to see journey times between southern and northern Norway reduced (as there had been scarcely any improvement between 1893 and 1914) suggested the creation of a fleet of vessels capable of 19 or 20 knots. In practice, journey times on the Hurtigruten were determined by the speed and capabilities of the slowest member of the fleet, so there was little incentive to build a vessel capable of more than 14 or 15 knots when there were still other steamers plodding along at a maximum of 11 or 12 knots. Various proposals for a two-tier service, stopping and limited-stop,

1922 turbine proposal
(Mike Bent)

The *King Edward*, the world's first turbine powered passenger ship on trials on the Firth of Clyde 1901
(Bruce Peter Collection)

failed to find much support, even though there were some experiments in this field, both in the 1930s and in the 1960s.

Coal fired triple expansion reciprocating engines had been the norm and now that fuel could be obtained from Svalbard instead of being reliant on imports from Britain, the situation had eased. However, these engines by their very nature took up a great deal of space and, in particular, their height affected the overall layout of a ship. The favoured design was the traditional layout of first class passenger accommodation aft and third class amidships, with cargo spaces concentrated forward. The only difference of opinion lay in the type of prime mover that should be installed.

1922 motorship proposal
(Mike Bent)

Two developments had been taking place since the turn of the century, the first being the introduction in 1901 of the *King Edward,* the world's first turbine powered passenger ship on the Firth of Clyde in Scotland. She was sleek, fast, smooth and quiet and set new standards in excursion ships. By the early 1920s, oil-fired turbine steamers were becoming quite commonplace, but they were not to find favour on the Hurtigruten. Any number of arguments were put forward against turbine propulsion: lack of manœuvrability in tricky coastal waters; operational difficulties because of the short distances between ports of call; heat below decks generated by the turbines, but it was hard to reconcile these claims as turbine steamers operated highly satisfactorily on the short cross-channel services between England and France as well as on the congested waters of the Clyde. Two ideas for turbine ships, one a twin funnelled version, were put forward but were destined not to leave the drawing board.

A second and parallel development came to the fore in February 1912 when the *Selandia,* the world's first true motor ship, made her maiden voyage from Copenhagen to Bangkok. Notwithstanding that the first

motor ships were noisy and rather slow, the major problem for the Coastal Express service was that they would be back to square one and dependent entirely on imported fuel, not a pleasant scenario if war were to come again. A proposed version for the Hurtigruten looked remarkably like a miniature version of the *Selandia* but in the end nothing really changed until after the Second World War, when in 1949 the second *Erling Jarl* became the first motorship specifically designed to serve on the Hurtigruten.

The m/s *Selandia* – the world's first true motor ship built in 1912 for the East Asiatic Company and its compact engine room (B & W Archive)

Risøyrenna

Until 1922 all Coastal Express services having called at Svolvær (Lofotens) then sailed to the east of Hinnøya via Lødingen, Tjeldsund and on to Harstad, marginalising the prosperous area of Vesteraalen and, in particular, Stokmarknes where Richard With, founder of the Hurtigruten had his headquarters. At Risøyhamn, where he lived, was a narrow shallow channel separating the islands of Hinnøya and Andøya. As a Member of the Storting (Parliament) from 1910 he began to petition the Norwegian Government to have this channel dredged so that it could take larger steamers. After protracted debate the finance was found and in July 1911 the work commenced to excavate the hard stony bed of the channel, but by 1913 it was increasingly evident that the dredger wasn't up to the job. They had to wait until the spring of 1920 before a new dredger, *Ekskavator 6,* had been built and was able to start work on the channel. It was finally completed and ready for opening in 1922 at a cost of around three million kroner.

The new channel was 5 km (3 miles) long, 50m (160 feet) wide with a minimum depth of 5m (15 feet). It was a magnificent achievement and one of national pride and importance. VDS's *Finmarken* was appropriately chosen to carry King Haakon, Norwegian President Jahren, Richard With and other dignatories from Trondheim to Risøyhamn. At 23.00 on 24th June 1922, leading a flotilla of more than 400 craft, the *Finmarken,* with Captain Hegge, Richard With, pilot Anders Holte and the official party on the bridge, steamed through the Risøyrenna Channel, her bow bursting through the 80m banners at either end amid a cacophony of ships' sirens and whistles, the 'star turn' being the *Ekskavator 6* which as a way of welcoming the distinguished guests noisily set all her machinery into motion.

From 1st July 1922, two of the five weekly coastal express services were

The opening of the
Risøyrenna on 24th June 1922
photographed by H. Johansen
(VDS archive/Hurtigruten
ASA)

diverted after Svolvaer to travel through the Raftsundet onto Stokmarknes, Sortland, Risøyhamn and Harstad. This gradually increased in frequency and today the Risøyrenna channel is now the norm for all Hurtigruten vessels. As compensation for the change a "replacement" route from Narvik via Lødingen to Svolvaer was put in place. Det Ofotens Dampskibsselskap, based in Narvik, secured the contract which began on 2nd July 1922 using the chartered ship *Torgtind*. This route connecting Ofoten with Lofoten lasted for 80 years, until it ceased in January 2003.

In 1957, further dredging work was needed to deepen the channel as well as widen it at the bends; it took until 1966 to finally complete this work. With new and larger ships now in service further deepening of the Risøyrenna was undertaken from September 1997 through to September 2001 when the *Narvik* (1982) officially reopened the channel. The need to further deepen the channel does not go away as the 'Millennium' class Hurtigruten ships are said to have only 200mm (8 inches!) under their keel when the tide is at its lowest. After the *Trollfjord* touched the bottom in 2011 further dredging is planned for the spring, summer and autumn of 2013, with the spoil being used in development of the Norwegian Coastal Authority's 'Pure Project' at Harstad.

Dredging is ongoing in the Risøyrenna Channel; here, it is in preparation for the new Millennium ships in September 2000. Note the narrowness of the channel (Mike Ryan/ Hurtigruten ASA)

Consolidation

1924–1939

In 1924, in order to give better continuity, a new six year contract was agreed, though with a reduction in service levels with only three sailings per week to Kirkenes from Bergen, one from Stavanger and one from Trondheim. However, journey times from Kirkenes to Trondheim were reduced by no fewer than eight hours. Trondheim had in 1921 strengthened its importance as an interchange between rail and steamer services when the new Dovrebanen, the direct railway line from Oslo via Dobås and Dovrefjell was opened, further cutting journey times between the two cities.

The next new ship from NFDS was to be the first new build on the Coastal Express service since the *Finmarken* in 1912. It was a radically improved version of BDS's *Midnatsol* and *Polarlys*, not surprising as they were now 15 years old. Built by the Fredrikstad Mek Shipyard the *Dronning Maud* was formally handed over on 3rd July 1925. Much larger at 1,505 gross tons (570 dwt) and with a length of 235 feet, she had two continuous decks with cargo holds fore and aft. With a non 'in house' interior designer being employed for the first time the ship had a totally different feel; first class was now amidships with large lounges on the main deck and each cabin had running hot and cold water. Above the first class dining room was a large observation lounge. Reputed to have cost just over 1 million kroner it was expensive but money well spent. Indeed, according to a popular tale, after the celebratory inaugural lunch held on board at Trondheim, a number of the NFDS directors and guests went aft and ensconced themselves in the 3rd class lounge, thinking that they were in the 1st class accommodation!

Below: The NFDS ship *Dronning Maud* just prior to launching at the Fredrikstad Mek Shipyard in June 1925 and (bottom) makes a fine sight at sea (Fredrikstad Museum Archive/Bård Kolltveit Collection)

The machinery was of the traditional triple expansion type developing 1,500 ihp, and her boilers were still coal-fired, reflecting that coal was still the cheapest and most readily available fuel, especially as they were also now able to source it from Svalbard. In trials she achieved 16.25 knots, though

her service speed was to be around 13 knots. From 1931 she was equipped with a radio telephone.

The *Dronning Maud* became an early victim of the 1939-45 war. On 1st May 1940, as a designated hospital ship, she approached the berth at Foldvik, Gratangen (north of Tromsø) and despite clearly displaying Red Cross signs and flags she was attacked by 3 German aircraft. The ship immediately caught fire, 18 people being killed and 31 wounded in the attack. A fishing boat managed to tow the burning wreck away from the wooden pier, the ship eventually running aground. It was a tragic end for such a well loved ship. *(see also War – For a Second Time)*

In 1926 Det Stavangerske Dampskibsselskab (DSD) ordered its first ever new ship to serve on the Hurtigruten from the International Shipbuilding & Engineering Co. Ltd, Danzig (Gdansk). Named *Sanct Svithun* in honour of Stavanger Cathedral's patron saint it was delivered on 30th June 1927 measuring 1,375 gross tons (734 dwt) and 225 feet in length. Designed as a

Hurtigruten Timetable – Summer 1925

Northbound			Southbound	
	Time		Time	
Day 1	12.00	Stavanger	00.00	Day 16
	15.00	Haugesund	21.00	
	22.00	Bergen	14.00	
Day 2	19.00	Bergen	05.00	Day 15
	03.00	Florø	21.00	
	06.00	Måløy	18.00	
	12.30	Ålesund	12.30	
	16.00	Molde	08.00	
	21.30	Kristiansund	03.00	Day 14
Day 3	06.00	Trondheim	18.00	
	12.00	Trondheim	08.00	Day 13
	23.30	Rørvik	20.30	
Day 4	04.30	Brønnøysund	15.30	
	09.00	Sandnessjøen	11.00	
	10.30	Nesna	08.00	
	12.00	Indre Kvarøy	06.00	
	14.30	Grønøy	03.30	Day 12
	19.30	Bodø	23.00	
Day 5	03.00	Svolvær	16.30	
	08.00	Lødingen/Evenskjaer/Melbu/Stockmarknes	10.30	
	09.30	Sortland	08.00	
	11.00	Risøyhamn	06.00	
	1430	Harstad	03.00	Day 11
	18.30	Finnsnes/Gibostad	20.30	
	22.00	Tromsø	15.00	
Day 6	01.00	Tromsø	13.00	
	06.30	Skjervøy	08.00	
	10.00	Øksfjord	04.00	
	1800	Hammerfest	00.00	Day 10
Day 7	00.00	Honingsvåg	15.00	
	04.00	Kjøllefjord	10.00	
	07.00	Mehamn	07.00	
	08.30	Gamvik/Finnkongkeila	05.00	
	11.00	Berlevåg	03.00	Day 9
	18.00	Vardø	22.00	
Day 8	00.00	Vadsø	16.00	
	03.00	Kirkenes	12.00	Day 8

Departures only unless otherwise shown. Not every day for each port. Stavanger service one per week two class ship, it had 82 first class berths amidships with 100 third class berths forward. The ship had a full promenade deck, a substantial boat deck above which was the chartroom and wheelhouse. Although still coal fired, the engine was a Lentz double compound machine generating around 1,650 ihp, giving her a 14 knot service speed. The *Sanct Svithun* was built at a cost of just over 1 million kroner, which was considerably cheaper than any of the more local Norwegian shipyards could quote and would prove to be a particularly good sea boat.

The *Sanct Svithun* served the Hurtigruten continuously for nearly 16 years, but on 30th September 1943 at around 18.45, in heavy seas crossing the Stadlandet between Florø and Ålesund, she was spotted by six British aircraft which attacked her with bombs and machine gunfire. The *Sanct Svithun* was hit forward of her funnel, the engine telegraph was put out of action and the ship was soon ablaze. Captain Alshager managed to run the ship aground on Købbeholmen, a few hundred metres from the mainland at Ervik. Despite the heroics of deckhand Olav Iverson, who managed to scramble ashore and attach a thick manila hawser around some rocks, so that 21 people could escape over this perilous route, no less than 57 people lost their lives. The ship was past salvaging and a few days later slipped off the rock into deep water. The ship's bell was later salvaged and can be seen as part of the memorial to the tragedy in the local church in Ervik. *(see also War – For a Second Time)*

Above: A postcard study of the DSD steamer *Sanct Svithun* in 1927 taken when new (Eric Hagger Collection/unknown)

By 1927 with business recovering, the Hurtigruten again expanded to six weekly round trips, with five from Bergen and one from Stavanger. BDS chose their 37 year old *Mira* built by A & J Inglis of Glasgow and dating from 1891 to join the service, hardly a move forward.

Built for North Sea trade as well as for cruising, her claim to fame was that in July 1906, after their coronation ceremony in Trondheim, the ship had the honour of taking Kong Haakon and Dronning Maud back to Oslo,

Left: *Sanct Svithun* wrecked off Ervik in 1943 (Fric Hagger Collection/unknown)

Top left: DSD's steamer *Mira* photographed off Odda in 1911 (Anders Beer Wilse)

Top right: A busy scene as the *Mira* departs Svolvær (Norsk Folkemuseum/unknown)

calling at many of the major towns on the way. She was no stranger to the Coastal Express, having previously sailed on it in a relief capacity between 1917 and 1921. Now measuring 221 feet and 1,112 gross tons (910 dwt) with a service speed of 12 knots, she was given another full refit at the Laksevåg Shipyard, Bergen where her interior was totally revamped before she took up her new role.

The *Mira* lasted longer on the Hurtigruten than anyone expected and it was not until 1937 that she was put into reserve having been replaced by BDS's new *Nordstjernen*. Layup didn't last for long as she was hastily reactivated to replace the *Irma* which had run aground off Kabelvåg, near Nesna.

With an increasing tonnage shortage the *Mira* was pressed back into Hurtigruten service in 1941. Her time was short as on 4th March 1941 she was sunk off Brettesnes (Lofotens) by HMS *Bedouin*. Seven people lost their lives; the others, including a German officer and 12 soldiers, were taken on board the destroyer and brought to Britain. *(see also War – For a Second Time)*

1927 would also see the introduction by VDS of the *Mosken* onto the Hurtigruten, albeit in a relief capacity, subsequently for the next five years. A small local steamer built in 1924 by Trosvik M/V of Brevik she measured

Another Wilse picture, this time of the VDS vessel *Mosken* also departing Svolvær (Lofoten) in 1928 (Norsk Folkemuseum)

only 410 grt with an overall length of 150.3 feet. The ship had a long career, including being used in the evacuation of civilians from Finnmark in 1944, before being sold firstly in 1957 to Sivert Bakke of Bergen and then again in 1960 to Britt Wadner, renamed as the *Cheetah II Gambia* for use as a pirate radio ship in the North Sea. Her last known whereabouts were as a floating hotel and restaurant ship at Bathurst (Banjul) in the Gambia. It is believed that she was scuttled following a fire, though there are no details as to when this happened.

The *Kong Gudrød* was another elderly ship to be cascaded onto the Coastal Express in a relief capacity. Built in 1910 at the Trondheim Mek shipyard for NFDS she was of 1,091 gross tons (1,000 dwt) with a hull length of 215 feet. When it became necessary in 1929 to withdraw the *Haakon Adalstein*, the *Kong Gudrød* with its 242 passenger certificate was the best option the company had even though the ship was not entirely suited to the Hurtigruten.

Her later career is probably the more interesting; sold in January 1936 to Pärnu Laeva AS, Estonia, the vessel was renamed *Estonia* and put in service on the Tallinn to Stockholm route. In the summer of 1940, Estonia was taken over by the Soviet Union but twelve months later it was under German occupation. The *Estonia* became a mother ship for German gun boats at Turku and then in 1943 an accommodation ship at Swinemünde (Kiel). May 1945 saw the ship in very poor condition and it was another four years before it was sold to Charles Waap of Kiel who did some remedial work before passing it on to S Stein of Hamburg. By 1954 it had been completely rebuilt, including the installation of a diesel engine, and renamed *Mönkedamm*.

In 1963 the ship was sold to Lübeck Linie A/G as the *Overbeck* for use as a car transporter between Germany and Sweden. In 1967 she was bought by Antwerpe Kustvaart, Antwerp and renamed as the *Boom*, almost immediately sold to Greek interests, renamed *Efthycia* and later as the *Phaedra* (1970). After this no one is very sure – it may have gone to the

More from the camera of A B Wilse, the *Kong Gudrød* in 1918, location unknown (Norsk Folkemuseum)

Phillipines in 1977 and was possibly in service during the 1990s; others indicate that the ship remained in Greece until 1993 before finally disappearing off the shipping registers in 1997! What a career!

The BDS ship *Mercur* was another Hurtigruten relief vessel throughout the 1930s, rather late in her career having been built in 1883 as the *Kong Dag* by Motala M/V, Göteborg, for Det Søndenfjeldske Dampskibsselskab. Of 989 gross tons (750 dwt) and 207.0 feet in length the ship's 1,040 ihp Motala two-cylinder compound engine, gave her a service speed of 11.5 knots. In August 1899, she was sold to BDS and renamed *Mercur*. The ship survived a number of almost obligatory groundings, including sinking on 23rd October 1919 off Nord-Leksen in Trondheimsfjorden. The *Mercur* was usually seen on the BDS Bergen to Newcastle service before finding employment on the more local routes. Drafted in as temporary replacement on the Hurtigruten after the sinking of the *Hera* in 1931, she was finally withdrawn in January 1939; the ship was sold to Einar Cook of Bergen, stripped down to become a barge before being sold on to Kristiania-Portland Cementfabrikk, Oslo, who renamed her *Else*. Another new owner, Johan Nilsen of Fredrikstad, purchased her in 1951, but quickly sold it on in February 1952 to Belgian interests.

BDS' *Mercur* (1883) was a great survivor despite her reputation for frequently going aground, pictured below off Bergen (unknown)

BDS had already earmarked the *Irma* to replace the *Hera* when the news of the tragic loss of the company's oldest vessel off Havøysund in March 1931 was announced. Dating from 1905 the *Irma* was built by Raylton Dixon & Co. Ltd. at Middlesbrough and was regarded as a good example of the 'kombinerte' ships of the time, measuring 1,322 gross tons (920 dwt) with an overall length of 244 feet. Her 1,500 ihp Dickinson triple expansion engine gave the ship a top speed of nearly 14 knots. Her stately interiors were designed with international travel in mind with smart lounges and berths for up to 140 passengers in different

Above, an early BDS postcard of the *Irma* of 1905 as seen with her white hull and left, an Anders Beer Wilse photograph of her at Åndalsnes on 13th June 1924 (Norsk Folkemuseum)

configurations depending on the season. In reality, she wasn't too good a sea-boat as she tended to dip into the waves, earning her the nickname of 'the submarine', and used mainly on the Nordkapp and Spitsbergen cruises until 1931 when she was scheduled to take over from the ill-fated *Hera*.

The *Irma* continued in Hurtigruten service throughout the war until on 13th February 1944 she was torpedoed by two Shetland based, Norwegian crewed MTBs as she traversed the Hustadvika between Molde and Trondheim, sinking almost immediately. Of the 86 people on board only 25 survived; 25 passengers and 36 crew members lost their lives. *(see also War – For a Second Time)*

Following the loss of the *Haakon VII* in 1929, NFDS immediately ordered a replacement ship from the Fredrikstad Mek Shipyard at a cost of 1.47m kroner. Named *Prinsesse Ragnhild* (after the daughter of Crown Prins Olav) she was introduced onto the Hurtigruten on 25th November 1931.

Of 1,590 gross tons (570 dwt), 236 feet in length with cabins amidships for 99 first class and 108 berths aft for third class passengers she had an air of modernism in her layout as well as in equipment, with sonar and an electronic log installed as standard. The shipyard's technical director, K G Meldahl, had designed a 'steam motor', a double compound engine capable of developing 2,500 ihp, giving a speed of 16.5 knots, not dissimilar to the Lenz compound engine fitted to the *Sanct Svithun* but much more powerful. Less modern was the fact that her boilers remained coal-fired although they were more fuel efficient.

The *Prinsesse Ragnhild* became an early casualty of the Second World War. She already had a lucky escape on 9th April 1940, when she managed to hide tight to the mountainside in Hjørundfjorden, near to Ålesund, as several German warplanes tried to sink her. However, on 23rd October 1940, whilst only 30 minutes out from Bodø off Landegøde on her way to Svolvær,

A Mittet postcard study of the NFDS steamer *Prinsesse Ragnhild* as new in 1931. The ship had a relatively short career being sunk by allied action in 1940

a powerful explosion ripped open her keel. Within a few minutes the ship had sunk. On board were least 400 passengers and a crew of 50. Two small coasters in the vicinity rescued 156 persons, but over 300 died. The cause was a mystery until many years later when it was revealed that her attacker was the British submarine HMS *Taku. (see also War – For a Second Time)*

Towards the end of the 1920s VDS ordered a replacement for the *Vesteraalen*, now 38 years old, from the Fredrikstad Mek Shipyard, at a cost of 1.3m kroner.

A long running industrial dispute delayed completion of the new *Lofoten* (1,571 gross tons, 760 dwt and 253 feet in length) until February 1932. The ship had two continuous decks, with accommodation in the standard arrangement of first class amidships and third class aft. For the first time all cabins had running hot and cold water. Refrigerated cargo holds for the carriage of fresh fish were both fore and aft. Rather than a 'steam motor', VDS preferred a more conventional 2,200 ihp FMV triple-expansion engine as propulsion, which enabled the ship to achieve 17.25 knots during trials.

Smoking furiously, the *Lofoten* is pictured on her inauguaral voyage
(Uwe Jakob Collection)

Under the watchful eye of Captain Alf Korneliussen the *Lofoten's* first departure from the Fortress Quay at Bergen was on 24th February 1932.

During the war the *Lofoten* continued to serve on the Coastal Express.

A classic 1932 study of the VDS steamer *Lofoten* off Bodø, in her second year of service (unknown)

In February 1942, she was requisitioned to take the Gestapo chief Heinrich Himmler and the Reichkommmissar for Norway Josef Terboven to Kirkenes and back. In the October the *Lofoten* was hit by a torpedo in Saltenfjørden but luckily it did not explode. Later on in October 1944 she was involved in the evacuation of Finnmark.

The *Lofoten* was one of only three active Hurtigruten ships in May 1945, the route limited to between Trondheim and Tromsø. On the evening of 25th January 1948, with 200 passengers on board, in poor weather conditions she experienced mechanical trouble off the Nordkyn peninsula and had to be towed into Honningsvåg. During the subsequent repairs in Trondheim, her boilers were converted to oil-firing. It wasn't until the late spring of 1949 that she was back in service.

After a further modernisation in 1958 at Aker Mek Oslo, the *Lofoten* continued in Hurtigruten service for another five years until 1963 when, with a new build on the way, her name was changed to *Vågan*. However, she was to continue in service until the new *Nordnorge* was delivered. After destoring at the BMV Laksevåg Shipyard, Bergen, on 23rd May 1964 she was handed over to Greek Cypriot buyers. Now registered under Cyprus Sea Cruises and renamed *Kypros,* she was given a total rebuild including a raked bow and streamlined funnel for service between Piraeus, Limassol and Haifa. On 10th November 1966 a fire broke out on board whilst the ship was on her way to Haifa. The master managed to run her aground about 200 metres from the shore; fortunately no one was injured. The *Kypros* was then towed to Haifa to be broken up.

Late in the spring of 1935, the Government entered into talks with the Hurtigruten companies as to whether there should be another service on the Coastal Express in order to make it daily. One of the issues was whether Narvik, an important transport, commercial and industrial centre, should be now included in the itinerary. Whilst this meant a lengthy detour it also provided the means by which the long running 'Nordland Tariff War' could

The *Nordnorge* (1924) was an elegant ship; from top to bottom, the perils of taking your car on board (the 'A' registration is for Oslo); arriving at Bodø in 1928; off Trondheim in 1936; after lengthening in readiness for Hurtigruten service (Anders Beer Wilse; Norsk Folkemuseum/ unknown/STFM/Fotosamling)

be resolved. Det Ofotens Dampskibsselskab (ODS) had in 1914 launched their version of an express service between Narvik and Trondheim. ODS saw this new daily Hurtigruten proposal as a threat to their wellbeing and knew that once this was introduced they would lose the subsidy for their existing service. Left with little choice they offered their flagship, *Nordnorge*, to become part of the Hurtigruten.

The *Nordnorge* was of classic proportions and dated from 1924, having been built at the Trondheim Mek Shipyard, designed specifically for the ODS Narvik to Trondheim service. As built, she was a three class ship of 873 gross tons and 181 feet in length, with a passenger certificate for 270 passengers. Her triple-expansion engine developed 1,000 ihp which gave her a 12 knot service speed.

When it became clear in 1936 that the ship would be engaged on the Coastal Express service she was sent to Trondheim for rebuilding and lengthening. She now measured 213 feet in length with a gross tonnage of 991. Second class was abolished and both the first and third class accommodation was modernised and enlarged. Refrigerated compartments were fitted in her holds, an observation lounge was built at the forward end of her promenade deck, the bridge and chartroom being moved one deck higher. New navigational aids were installed including an echo sounder, electric log and radio telephone. Whilst externally she was a very imposing vessel, some felt that internally she had lost some of her former elegance. The *Nordnorge* proved to be ideally suited to the Hurtigruten and what she lacked in speed was offset by her handling capabilities which enabled her to get alongside quays very quickly.

The *Nordnorge* continued on the Coastal Express until 7th May 1940, when it was requisitioned and her crew replaced by German naval personnel. Two days later, she went north with troops to Hemnesberget, close to Mo i Rana, with orders to secure the area. She was spotted off Rørvik and the information relayed on to the British Military Command. As the troops disembarked she came under fire and not wanting the ship to fall into the hands of the Allies her crew opened the sea cocks, as well as throwing grenades into the bilges. Two British destroyers (HMS *Carlisle* and HMS *Zulu*) then appeared and after almost simultaneous explosions the *Nordnorge* drifted away from the quayside and sank in deep water. *(see also War – For a Second Time)*

The Nordland Tariff Battle

During the inter-war years, as the economy gradually recovered, the Coastal Express route between Trondheim, Bodø and Harstad became a battleground between various competing companies. This stretch of the coastline is by far the most profitable in terms of the amount of freight it generates. With roads almost impassable in winter and no direct railway between Trondheim, Narvik and Bodø the coastal steamers represented the best means of communication between the ports. A number of local companies vied for trade along this coastline and saw the Hurtigruten as a rival to their wellbeing. Matters came to ahead with a price war breaking out as Det Ofotens Dampskibsselskab (ODS), Det Saltens Dampskibsselskab (SDS) and Det Helgelandske Dampskibsselskab (HDS) who jointly ran the services along the Nordland area of the west coast (Sandnessjøen, Bodø, Narvik and Harstad), took on the Hurtigruten, undercutting them through use of the subsidies they were getting for their local services. The Hurtigruten companies argued that this was unfair as they were contracted not just to serve these areas but also the less profitable regions of Troms and Finnmark and that trade should be on an equal footing with companies not able to 'cherry pick' only the lucrative elements (shades of today's competitive tendering processes!). BDS, NFDS and VDS had all been forced to slash their freight rates by up to 50 % as well introduce new, competing and unprofitable services. Nobody benefited, and the dispute rumbled on until 1935 when all parties came together at the Heim Hotel in Mo i Rana over 9th/10th August 1935 to thrash out an agreement under which local operators could not start up new routes which were in direct competition with those provided by the Hurtigruten. With the Norwegian Government also proposing that a daily Hurtigruten be introduced ODS, realising that once this happened they would lose the subsidy for their existing services, offered their flagship, *Nordnorge*, to the Hurtigruten. As part of the deal a weekly call at Narvik was introduced.

Ofotens, Helgelandske and Saltens flags

Ship to Shore Communications

During the 1920s communications to and from ships on the Coastal Express were, in the main, reliant on telephone calls from one port to another. Although by 1927 the Norwegian Government had set up a network of coastal radio stations along the whole of the coastline a degree of complacency still reigned and whilst it was not unusual for Hurtigruten ships to be delayed in poor weather, nobody actually knew where they were, creating anxiety for those waiting for their arrival.

In 1929 two incidents happened, firstly in January when the *Haakon VII* was delayed by over eight hours whilst trying cross the Østhavet in a severe gale en route to Vardø. The second incident came at the end of the year when the *Dronning Maud* was a day late arriving at the same port and nobody knew what had happened and feared the worst.

However, it was the *Polarlys* incident on 13th February 1930 that really jolted the conscience of the Coastal Express companies. The ship was en route to Trondheim and having departed Rørvik was crossing the Folla (Folda) in deteriorating weather conditions. The *Polarlys* had

Agdenes Lighthouse, Trondheimsfjorden (Author's Collection)

NFDS ship *Dronning Maud*, the first Hurtigruten ship to have radio telephone in 1931 (Anders Beer Wilse/Norsk Folkemuseum)

been passed by the northbound *Finmarken* when at around 23.45 a freak wave smashed in the starboard door to the first class foyer, flooding several cabins. By midnight it was becoming increasing difficult to steer the ship in almost nil visibility. Both Captain Norlie and his pilot, Alfred Petersen, became increasingly uncertain as to their position. They decided to steam west in order to ride out the storm. The *Polarlys* was due to arrive at Trondheim at 06.00 the next morning. By the afternoon, with no sign of her, the local newspaper, *Arbeider-Avisen*, was carrying the headline 'Polarlys lost on Folla overnight?' Early in the evening, the weather began to abate enough for the *Polarlys* to attempt to claw her way towards Trondheim. She was spotted passing the Agdenes lighthouse at the end of Trondheimsfjorden around 23.00, finally arriving at Trondheim in the early hours of the next morning (15th). The Captain and crew were feted as heroes, but the incident didn't go away.

Pressure from the Norwegian Seamen's Union, businessmen and the media took up the cause so effectively that by the end of the year the *Dronning Maud* was fitted with a radio telephone. It was first used on 3rd January 1931 when a call was made by *Arbeider-Avisen* newspaper to the ship as she crossed the Folla en route to Rørvik.

It was an unqualified success; not only was the safety of Hurtigruten operation enhanced through better ship to shore communications, but up to date information on weather conditions and of possible delays together with passenger and cargo needs. By 1936 all Coastal Express steamers were equipped with radio telephones.

The Blue Riband of Vestfjord

The area between Svolvær (Lofotens) and Bodø (Nordland) is known as the Vestfjord and involves a 70 mile sea passage. Traditionally, whenever a new vessel took up service on the Hurtigruten the crossing of this open stretch of water gave ships' masters the chance to show just what their new charge could do. Any passage time close to four hours was considered to be excellent. Gradually the *Dronning Maud*, *Haakon VII* and *Finmarken* reduced it until in 1930 the *Prinsesse Ragnhild* broke the 'four hour barrier' with a time of 3 hours 56 minutes. In 1932 the *Lofoten* further lowered this to 3 hours 51 minutes only for the *Prinsesse Ragnhild* to regain the unofficial 'Blue Riband' with a time of 3 hours 41 minutes. This feat put any further attempts to lower the mark well out of reach until the spring of 1950 when NFDS's new motorship, *Erling Jarl,* cut another six minutes off the time bringing it down to 3 hours 35 minutes.

A NFDS postcard of the *Erling Jarl* (1949) which took the Blue Riband of Vestfjord in 1950 (David Parsons Collection)

To the Land of the Midnight Sun

PART 2 TO 1939

In the years immediately after the Great War, summer tourism was showing some encouraging signs of recovery. However, the emphasis was changing as large foreign registered cruise liners began to dominate the Nordkapp cruise scene during the 1920s, bringing in both European and North American visitors who generally chose to travel on ships registered at European ports, since the USA's prohibition laws ensured that their own vessels were 'dry'.

As far as the Coastal Express companies were concerned, with six round trips scheduled on the Hurtigruten each week, they were now finding it difficult to release ships suitable for the summer cruises from Bergen to Nordkapp. In order to stand a chance of competing in this market they would have to adopt completely new strategies.

Nordkapp and the Land of the Midnight Sun; 1939 NFDS poster depicting their *Dronning Maud*, *Prins Olav* and *Princesse Ragnhild* (Bård Kolltveit Collection)

BDS had the *Stella Polaris* built specifically for cruising, below and lower left at Narvik in 1927, lower right at Naerøyfjorden in 1928 (unknown/Anders Beer Wilse/ Norsk Folkemuseum)

BDS

In 1921, BDS restarted their cruises using the former HAPAG cruise liner *Meteor*. On account of the prohibitive Norwegian laws concerning the sale of alcohol, for the first year she sailed under the Red Ensign. This venture became so successful that in 1925 BDS ordered a larger and even more luxurious cruise liner, the *Stella Polaris*.

The Gothenburg built ship (5,208 gross tons) was at the time the largest vessel to have been built in a Scandinavian shipyard and cost 4.5 million Swedish kroner. However, in spite of her size, the diesel powered ship had cabin accommodation for just 200 passengers. On 8th June 1927 the *Stella*

Polaris made the first of a series of summer cruises to Nordkapp and Svalbard. Off season, she cruised mainly in the Mediterranean but in winter she was laid up, though in the winter of 1928/9 the *Stella Polaris* made a 106-day cruise to the Far East and in 1931/2 she did a three and a half month world cruise. From then on the ship settled into a regular pattern of cruises mainly around Northern European waters.

NFDS

With the *Irma* and *Haakon VII* no longer needed on NFDS's North Sea services, they too restarted their popular 14-day cruises from Bergen to Nordkapp in the summer of 1922. Additionally, that summer the *Irma* undertook a three-week cruise to Svalbard. Both ships, however, were not ideal for the up market clientele their owners were keen to attract to Norway. A more luxurious ship was needed, of similar size in order the ship could visit those out of the way and confined places barred to the larger cruise liners.

The solution for NFDS was to purchase the Royal Yacht *Alexandra* in 1925. Built by A. & J. Inglis of Glasgow, she had been launched in 1907 and was intended to be Edward VII's private yacht as well as for informal use by the Royal Family. A graceful vessel, she boasted three masts, a clipper bow complete with bowsprit and two imposing bell topped funnels and measured 1,728 gross tons and 293.4 feet in length. Powered by three Parsons turbines, with a combined output of 4,500 ihp, she had a service speed of between 17 and 18 knots and a voracious appetite for coal.

Renamed *Prins Olav*, its first Nordkapp cruise commenced from Bergen on 5th July 1925. But the ship was to make only two cruises that summer as it was then sent to Fredrikstad M/V for a more substantial refit.

The recession, which set in during the early 1930s, coupled with

The *Prins Olav* was originally the Royal Yacht *Alexandra* built for Edward VII. Purchased by NFDS in 1925 she was photographed that same year at Åndalsnes by Anders Beer Wilse (Norsk Folkemuseum)

increasing competition from foreign 'floating hotels' and her own high operating costs, all conspired together to hammer nails into *Prins Olav*'s coffin as far as cruising was concerned. In 1936/1937 the former Royal Yacht underwent another major facelift, this time for a new career as a Hurtigruten ship. The transformation had to be seen to be believed.

VDS

VDS, however, were not to return to cruising until 1927 when they introduced the local steamer *Mosken*, built in 1924 by Trosvik M/V of Brevik (410 gross tons) on weekly departures from Narvik to Nordkapp. The same year the three major Coastal Express companies, in partnership with the Finnmark Turistforening (Tourist Board) and the travel agencies of Thomas Bennett, Thomas Cook and Berg-Hansen had created Nordkapps Vel to promote tourism in that area. The new company built a landing stage at Hornvika at the foot of the 300 metre high cliffs of Nordkapp, a new pathway up to the plateau together with a pavilion and post office.

By the end of the 1932 season, the *Mosken's* cruises were no longer financially remunerative. However, the publicity for these trips had not been wasted as it had also generated a considerable number of additional bookings by foreign tourists on the Hurtigruten steamers.

Other initiatives included using NFDS's *Tordenskjold*, which in the late 1920s was introduced onto a new Trondheim to Hammerfest freight service. In the summer months this was extended to Honningsvåg for Nordkapp. This became very popular with freelance tourists as a cheap cruise, known as the 'ilgodsruten'. Later, the ship was to have spells of relief work on the Hurtigruten.

It was the Hurtigruten, in the difficult economic climate of the 1930s, which provided the answer to how best to cater for those growing numbers of tourists who wanted to see Norway close up rather from the remoteness of the decks of a 'floating hotel'. Together with the major

Left: The *Mosken* undertook short cruises for VDS from Narvik to Nordkapp between 1927 and 1932 - photographed off Åndalsnes (Anders Beer Wilse/Norsk Folkemuseum/

Below: Hornvika and the only way is up to Nordkapp! (unknown)

travel agencies, they petitioned the Storting's (Norwegian Parliament) Tourism Committee for permission to advertise package holiday round trips on the Hurtigruten.

Significantly, they also requested that in summer vessels could sail north of Magerøy and call at Hornvika to enable passengers to visit Nordkapp. By 1934, with permission granted, the Hurtigruten began to attract passengers in even greater numbers from all over the world. Colourful brochures were produced to publicise the 'new' service and even canvas swimming pools were erected on the promenade decks if space permitted!

The tourist shop at Hornvika, note the VDS flag (unknown)

Svalbard Adventures

TO 1939

It was not until 1933 that the Storting agreed to financially support a regular passenger and mail service to Svalbard during the summer months, for which Troms Fylkes Dampskibsselskap (TFDS) would receive an annual subsidy of 20,000 kroner using their largest and newest steamer, *Lyngen* (489 gross tons; 161.3 feet), built in 1931 by Trondheim M/V.

Posters and luggage sticker advertising Nordkapp and Svalbard, with (bottom left), a view of Longyearbyen (Spitsbergen) taken in 1935 showing the bleak landscape with glacier in background (Bård Kolltveit Collection/UNIS)

Starting from Tromsø calls were made at Bjørnøya, Longyearbyen and Ny-Ålesund to deliver supplies and mail. On the five round trips she made in 1934 she carried 181 passengers, of whom 51 were round-trip tourists, 45 were travelling to or from Svalbard on business and 85 were using the steamer between intermediate ports on the Norwegian coast.

In 1935, 285 passengers were carried, while freight traffic was boosted following the opening of a new fishing base at Ny-Ålesund. Each round trip lasted fourteen days. In both 1938 and 1939 the number of foreign tourists began to show signs of dwindling, reflecting the deteriorating international situation in Europe.

The outbreak of war would put an end to regular Svalbard sailings for another twelve years.

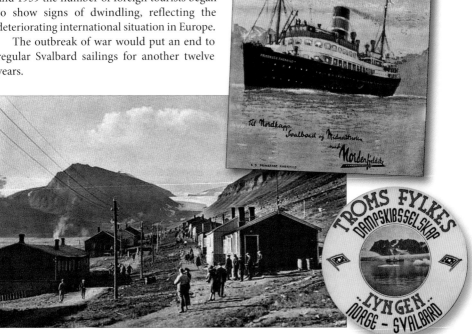

A Daily Hurtigruten

The proposed 1936 contract was to be of six years' duration, with fourteen steamers being required to run it. VDS were to use their *Loften*, *Richard With* and *Finmarken*; NFDS would supply no less than five vessels, *Prinsesse Ragnhild*, *Dronning Maud*, *Sigurd Jarl*, *Kong Harald* and *Erling Jarl*, whilst BDS would provide their *Mira*, *Irma*, *Polarlys* and *Midnatsol* with SDS and ODS contributing the *Sanct Svithun* and *Nordnorge* respectively. In addition, there would also be a number of relief ships most of which had seen service on the route previously. Each week there were to be five departures from Bergen to Kirkenes and one each from Stavanger and Trondheim to Kirkenes, the latter service including a call at Narvik using the *Nordnorge*. This new proposal wasn't greeted with universal acclaim, particularly from those based in Troms and Finnmark, singling out the shortened Trondheim service for criticism. They argued that if this were

Hurtigruten timetable for summer 1935

Northbound	Day	Monday	Tuesday	Wednesday	Thursday	Friday	Saturday	Sunday
Stavanger	0		09.00			09.00		
Haugesund	0		12.00			12.00		
Bergen	0		18.00			18.00		
Bergen	1	19.00	19.00	19.00	19.00	19.00	19.00	22.00
Florø	2	03.00	03.00	03.00	03.00	03.00	03.00	04.30
Måløy	2	06.00	06.00	06.00	06.00	06.00	06.00	07.00
Ålesund	2	12.30	12.30	12.30	12.30	12.30	12.30	13.30
Molde	2	16.00	16.00	16.00	16.00	16.00	16.00	17.00
Kristiansund	2	21.30	21.30	21.30	21.30	21.30	21.30	21.30
Trondheim	3	06.00	06.00	06.00	06.00	06.00	06.00	06.00
Trondheim	3	10.30	10.30	10.30	10.30	10.30	10.30	
Rørvik	3	20.30	21.30	20.30	20.30	21.30	20.30	
Brønnøys'nd	4	00.30	02.00	00.30	00.30	02.00	00.30	
Sandn'sjøen	4	04.00	05.45	04.00	04.00	05.45	04.00	
Nesna	4		07.15					
Indre Kvarøy	4	06.30		06.30	06.30		06.30	
Grønøy	4		11.15			11.15		
Ørnes	4	09.15		09.15				
Bodø	4	12.30	15.00	12.30	12.30	15.00	12.30	
Bodø	4	13.30	16.00	13.30	13.30	16.00	13.30	
Stamsund	4	18.15		18.15	18.15			
Svolvær	4	20.00	21.30	20.00	20.00	21.30	20.00	
Svolvær	4	21.30	23.00	21.30	23.00	23.00	21.30	
Lødingen	5		03.00		03.00	03.00		
Evenskjær	5				04.30			
Melbu	5			00.45			00.45	
Stokmarknes	5	01.15		01.15				
Sortland	5	02.45		02.45			02.45	
Risøyhamn	5	04.30		04.30			04.30	
Harstad	5	06.45	06.00	06.45	06.00	06.00	06.45	
Harstad	5	07.30	07.00	07.30	07.00	07.00	07.30	
Finnsnes	5	11.00	11.00	11.00	11.00	11.00	11.00	
Gibostad	5				11.45			
Tromsø	5	14.30	14.30	14.30	14.30	14.30	14.30	
Tromsø	5	17.00	17.00	17.00	17.00	17.00	17.00	
Skjervøy	5		22.00	21.30	21.30		21.30	
Øksfjord	6	00.00				01.00		
Hammerfest	6	03.30	05.00	03.30	03.30	05.00	03.30	
Hammerfest	6	05.00	06.30	05.00	05.00	06.30	05.00	
Havøysund	6				08.00			
Honningsvåg	6	10.30	12.30	10.30	10.30	12.30	10.30	
Kjøllefjord	6	13.00			13.00		13.00	
Mehamn	6	15.30			15.30		15.30	
Gamvik	6		17.00			17.00		
Berlevåg	6	19.00		16.30	19.00		19.00	
Båtsfjord	6				19.00			
Vardø	6/7	23.00	00.00	23.00	23.00	00.00	23.00	
Vardø	7	00.00	01.00	00.00	00.00	01.00	00.00	
Vadsø	7		05.00		04.00			
Kirkenes	7	04.00	07.00	04.00	06.00	05.00	06.00	

Southbound	Day	Monday	Tuesday	Wednesday	Thursday	Friday	Saturday	Sunday
Kirkenes	7	06.00	08.00	06.00	08.00	06.00	08.00	
Vadsø	7		08.30			08.30		
Vardø	7	12.00	12.45	12.00	12.00	12.45	12.00	
Vardø	7	13.30	14.00	13.30	13.30	14.00	13.30	
Båtsfjord	7				17.00			
Berlevåg	7	18.00		18.00		18.30	18.00	
Gamvik	7		20.30					
Mehamn	7	22.00		22.00	22.00		22.00	
Kjøllefjord	8	00.30		00.30	00.30		00.30	
Honningsvåg	8	04.30	03.00	04.30	04.30	03.00	04.30	
Havøysund	8	06.30						
Hammerfest	8	09.30	08.30	09.30	09.30	08.30	09.30	
Hammerfest	8	11.00	10.00	11.00	11.00	10.00	11.00	
Hasvik	8				14.40			
Øksfjord	8			14.30			14.30	
Skjervøy	8	17.15	16.45			17.15	16.45	
Tromsø	8	22.00	21.30	22.00	22.00	21.30	22.00	
Tromsø	9	00.30	00.30	00.30	00.30	00.30	00.30	
Gibostad	9				03.00			
Finnsnes	9	03.45	04.00	03.45	04.00	04.00	03.45	
Harstad	9	07.30	08.00	07.30	08.00	08.00	07.30	
Harstad	9	08.30	09.00	08.30	09.00	09.00	08.30	
Risøyhamn	9	11.00		11.00			11.00	
Sortland	9	12.45		12.45			12.45	
Stokmarknes	9			14.45			14.45	
Melbu	9	14.45						
Evenskjær	9				10.30			
Lødingen	9		12.30		12.30	12.30		
Svolvær	9	18.00	16.00	18.00	16.00	16.00	18.00	
Svolvær	9	19.30	18.00	19.30	18.00	18.00	19.30	
Stamsund	9	21.30		21.30	20.30			
Bodø	9/10	02.00	23.30	02.00	02.00	23.30	02.00	
Bodø	10	03.00	00.30	03.00	03.00	00.30	03.00	
Ørnes	10		04.00		06.15			
Grønøy	10	06.30					06.30	
Indre Kvarøy	10			08.30		06.30	08.30	
Nesna	10	10.15		10.15				
Sandn'sjøen	10	12.30	10.30	12.30	12.30	10.30	12.30	
Brønnøys'nd	10	16.00	14.30	16.00	16.00	14.30	16.00	
Rørvik	10	20.00	19.00	20.00	20.00	19.00	20.00	
Trondheim	11	06.00	06.00	06.00	06.00	06.00	06.00	
Trondheim	11	17.00	17.00	17.00	17.00	17.00	17.00	17.00
Kristiansund	12	02.00	02.00	02.00	02.00	02.00	02.00	02.00
Molde	12	07.00	07.00	07.00	07.00	07.00	07.00	07.00
Ålesund	12	12.00	12.00	12.00	12.00	12.00	12.00	12.00
Måløy	12	17.30	17.30	17.30	17.30	17.30	17.30	17.30
Florø	12	20.30	20.30	20.30	20.30	20.30	20.30	20.30
Bergen	13	04.30	04.30	04.30	04.30	04.30	04.30	04.30
Bergen	13		11.00			11.00		
Haugesund	13		18.00			18.00		
Stavanger	13		21.00			21.00		

extended to Bergen and the Stavanger service truncated at Bergen you could have a much more balanced service, as well as eliminating the unpopular transfer of cargo, passengers and mail at Trondheim. Stavanger could be served by other means. In fact this is what happened in October 1936 and forms the basis of the service we have today.

During the negotiations for a daily Hurtigruten, both BDS and NFDS had committed themselves to the ordering of new tonnage for the route. NFDS then took the decision, rather than have a new ship, it would be more cost effective to rebuild their cruise steamer, the *Prins Olav*.

More than a few eyebrows were raised at the announcement as many felt that the money would be better spent on a new ship rather than a costly rejuvenation of one that was now approaching 30 years old. The *Prins Olav*'s emergence in the spring of 1937 from this 1.25m kroner rebuild at Trondheim revealed that the ship had been totally transformed. The profile had been totally changed with the superstructure radically altered, the former clipper bow replaced by a raked 'soft nose' bow and the previous two bell topped funnels replaced by one large modern version. The *Prins Olav* now measured 2,147 gross tons (650 dwt), its length increased to 284.3 feet, whilst down below the turbine machinery had been replaced by a 3,500 ihp FMV double compound engine giving her a service speed of 17 knots. Two cargo holds, one forward and one aft had been created giving a refrigerated capacity for 5,000 cases of fresh fish. The accommodation was to a very high standard with the ship now configured as a two class vessel certificated for 450 passengers.

The *Prins Olav*'s Hurtigruten career was to be very short

Below: NFDS pre war suitcase stickers for the *Prinsesse Ragnhild* (Nordkapp and Trondheim) and *Prins Olav* (Nordkap and Spitsbergen) cruises (Bård Kolltveit Collection)

Bottom: The *Prins Olav* on Hurtigruten service 1937 (Bård Kolltveit Collection)

lived, less than three years. In May 1940, having been requisitioned by the Norwegian military it was ordered to set sail to Britain for safety. On 9th June, in company with the hospital ship *Ariadne* and en route to Torshavn (Faroe Islands) about 80 miles west of the Lofotens, the ship suffered a sustained attack from six enemy bombers. Despite increasing speed and constantly changing course the *Prins Olav* was unable to escape. Given the ferocity of the attack, fatalities were very low, just one on the *Prins Olav* and nine on the *Ariadne*. The two crews managed to get away in four lifeboats before being picked up early the following morning by the British destroyer, HMS *Arrow*. Both ships were left to sink. *(see also War – For a Second Time)*

BDS's first new Hurtigruten ship since 1912, the *Nordstjernen* was launched at Fredrikstad in 1936, her powerful lines very evident in these images. Sadly, her career ended in 1954 when she struck rocks in the Raftsundet and sank with the loss of five lives (Fredrikstad Museum Archive/unknown)

Unlike NFDS, Det Bergenske Dampskibsselskab opted for new tonnage in 1936 signed a 1.9m kroner contract with the Fredrikstad Mek Shipyard for its construction. It was to be the company's first new build for the Coastal Express since 1912. The delivery of the *Nordstjernen* (1,919 gross tons; 535 dwt; and 250 feet long) was delayed by a couple of months owing to a small fire on board whilst being fitted out and so it was not until 15th June 1937 that she was formally handed over.

Her engine was a 2,645 ihp FMV double compound 'steam motor' giving a service speed of 16 knots, still coal fired with sufficient bunker capacity to do a complete Bergen – Kirkenes round trip. With a passenger certificate for 590 most of the first class accommodation was to be found on the shelter deck with single and two berth cabins for 63 occupants, whilst third class had room for 92 in two and four berth cabins. All cabins had wash basins with hot and cold running water and the ventilation was provided by the new 'Thermotank' forced air system.

The crew accommodation was substantially improved with comfortable two and three berth cabins. Their working conditions were also enhanced as the ship had electric winches for cargo handling. An indicator of the changing needs of travellers was the provision of space for the carriage of cars. On Monday 21st June 1937, under the command of Captain Michael Kobrø, she made her first Hurtigruten sailing.

The *Nordstjernen* was to remain on Hurtigruten service throughout most of the Second World War until 20th September 1944, when requisitioned by the German Government to assist in the evacuation of Finnmark.

After a major refit in November 1945 the *Nordstjernen* returned to service in February 1946. Eighteen months later in the autumn of 1947 she was sent to the BMV Laksevåg shipyard at Bergen for conversion to oil burning. Despite

now having radar equipment, in September 1948 she still managed to run aground at Brønnøysund in poor visibility, sustaining a four feet long gash in her bow, the repairs being carried out at Rosenberg Shipyard, Stavanger.

This beautiful and well loved ship met an all too early end as on 20th September 1954 at 0210, whilst in the Raftsundet, on her way north from Svolvaer to Stokmarknes with 204 passengers on board, she struck rocks which ripped open her hull, flooding the cargo spaces and boiler room. The sudden ingress of cold water caused the ship's boilers to explode and the ship sank in 160 feet of water within 20 minutes. Five people lost their lives in the incident.

The daily service to Kirkenes from Bergen finally became reality as from 5th December 1939 when BDS introduced their *Ariadne* to the route. Her new career was to last a mere six months. The *Ariadne* (2,028 gross tons; 2,000 dwt and 271 feet long) had been built in 1930 at the Nylands Shipyard, Oslo, for their Trondheim/Bergen to Rotterdam service as a combined cargo and passenger ship.

In April 1940, she was requisitioned by the Norwegian authorities to serve as a troop transport before becoming a hospital ship and marked as such according to international rules. After the German invasion on 8th June, with 54 people on board, she headed west from Tromsø to try to reach Britain. Joined by the *Prins Olav* both ships were suddenly pounced on by six German bombers. Despite the fact that the *Ariadne* was protected by the Geneva

Left: The *Ariadne* (1930) was transferred from the BDS Rotterdam service in December 1939 but only six months later was sunk in June 1940 despite carrying hospital ship markings.

Below left: *Ariadne* seen as new in 1930 at Nyland, Oslo (Hurtigrutemuseet/NMM)

Convention, she was the first to be attacked, receiving direct hits on the bow and funnel casing, and began to sink. Eight were killed in the attack (another later died from their wounds) but the crew and passengers were able to get into two lifeboats meeting up with the survivors of the *Prins Olav* which had also suffered the same fate. Early the following morning, the British destroyer HMS *Arrow* arrived to pick them up. *(see also War – For a Second Time)*

In 1939, Det Vesteraalens Dampskibsselskab ordered a new ship from Moss Værft og Dock, intended for their local Lofoten and Vesterålen services. Delivered in October 1940 the *Hadsel* was a motor ship, with a very smart modern streamlined profile. Although relatively small and of only 406 gross tons and 145 feet in length, she set new standards. A smaller version of the larger local ships, she had two decks, cargo holds fore and aft and some cabin space. Notwithstanding her propulsion unit (a 6-cylinder MAN of 540 bhp, giving a service speed of 11 to 12 knots), it was the high degree of manoeuvrability that her Ka-Me-Wa variable pitch propeller afforded which caught the eye. It was a major advance and well ahead of her contemporaries on coastal services.

In 1940 with NFDS already having lost its top three ships, *Dronning Maud, Prins Olav* and *Prinsesse Ragnhild,* later followed by the loss of the *Sigurd Jarl* and the chartered *Ryfylke* from DSD, the *Hadsel* was chartered from VDS in April 1941, and was to become closely associated with the route throughout the next decade.

The *Hadsel* would serve on the Hurtigruten until September 1941 when the situation in Finnmark became too hazardous. She is recorded as being the last Coastal Express ship to leave Kirkenes. Tromsø now became the northern endpoint and the *Hadsel* served between there and Trondheim until the autumn of 1944 when, because of oil shortages, she was laid up at Mosjøen, near Nesna.

When the Hurtigruten resumed in the summer of 1945, the *Hadsel* was reinstated on the Trondheim - Tromsø leg, but with conditions improving the *Hadsel* became a regular ship on the Kirkenes service. After 1947 she alternated between the Hurtigruten and local coastal routes before finally bowing out at Bergen on 31st March 1950, being replaced by the new *Vesteraalen*.

On 29th January 1958, in bad weather and in an area of strong currents, the *Hadsel* struck rocks off Nakkmean tearing the bottom out of her engine room. Everyone, 20 passengers and 26 crew members managed to get away safely in the lifeboats. The ship then slid off the rocks and sank within three minutes.

The *Hadsel* (1940) was VDS' first diesel engined ship and later in 1941 was chartered to NFDS for Hurtigruten service. Below left, off Trondheim in 1941 and below right departing Stokmarknes in the early 1950s (STFM/Hurtigrutemuseet)

War
FOR A SECOND TIME

The high and heady days of 1930s idealism ended abruptly in the stark reality of 1st September 1939 when Germany invaded Poland. The next six years would markedly affect the whole world including the world of the Hurtigruten. No less than 14 ships on the Coastal Express were to be lost including a number which had replaced others. This is their story.

1939 In early October the Hurtigruten services were reduced by two per week, leaving the *Midnatsol, Richard With, Kong Harald and Sigurd Jarl* laid up. Howls of protest, particularly from businesses based in Northern Norway, left the Ministry of Trade in no doubt as to the popularity of their decision and of the effects it would have, particularly on the fishing industry. By the end of October both the *Midnatsol* and *Kong Harald* were back in service, followed by the *Sigurd Jarl* a month later and the *Richard With* in mid December. The *Dronning Maud* and *Polarlys* spent several weeks making round trips from Trondheim to Tromsø. The *Polarlys* was then requisitioned by the Government and temporarily laid up at Bergen pending conversion into a hospital ship. As a result BDS introduced their *Ariadne* (dating from 1926) on 4th December 1939 to help cover the six weekly round trip service then in force.

The *Nova* was drafted in as an extra ship on the Hurtigruten for the winter of 1939/40, but in June 1940 was ordered to escape to Britain to join the Nortraship (Norwegian Shipping and Trade Mission) fleet. Built by Ateliers et Chantiers de la Seine Maritime, Worms & Cie. of Le Trait, France, for BDS and delivered in July 1925, the ship measured 1,382 gross tons and had an overall length of 246.4 feet. Prior to 1939, the *Nova* was normally to be found on the BDS Bergen to Tórshavn and Reykjavik service. The *Nova*  returned to Norway in the spring of 1945 and was placed on the company's

Photographs of the *Nova* are difficult to source; these both date from 1925, including her launching for BDS at Ateliers et Chantiers de la Seine Maritime, France (unknown)

Bergen to Rotterdam and Antwerp services. En route from Antwerp to Stavanger on 19th December 1949 she stranded off Jæren and was declared a constructive total loss, being scrapped where she lay.

1940 Norway's neutrality went by the board as soon as the war started. The unthinkable happened when on 9th April the country was invaded by Germany and the King and Parliament had to flee. Bergen was under siege, with three Hurtigruten steamers (*Polarlys*, *Mira* and *Lofoten*) trapped at the port. The *Mira* became an accommodation vessel, the *Polarlys* likewise, having the ignominy of being renamed *Satan*, thankfully soon shortened to *Tan* before reverting back to her original name by the end of the year.

The first Coastal Express casualty of the war was the *Sigurd Jarl*, which had been operating in the Ålesund, Bolsøy and Molde region unloading food supplies when she was subjected to attacks by German planes, firstly on 21st April and then again two days later. This time she was sunk in shallow water in Vågseterbukta, near Molde, thankfully without loss of life. It was not until November 1942 that the ship was raised. NFDS considered putting her back in service but the ship was beyond economic repair.

Only eight days later there was a further casualty on 1st May 1940. As the *Dronning Maud* approached the berth at Føldvik, Gratangen (Troms) and despite clearly displaying Red Cross signals and flags she was attacked by 3 German aircraft. Two bombs hit the forward hold and another crashed in between the bridge and funnel. The *Dronning Maud* immediately caught fire with 18 people being killed and 31 wounded in the attack. The burning

The *Dronning Maud* on fire off Føldvik, Gratangen on 1st May 1940 (unknown)

The *Dronning Maud's* engine room where many of the crew died (Fredrikstad Mek Archive)

wreck was towed away from the wooden pier before finally running aground and rolling over.

Despite stiff opposition from both Norwegian and British Armed Forces the German Army was gradually gaining ground so that by May the southern terminus for the Hurtigruten was now at Bodø.

At that time the *Finmarken,* under the command of Captain Falck, was involved with troop transports to Nordfjord (Bodø). On the night of 7th May, painted in wartime grey, she made an audacious attempt under the cover of fog to escape to the Shetlands with just a crew of seven, but her fuel reserves were too low and she only got as far as Stokmarknes.

Worse was to come on May 10th, when Det Ofotens Dampskibsselskab's *Nordnorge* was lost. The ship had continued in Hurtigruten service until 7th May 1940 when she was requisitioned and her crew replaced with German naval personnel. Two days later, the *Nordnorge* went north from Trondheim with troops to Hemnesberget, close to Mo i Rana. She had been noted off Rørvik and this news was quickly passed on to the British Military Command. She came under fire as she disembarked her troops and with the Germans not wanting the ship to fall into the hands of the Allies, the sea cocks were opened and grenades thrown into her bilges, leaving her to sink. At 19.30 two British destroyers (HMS *Carlisle* and HMS *Zulu*) appeared and after almost simultaneous explosions, the *Nordnorge* drifted away from the quayside and sank in deep water.

By 6th June it was clear that Norway would have to capitulate. For this eventuality, Ole Siem, Shipping Director for Free Norway (and also Chairman of VDS) had prepared a plan to send to Scotland or Shetland all steamers not essential for the maintenance of the Coastal Express. Each ship would need to take on coal and provisions for at least ten days' sailing.

Overnight, on 7th/8th June, various ships slipped out of their hiding places and steamed westwards to Britain. Among them was the *Finmarken,*

A Schrøder postcard of the
Finmarken taken before the
war (Author's Collection)

which had sailed from Hekkingen. She was somewhere between 100 and 150 miles from the Norwegian coast when she was spotted by a German bomber which managed to score a hit on one of her lifeboats. Such was the force of the explosion that it sprang a leak in her hull. Making water, she was forced to turn back.

The loss of three ships in 17 days had already been acutely felt, but on 9th June 1940, less than a month later, came a double whammy.

Both the *Prins Olav* and *Ariadne* were to have very short careers on the Hurtigruten, as whilst not new ships they had not come onto the Coastal Express until 1937 and 1939 respectively. The *Prins Olav* had been requisitioned in May 1940 by the Norwegian military to assist in the evacuation of Helgeland and then later to convey troops from Kirkenes to Gratangen (north of Tromsø). The ship received fresh orders on June 7th to sail to Britain and headed to Hammerfest for bunkering. Likewise the

The *Prins Olav* northbound off
the Seven Sisters approaching
Sandnessjøen in 1937
(unknown)

An aerial shot of the *Prins Olav* departing Trondheim with Munkholmen in the background in happier days (unknown)

Ariadne previously requisitioned by the Norwegian authorities to serve as a hospital ship and marked as such according to international rules. On 8th June with 54 people on board she headed west from Tromsø to try to reach Britain. The next day the two ships joined up and set course for Torshavn in the Faroe Islands. That evening around 22.30 and 80 miles west of the Lofotens both ships suffered a sustained attack from six enemy bombers. Despite the fact that the *Ariadne* was protected by the Geneva Convention, she was the first to be attacked receiving direct hits on the bow and funnel casing and began to sink. Eight were killed in the attack but the crew and passengers were able to get into lifeboats. The *Prins Olav* with its superior speed tried to escape through repeated course changes but failed to do so. Given the ferocity of the attack, fatalities were very low with just one on the *Prins Olav*. Four lifeboats, two from each steamer, managed to link together. As the lifeboats from the *Prins Olav* were larger than the *Ariadne's*, survivors were exchanged between them, to improve buoyancy and reduce crowding. The cook from the *Ariadne*, severely injured, died shortly afterwards.

At about 03.00 on 10th June, the lifeboats were intercepted by the British destroyer HMS *Arrow* and the survivors were taken to Scapa Flow. The same day the capitulation of Norway officially took place, when German storm troopers entered Tromsø.

Hurtigruten sailings did not properly resume until early July 1940. There was some optimism that the tonnage situation would soon be eased as that summer, with the NFDS fleet now quite depleted, they managed to purchase the modern Copenhagen to Rønne overnight ferry, *Bornholm* to help fill the gap. However, it would be another two years before she was ready to enter service as the *Ragnvald Jarl*. VDS had the luxury of a new build, the *Hadsel*, which was delivered in October 1940, but straight away it was chartered to NFDS as their needs were greatest. Det Nordlandske Dampskipsselskap (NDS) also purchased a ship from Sweden, the *Hansa*, which became their *Skjerstad* entering service in December 1940.

After a relative lull in events, war losses again hit the Coastal Express on 23rd October 1940, when the *Princesse Ragnhild* became the first Hurtigruten steamer to be lost while on an ordinary service. She already had a lucky escape on 9th April 1940 at Ålesund when she had managed to hide in the nearby Hjørundfjorden, whilst several German planes tried to sink her. But her luck ran out when northbound from Bodø to Svolvaer, off Landegøde, a powerful explosion ripped open her keel. Within a few minutes the ship had sunk. On board were least 400 passengers and a crew of 50. Two small coasters were in the vicinity and rescued 156 persons, but over 300 perished. The precise cause was a mystery until many years later when it was revealed that her attacker was the British submarine HMS *Taku*.

Hurtigruten Services - autumn/winter 1940/1

NORTHBOUND						SOUTHBOUND				
1	2	3	4	Day		Day	1	2	3	4
12.00		12.00		1	Bergen	16	07.00	07.00		
20.30		20.30			Florø		22.30	22.30		
23.00		23.00			Måløy		19.00	19.00		
06.00		06.00		2	Måløy					
12.00		12.00			Ålesund		13.00	13.00		
19.30		19.30			Kristiansund	15	06.00	06.00		
06.00		06.00		3	Trondheim		20.00	20.00		
23.00	23.00	23.00	23.00		Trondheim	14	00.00	00.00	00.00	00.00
05.00	05.00			4	Stokksund			17.00		17.00
			06.30		Bessaker					
12.00	12.00	12.00	12.00		Rørvik		11.00	11.00	11.00	11.00
17.00	17.00	17.00	17.00		Brønnøysund		06.00	06.00	06.00	06.00
22.30	22.30	22.30	22.30		Sandnessjøen	13	01.30	01.30	01.30	01.30
		00.15		5	Nesna					23.30
01.30	01.30				Indre Kvarøy		21.30	21.30		
		05.00			Grønøy		18.30			
04.30	04.30		04.30		Ørnes			18.30	18.30	18.30
09.00	09.00	09.00	09.00		Bodø		14.30	14.30	14.30	14.30
10.00	10.00	10.00	10.00		Bodø		14.00	14.00	14.00	14.00
16.00	16.00		16.00		Stamsund		08.30	08.30	08.30	08.30
18.00	18.00	16.00	18.00		Svolvær		06.00	06.00	06.00	06.00
20.00	20.00	17.00	20.00		Svolvær		04.30	04.30	04.30	04.30
		23.30			Narvik					
		00.30		6	Narvik					
		04.00			Lødingen					
23.30					Melbu		01.00	01.00		
	23.30		23.30		Stokmarknes	12			01.00	01.00
01.30	01.30		01.30		Sortland		23.00	23.00	23.00	23.00
04.00	04.00		04.00		Risøyhamn		21.00	21.00	21.00	21.00
07.00	07.00	07.00	07.00		Harstad		18.00	18.00	18.00	18.00
08.00	08.00	08.00	08.00		Harstad		16.00	16.00	16.00	16.00
12.30	12.30	12.30	12.30		Finnsnes		11.30	11.30	11.30	121.30
16.00	16.00	16.00	16.00		Tromsø		08.00	08.00	08.00	08.00
19.00	19.00	19.00	19.00		Tromsø	11	04.00	04.00	04.00	04.00
00.30	00.30		00.30	7	Skjervøy		22.00	22.00		22.00
05.00		05.00			Øksfjord		18.00		18.00	
09.00	09.00	09.00	09.00		Hammerfest		14.30	14.30	14.30	14.30
11.00	11.00	11.00	11.00		Hammerfest		13.00	13.00	13.00	13.00
					Havøysund		09.30			09.30
18.00	18.00	18.00	18.00		Honningsvåg		06.30	06.30	06.30	06.30
21.00	21.00	21.00			Kjøllefjord	10	02.00	02.00	02.00	
	23.30	23.30	23.00		Mehamn		23.00			23.00
			00.30	8	Gamvik			21.30		21.30
	03.30	03.30	03.30		Berlevåg		19.00	19.00	19.00	19.00
05.00					Båtsfjord		16.00	16.00	16.00	16.00
09.00	09.00	09.00	09.00		Vardø		11.00	11.00	11.00	11.00
10.30	10.30	10.30	10.30		Vardø		09.00	09.00	09.00	09.00
14.30	14.30	14.30	14.30		Vadsø		05.00	05.00	05.00	05.00
15.30	15.30	15.30	15.30		Vadsø		04.30	04.30	04.30	04.30
18.00	18.00	18.00	18.00		Kirkenes	9	02.00	02.00	02.00	02.00

Departures:- Bergen - Mondays and Thursdays; Trondheim - Mondays, Wednesdays, Fridays, Saturdays
Departures from Kirkenes - Tuesdays, Thursdays, Fridays and Sundays

During 1940/1 the Hurtigruten service was reduced to four weekly trips, with only two south of Trondheim

The *Prinsesse Ragnhild* seen here at Melbu, was the first Hurtigruten steamer to be lost in ordinary service, on 23rd October 1940 (Anders Beer Wilse/Norsk Folkemuseum)

1941 In January 1941, daily Hurtigruten sailings between Trondheim and Hammerfest were resumed as both the *Polarlys* and *Mira* had been returned to service. Whilst there were only two extended services to Bergen each week, Kirkenes fared better with a near daily service.

With the sinking of the *Prinsesse Ragnhild*, NFDS had now lost four of its five Coastal Express ships vessels in just over a year. They now chartered the *Ryfylke* from their fellow Hurtigruten partner, Det Stavangerske Dampskibsselskab (DSD).

The *Ryfylke* was not new, having been built in 1917 for the East Asian Kompagniet at Copenhagen as the *St. Croix* for inter-island services in the West Indies, subsequently being passed on to the London-based United Baltic Corporation, who renamed her *Baltriger* and later sold her in September 1931 to DSD for £11,000.

Originally measuring 1,143 gross tons and 220 feet in length, the ship had plenty of cargo space but limited passenger cabins. On being purchased she was renamed *Ryfylke* and underwent a thorough refit, including conversion to oil firing. Normally on the Stavanger to Oslo express service, she was requisitioned by the Germans in early 1940 for use as an accommodation ship in Stavanger before being released in November 1940, whereupon SDS immediately leased the ship to NFDS for Hurtigruten service.

It was a short and unhappy Hurtigruten career. On her first sailing northwards from Trondheim she grounded near Ørland. Only two round trips later on 5th February 1941, just north of Måløy off Stad, she was sighted by the British submarine, HMS *Sealion*, which came in so close to her that those on board could read its number clearly. A warning shot was fired across her bows. Once the *Ryfylke* had lost way, the British commander ordered her crew to lower the boats and abandon ship. Having done so, the submarine promptly sent the *Ryfylke* to the bottom with 25 rounds of

The *Ryfylke* dated from 1917 and only came to DSD in 1931. In November 1940 the ship was leased to NFDS to cover their war losses on the Hurtigruten, but was sunk just two months later (DSD/Postal)

cannon fire. All passengers and crew passengers eventually found safety.

Just a month later early on the morning of 4th March 1941, the *Mira* was northbound on her way to Harstad from Svolvær when she was intercepted by the British destroyer HMS *Bedouin* at the entrance to the Raftsundet. A warning shot was fired across *Mira*'s bows, but she continued at full speed. A second shot, fired into the forward part of her hull, failed to produce any response from those on her bridge. The inevitable then happened and the destroyer let fly a whole volley of shots, one of which struck the ship just below her funnel, rupturing vital pipework. Coming to a stop, she was then evacuated and once her lifeboats were clear the destroyer fired another salvo sending the *Mira* to the bottom. Seven people died as a result of this incident. The wounded were taken by HMS *Bedouin* to Aberdeen for hospital treatment. It transpired later that a German officer had run up to the bridge and held the *Mira*'s captain at gunpoint to ensure he didn't obey the destroyer's commands.

Operating the Hurtigruten in wartime was not easy, as in an attempt to

A Mittet postcard dating from the 1930s of the *Mira* which was sunk by HMS *Bedouin* on 4th March 1941

confuse German convoys many lighthouses, channel markers and lighted buoys had been deliberately put out of action. As a result, sailings were restricted to daylight hours as was cargo handling so as not to contravene the blackout regulations. It was also deemed prudent that when crossing open stretches of water such as the Lopphavet, Hustadvika or Stadhavet ships should do so in convoys although this led to some Hurtigruten vessels being used as 'shields' in case of attack from Allied aircraft.

On 30th August 1941 the *Midnatsol* was en route from Hammerfest to Tromsø and approaching Øksfjord. It was a fine, sunny afternoon with a calm sea and a German convoy had been observed approaching from the opposite direction. At 15.30 there was a violent explosion and one of the supply ships, the *Donau*, was enveloped in smoke. This was followed by a second explosion as the ship following her, the *Bahía Laura*, was also torpedoed and caught fire. The *Midnatsol*, barely half a mile away, stopped and lowered all four of her lifeboats. The sea was filled with bodies and wreckage and it was difficult for the boats to force a passage through to reach survivors. The *Midnatsol* rescued around 200 survivors and unconfirmed reports suggested that between 1,000 and 2,000 others were killed or drowned. The attack was presumed to have come from a British or Russian submarine.

The 13th September 1941 was another day of double losses on the Coastal Express, though this time it was in separate incidents.

The first sinking on this day was off the Nordland coast. After the loss of the *Nordnorge* on 1st April 1940, Det Ofotens Dampskibsselskab had been using the smaller *Barøy* on the Hurtigruten from Trondheim to Narvik. She had been built by the Trondheim Mek Shipyard in 1929 for the ODS route from Narvik to Svolvaer via Lødingen. She was a classic local routes boat of 424 gross tons (234 dwt) and 143 feet in length, with two holds and a passenger certificate for 200.

ODS's *Barøy* (1929) was a regular relief vessel on the Coastal Express. Pictured here at Lødingen in 1930 by Anders Beer Wilse, with the *Dryo* in the background, she became a victim of war when mistakenly sunk by allied aircraft in 1941 (Norsk Folkemuseum)

A Norwegian stamp depicting the sinking of the *Barøy* by an allied torpedo in 1941

Involved in trooping duties in the first phases of the war, by August 1941 the *Barøy* was back on the Coastal Express again when the fifth weekly departure from Trondheim was reinstated. On the morning of 13th September 1941 at 03.50 on her way north from Skutvik towards Tranøy on the Nordland coast, she was hit on the port side by a torpedo from a British aircraft operating from HMS *Victorious*. The ship sank almost immediately. Unconfirmed figures suggest that there were 68 Norwegian and 37 German passengers together with 26 crew on board. Whilst there were no actual witnesses to the incident, it was fortunate that the steamship *Skjerstad* was nearby and observing unusual flotsam in the dark managed to stop and pick up 19 survivors. Later that day a BBC broadcast from London stated that a 'large transport ship' had been bombed and sunk off Nordland. It would seem that the *Barøy* had been mistaken for another vessel which had been in the area a few hours before.

The second incident concerned one of the Hurtigruten's most loved ships and happened a few hours later. The *Richard With,* with nearly 40 years of service under the belt, was southbound from Honningsvåg en route to Hammerfest. The ship had arrived the previous day but was ordered not to proceed any further in the direction of Kirkenes because of high levels of submarine activity. Around 11.00 whilst passing Rolvsøya, the ship was rocked by an explosion and immediately began to sink stern first. Only able to launch one lifeboat, passengers and crew just had to grab anything buoyant they could find. Eye witness accounts say that she sank within 50 seconds.

Fortunately the fishing vessel *Skolpen* was close by and managed to pick up 32 survivors. Officially 65 passengers and 28 crew lost their lives but it is likely that this is an underestimate. The blame for this was put on a marauding Russian submarine, but years later it was revealed the perpetrator was the British submarine HMS *Tigris*.

When news of the sinking reached the VDS head office in Stokmarknes an emergency meeting of directors was held. They decided to suspend all

The *Richard With* at full speed – she was sunk by HMS *Tigris* on 13th September 1941 (unknown)

The *Vesteraalen* seen here in a Mittet postcard from 1933 was also sunk by a submarine, this time by the Russian SHCH-402

Hurtigruten services north of Hammerfest as the risk for large steamers was now too great. A substitute service, (the 'Erstatningshurtigruten') to Kirkenes would be set up using smaller vessels until matters improved – which they didn't. *(see separate article)*

As a temporary measure Finnmarkens Fylkesrederi (FFR) offered to provide a service using the *Tanahorn* (built 1910, 326 gross tons) and the *Alta* (ex *Alten* built 1906). The last Hurtigruten steamer to sail from Kirkenes was the *Hadsel*, an ODS ship under charter to NFDS. The *Lofoten* remained at Mehamn until 23rd September 1941 and so technically was the last Hurtigruten steamer to leave the area.

There was a subsequent change of plan and all normal Hurtigruten sailings were now to be terminated at Tromsø. From there to Skjervøy, Øksfjord and Hammerfest, the *Vesteraalen* was rostered to provide a fast connecting shuttle service. It was a high risk decision as it involved crossing the Lopphavet.

On 17th October 1941 the *Vesteraalen* was to go the same way as the *Richard With*. With 39 passengers on board, the ship had safely arrived at Skjervøy having left Tromsø earlier that afternoon and was now closing in on Øksfjord. Around 15.30 there was a loud explosion and the ship broke in two, the bow sinking almost immediately and the rest of the ship doing so about thirty seconds later. The disaster was witnessed by Sverre Isaksen who was working on the roof of his house in the nearby village of Samuelsnes in Nuvafjorden. He was certain that he saw the wake of something moving towards her. Then came the explosion. It took him and his stepfather about thirty minutes to row their boat to the scene of the *Vesteraalen's* sinking. There were only seven survivors, one of them being Ragnar Alvær, the *Vesteraalen's* pilot, whilst 60 others lost their lives. The death toll was made worse by the fact that nearly everyone was below decks at the time of the attack. It was later confirmed that the *Vesteraalen* had been torpedoed by the Russian submarine SHCH-402.

There were, thankfully, to be no more Coastal Express losses for another 15 months.

The NDS vessel *Skjerstad* had the unenviable task of transporting teachers to the infamous Todt labour camp near Kirkenes in April 1942 (Mike Bent)

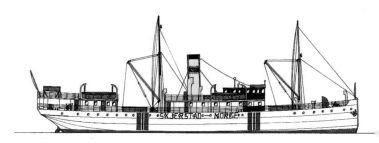

1942 Under the occupying powers many sections of Norwegian society were subjected to harassment and persecution if they did not conform to doctrines and edicts. Academics, teachers, clergy and the press in particular were singled out and many were arrested. Among the decrees passed was one making it compulsory for teachers to join the Nazi-controlled Lærersamband (Teachers' Union). Out of Norway's 14,000 schoolteachers, some 12,000 declared in writing that they would have absolutely nothing to do with such an organisation. The upshot was the arrest of many of them.

On Sunday 12th April 1942, 498 arrested teachers were brought on board the NDS vessel *Skjerstad* (passenger certificate 250) under armed guard. They sailed north for Kirkenes, where for part of the journey the *Skjerstad* acted as a shield for the German transport ship *Santos*. With numerous delays along the way and after enduring inhuman conditions for nearly 17 days the prisoners were finally landed. Their reward would be to work at one of the infamous Organisation Todt camps scattered around Festning (Fortress) Kirkenes. The teachers, physically exhausted, sick, and half-starved, were housed in barracks together with Russian prisoners of war and put to heavy manual labour. News of this spread rapidly throughout the country with the consequent tide of anger and wave of protests so great that six months later the teachers were released and sent south.

There was a sequel to this story when, in the summer of 1950, many of the teachers who in 1942 had been arrested and forcibly sent to Kirkenes returned to do the same journey in the same boat, this time as an act of pilgrimage.

Matters began to improve when in July 1942 the new NFDS ship *Sigurd Jarl* finally entered service over a year late owing to delays in obtaining materials.

In 1939, NFDS had ordered a new cargo ship for their Bergen, London and Mediterranean Sea service, but with war losses it was decided in November 1940 to have this completed as a vessel suitable for the Hurtigruten. The hull and machinery were to remain the same. Difficulties in obtaining construction materials meant that it was not until July 1942 that it was finally delivered from the Fredrikstad Mek Shipyard.

The *Sigurd Jarl* was the largest Hurtigruten ship to date, of 2,335 gross tons, with a high load capacity of 1,200 dwt and 289.5 feet in length, two full length decks and cabins for 63 passengers in first class and 120 in third class, all placed amidships. Crew accommodation was fore and aft. However, it was still very much a converted freighter. The *Sigurd Jarl* was powered by a coal-fired 239 ihp Fredrikstad 'steam motor', which produced a service speed of

14 knots. Although rather slower than other Hurtigruten steamers built between the wars, the ship was ideal for the service at this period, when capacity was far more important than speed. Costing NFDS 2,557,000 kroner and only in service for four months, the vessel was requisitioned and used for the next two years as a recreation ship for the occupying forces.

The *Sigurd Jarl*, delivered for NFDS in 1942, is seen here with her wartime hull markings (Hurtigrutemuseet)

In the autumn of 1944 the *Sigurd Jarl* resumed on the Coastal Express service between Trondheim and Tromsø, whilst by May 1945 it was a regular performer on the Lofoten to Finnmark sector.

In November 1947, after grounding near Florø, she was sent to her builders for a refit which included her boilers being converted to oil firing. A repeat of the same grounding feat on 9th August 1950, near Bygnes in Vesterålen, found the ship being stuck on the sandy bottom for nearly four days before being refloated.

The *Sigurd Jarl* was a very useful Hurtigruten steamer in that it had cavernous holds; however, this was double-edged. On one occasion the ship spent a whole day loading fish at Svolvær, but when on arrival at Trondheim there was insufficient space in the transit sheds for such a cargo she had to be diverted to Stavanger. This was ok when there was still a great deal of slack in the schedules but with new ships arriving on the Hurtigruten the sedate 13

A Schrøder post war picture of the *Sigurd Jarl* taken off Trondheim in 1947 (STFM)

or 14 knots service speed was becoming an issue. When NFDS ordered a replacement from Trondheim Mek in February 1959 the end was near.

The *Sigurd Jarl's* last sailing on the Hurtigruten was northbound on Sunday 12th June 1960 from the Brattøra Quay, Trondheim, after which it was replaced by the new build *Harald Jarl*. After unloading, the ship went to Mjellem & Karlsen in Bergen for a quick refit and renaming as the *Xin Hua* before being formally handed over to the People's Republic of China. Transferred to the China Ocean Shipping Company in 1974, nothing is known as to the ship's subsequent career though it is said to have been observed in Dalian Xiangang region as late as 1990.

The other 'new' NFDS ship the *Ragnvald Jarl* (ex *Bornholm*) entered service on 30th October 1942. It too was comparatively slow, which in post war years was to become a major handicap.

The war had badly decimated the NFDS Coastal Express fleet, but the company managed to purchase the Danish overnight motor ship *Bornholm*, owned by Bornholm Dampskipsaktieselskapet, Rønne as a replacement. The *Bornholm* dated from 1930 and had been built by Burmeister & Wain, Copenhagen. In September 1940, the ship was sent to the Fredrikstad Mek Shipyard to be made more suitable for the Hurtigruten service. After rebuilding she now measured 1,789 gross tons (570 dwt), with a length of 236 feet. The ship's 6-cylinder 1,600 bhp Burmeister & Wain diesel engine enabled a 13 knots service speed.

Difficulties in obtaining materials meant that it was not until October 1942 that the conversion was complete. The ship, now named *Ragnvald Jarl*, reappeared as a compact, simple and modern addition to the Coastal Express, sailing between Trondheim and Tromsø. After nearly two years on the route,

A post war NFDS postcard of the *Ragnvald Jarl*, seen here rounding Nordkapp, with (inset) an early 1950's view of the *Ragnvald Jarl* loading at Hammerfest. Note the cart being pulled by a Fjord horse (Bård Kolltveit Collection)

on 21st September 1944 the vessel was requisitioned by German authorities as a transport ship for the wounded during the evacuation of Finnmark.

On 6th July 1945 the *Ragnvald Jarl* was ready, together with the *Nordstjernen*, *Lofoten* and *Sigurd Jarl* to begin service on the post war Coastal Express. Whilst the *Ragnald Jarl* had many good qualities, speed and manoeuvring ability were not amongst them! With new boats having been delivered from both Italy and Denmark in the period 1949 – 1952, and further new tonnage planned, the decision was taken to sell her.

In February 1956, the ship was renamed *Harald Jarl* and put up for sale. Sold in July 1956 for 3m kroner to Lübeck Linie GmbH, Germany, it was renamed *Nordland* for a new cruising role, around the Baltic Sea and Norwegian coastline.

In 1970, now forty years old, the ship was sold to Karelia Lines O/Y, Helsinki for further cruising and renamed *Suvetar*. In April 1974 the ship was scrapped at Bilbao.

1943 For almost two years no further Hurtigruten ships had been lost through military action but on the last day of September, disaster! On Thursday 30th September 1943 the *Sanct Svithun* departed southbound from Ålesund into a strong southwest wind and heavy sea forcing the ship to reduce speed. At 18.45, off Kjerringa, six planes swept low across her, dropping five or six bombs and strafing the decks with machine gunfire. Captain Alshager rang down for the engine to be stopped, but as he did so a bomb landed close to the funnel, wrecking the telegraph wiring and destroying the main electricity switchboard, plunging the interior of the ship into darkness.

The *Sanct Svithun* was immediately ablaze amidships; so fierce was the heat that the lifeboat davits melted. However, with the engine still running and steering gear undamaged, Captain Alshager ordered the helmsman to steer for land, almost making it but fetching up on Kobbeholmen, a rocky islet, a couple of hundred metres from the shore, her bows held fast. Olav Iversen, a deckhand, crawled along a steel hawser, which was hanging slack with the waves breaking over it. He took a lightweight hauling line, which in turn was attached to a ten-inch thick manila hawser with a large eye, which he was able to loop over a rock. This escape route was extremely difficult as the hawser would change from taut to slack in an instant. In all, 21 people crossed to safety by this means. Of the 121 people known to have been on board 41 lost their lives including 19 members of the crew.

The *Sanct Svithun* (below left) in peacetime service and (below right) the wreck of the DSD ship being pounded by the waves at Kobbeholmen off Ervik on 30th September 1943 (unknown)

The stamp issued by the Norwegian Post Office commemorating the sinking of the *Sanct Svithun*

The ship was beyond salvaging and some days later she slid off the rocks, floated out into deeper water and sank. Her bell was salvaged and placed in Ervik Church as a memorial to the events of that night. The inscription reads:

"To the people of Ervik in appreciation of the rescue of human lives when s/s '*Sanct Svithun*' went down on 30th September, 1943".

1944 On Sunday 12th February 1944, after making her usual calls at Florø, Måløy and Ålesund, the BDS vessel *Irma* proceeded across the Hustadvika at full speed. On board were 47 passengers and 46 crew members.

A tremendous explosion ripped the bows off the ship, her foremast crashing down across her bridge. A second explosion came from the vicinity of the engine room and the *Irma* heeled over to port, sinking fast. There was no time to launch the lifeboats but the six life rafts floated to the surface as she went down. The cargo ship *Henry* was nearby and managed to lower two lifeboats before she too was torpedoed and sunk.

The inquest into the loss of *Irma* was held in Bergen on 24th April 1944. Both she and *Henry* had been carrying lights to illuminate their neutrality markings. 36 crew and 25 passengers were killed and only 25 survived.

Subsequently it was revealed that the *Irma* had been spotted by two Shetland based, Norwegian crewed MTBs (MTB 653 and MTB 627) with orders to sink any cargo shipping in that area. Why they didn't observe their neutrality markings is not understood.

Thankfully this would the last loss the Hurtigruten would suffer during the conflict.

Another stamp in the series depicting shipping losses issued by the Norwegian Post Office, this time remembering the *Irma* torpedoed in 1944

Two months later at 08.40 on 20th April 1944 Bergen was rocked by a massive explosion after a cargo of dynamite on board the Dutch ammunition ship *Voorbode* erupted, killing 23 people and injuring many more. The ship had berthed without permission and was not flying a red flag to indicate that she was carrying a dangerous cargo, in this case 120 tons of dynamite.

Moored next to the *Voorbode* was the Hurtigruten ship *Kong Sverre*, the name having been changed from *Kong Haakon* in 1942 on the orders of Quisling's Nasjonal Samling (Quisling's Government). She was badly damaged and had to go to the SDS shipyard in Stavanger for repairs. She did not return to Coastal Express service until January 1946.

As a result of the *Voorbode* incident, DSD drafted in the elderly *Christiania* as a replacement for the *Kong Sverre (Kong Haakon)* on the Hurtigruten. Dating from 1895 the *Christiania* had been built as a two funnelled steamer at Helsingør for Kristiania Kyst Dampskibsselskap, for service between Oslo and Bergen. Of 646 gross tons and 180 feet long, her 1,100 ihp triple expansion engine gave her a service speed of 12 knots.

In 1898 she was sold to DSD who had her repaired at the Nyland Shipyard in Oslo and repainted in their distinctive funnel colours of three red rings on black before resuming service on the same route as before. Managing to go aground and sink off Jomfruland, south of Sandefjord, on 17th February 1926 she was raised, repaired and modernised at Stavanger.

In the spring of 1944, now with only one funnel, she joined the wartime

The *Christiania* (1895) was drafted onto the Hurtigruten by DSD in 1944 to help cover war losses. She is photographed in earlier times at speed off Grimstad in 1934 by Anders Beer Wilse (Norsk Folkemuseum)

Coastal Express. It was to be a very short stint as on 19th October 1944 she struck a mine near Ålesund and was laid up. She returned to the Hurtigruten for the summer of 1945 and then reappeared in 1947 and 1948 on charter to NFDS when their *Sigurd Jarl* ran aground off Florø and was out of action for five months. After 53 years of service, she was laid up in August 1952 and sold for scrapping that November at Michael Brecker & Co.'s scrap yard in Granton, Scotland.

From 20th June 1944 there were to be five Hurtigruten services per week, two from Bergen and three from Trondheim, all terminating at Tromsø. The service had inevitably become less and less reliable as the fortunes of war changed in Finnmark.

The retreat from Finnmark began to gain momentum from the end of the summer. The *Nordstjernen*, which had already been requisitioned for trooping duties (her Norwegian crew paid off) was ordered on 20th September to Øst-Finnmark. The following day the *Ragnvald Jarl* was requisitioned, which was a mistake since there was a severe shortage of diesel fuel in Norway. The ship was laid up at once. The *Lofoten* was requisitioned on 21st October and adapted into a floating field hospital. She was allowed to retain her Norwegian crew.

Final Days

Although the war in the far north was over, further south, shipping still ran the gauntlet of frequent Allied attacks. On 4th October 1944 there was a massive air raid on the submarine depot at Bergen. Many were killed, including 60 children at a school not far from the installation. The *Kong Harald* which was being overhauled at Bergens Mek Shipyard sustained some damage, whilst the *Polarlys*, taking on bunkers, came under machine gun fire.

On 19th October, the *Christiania* struck a mine in the Åramsundet. Fortunately there were no casualties, but the ship was badly damaged and she had to be run aground in Hjørundfjorden, near Ålesund, remaining there until the war was over.

1945 The New Year of 1945 brought with it further severe coal and oil shortages and one steamer after another had to be laid up. The first victims of the oil fuel crisis had been *Ragnvald Jarl* and *Hadsel*, in the previous autumn. By February 1945 the *Kong Sverre (Kong Haakon)* had been repaired, but only sufficient coal could be scraped together for her to sail from the DSD shipyard in Stavanger to Vatlandsvågan, where she was laid up.

By March, the fuel crisis meant that the Hurtigruten had only weekly departures in each direction using the three ships still operational, the *Sigurd Jarl*, *Lofoten* and *Finmarken;* alternate weeks from Trondheim to Tromsø by the VDS vessels and one every three weeks by the *Sigurd Jarl* from Bergen.

On 7th May the occupying forces surrendered and, amidst great rejoicing, the rightful Norwegian administrative and political organisations assumed responsibility for the day-to-day running of the country once again. Crown Prince Olav returned from London on 13th May, accompanied by most of the members of the exiled Norwegian Government. There were even greater celebrations when King Haakon returned to the capital on 7th June.

Looking forward to happier days, the *Ragnvald Jarl* arriving at Bergen in the early 1950s (Bruce Peter Collection)

Already, the Hurtigruten companies were making plans for revival and recovery once peace eventually returned to Europe.

Erstatnings-hurtigruten

(THE COMPENSATION OR REPLACEMENT ROUTE)

The loss of the *Richard With* in 1941 had highlighted just how dangerous it was for Hurtigruten vessels to sail between Tromsø and Kirkenes and that an alternative means was needed. With the co-operation of the three main Hurtigruten companies, (VDS, BDS and NFDS) the Ministry and German Military agreed to a 'replacement service' using smaller vessels, particularly those which had a reasonable hold capacity.

The Erstatningshurtigruten, to give it its official title, initially operated between Vadsø and Hammerfest (later extended to Tromsø). For the short crossing across the Varangerfjord to Kirkenes two larger vessels were retained as it was felt it would give some sense of normality and not arouse unwanted curiosity from the Russian batteries sited opposite on Fiskarhalvøya.

Det Vesteraalens Dampskibsselskab had overall control of the operation and the vessels used were generally between 40 and 130 gross tons. The *Skandfer* at 36 gross tons was the smallest and the *Grinnøy* at 135 grss tons was the largest. From just six vessels chartered in November 1941 this had increased to no less than 27 vessels by May 1943. Fixed itineraries were established with six departures from Tromsø; two to Vadsø, two to Båtsfjord and two to Hammerfest each week. In addition the Post Office also chartered a number of small craft exclusively for the carriage of mail.

During its three years of operation it is estimated the Erstatningshurtigruten vessels carried more than 25,000 passengers, 181,673 mailbags northbound and a further 50,696 mailbags southbound. The *Grinnøy,* alone,

The *Grinnøy* was a new wooden hulled ship built in 1941 and around 100 feet in length. She is reputed to have made 55 trips between Hammerfest and Tromsø between 1942 and 1944. Seen here off Linesøya, Åfjord (Author's Collection)

is said to have made 55 trips between January 1942 and October 1944 mostly to Vardø, carrying 90,000 sacks of mail.

The 'prize' for the most valuable cargo probably went to the *Polarfjell*, captained by Hans Sorensen, when she carried over two million krone in banknotes from the Norges Bank bound for Vadsø. One of the crew, Andreas Johnsen, concealed it under the mattress of his bunk, thinking it safer than being in with the mail bags. Probably the nearest he came to being a millionaire!

It was a challenging route to operate on given the circumstances as they sailed in any weather along an open coastline without lights and beacons, having to run the gauntlet of marauding British or Russian submarines and avoid the ever dangerous floating mines. Whilst several vessels came under attack, there were only three recorded as lost, the *Vaaland* in January 1942, the *Moder II* and *Uløya* in May and July 1944 respectively.

As they abandoned Finnmark in the autumn of 1944 the German troops employed a 'scorched earth' policy in order to hinder the Russians. Every settlement, every building and quayside was destroyed and lines of communication, roads and telegraph wires cut. It was also decided that the civilian population should be evacuated, not for its own safety but so that no support or shelter would be on hand for the Russians as they advanced westwards.

The Erstatningshurtigruten now had to be abandoned as it was too dangerous to continue; the last sailing was, appropriately, by the *Skandfer*. She reached Tromsø at 21.00 on Sunday 29th October. A few Erstatningshurtigruten boat owners organised their own evacuations; the owner of the *Morild II* on the morning of 14th November sailed into Kvalfjord, emptied his house, loaded all his furniture and belongings onto the boat, and headed off south. Later that same day the building was burnt to the ground.

The war was now almost over.

Above: The *Morild II* was even smaller at 49 grt/76 feet; built in Hamburg in 1904 (Author's Collection)

Right: Dating from 1893 the *Ethel May* was a Brixham cutter only 67 feet in length fitted with a small 78 bhp engine (Author's Collection)

Post War Relief

In November 1945 Det Nordlandske Dampskipsselskap (NDS) became a member of the Hurtigruten consortium. The company dated from 1927 and generally operated out of Bodø in the Nordland region. Their original *Skjerstad* had been sunk in 1940 so the company purchased the *Hansa*, a ship dating from 1925 which had been built by Hallands Ångbåts of Halmstad, Sweden for services to Lübeck from the west coast of Sweden.

On 27th December 1940 NDS completed the purchase of the ship for 650,000 kroner, renaming it *Skjerstad*. Used mainly on the Bodø – Trondheim service the *Skjerstad* came through the war relatively unscathed though, when off the Nordland coast on the night of 13th/14th September 1941, the ship was able to rescue 19 survivors from the *Barøy* after she had been hit on the port side by a torpedo from a British aircraft operating from HMS *Victorious*.

In April 1943 NDS proposed the *Skjerstad* should have an extensive rebuild; not because it was an urgent priority but because sending her to a shipyard for a couple of years was less risky than keeping her in service. It was predicted, quite correctly, that once the war was over there would be a severe shortage of tonnage on the coastal services. An estimate of 425,000 kroner was received from Pusnes Mek of Arendal, Southern Norway, and early in February 1944 the *Skjerstad* sailed south for her rebuild.

Her rebuild was a protracted one and it wasn't until mid-May 1945 that the work really started in earnest. Once the Norwegian Ministry of Labour

A Schrøder image of the *Skjerstad* after she was rebuilt in 1945 for Hurtigruten service (Erik Hagger collection)

(*Arbeidsdepartement*) learned what was going on, NDS received a request that *Skjerstad* should be placed on the Hurtigruten, as ODS were unable to provide suitable tonnage. Completely transformed, the *Skjerstad* was handed back to her owners on 17th November 1945, her rebuild having nearly doubled in cost to 710,000 kroner. She now sported an enclosed superstructure, an observation saloon at boat deck level, with her bridge and wheelhouse now one deck higher. Her accommodation had been completely refurbished, and all her cabins had washbasins with running hot and cold water. Her reconditioned engine powered her at 12.8 knots on trial and she now measured 930 gross tons. Bodø now, at last, had its own 'Hurtigruten' ship.

Her first few years as a Hurtigruten steamer were quite eventful, as on 3rd July 1946 the *Skjerstad* went aground near the lighthouse on Grinna Folla in fog. All 420 passengers were safe but repairs took three months. In December 1947, she was sent to the Trondheim Mek Shipyard for her boilers to be converted to oil firing. Ready to resume service on 26th January 1948 she was berthed outside the entrance to the shipyard, where she was joined by Fosen Dampskibsselskab's steamer *Yrjar*, which was about to be drydocked. The next morning revealed that the *Yrjar* had heeled over (could she have been leaking?) and dragged *Skjerstad* with her. Both ships had sunk and were lying on their sides half submerged. Whilst it did not take long to raise them again, the *Skjerstad* now needed an even more extensive refit and was not ready to return to the Hurtigruten until early July.

In the early 1950s NDS were told that if they wished to remain in the Hurtigruten consortium they would have to provide new tonnage as the *Skjerstad* was no longer suitable for the demands. A number of plans were drawn up but none came to fruition. In September 1958 the ship was withdrawn from service to be temporarily replaced by the *Salten*.

In 1959, the *Skjerstad* was sold to the Holiday Line Inc, Panama for 600,000 kroner and renamed *Holiday* for service between Miami and the islands of the West Indies. Laid up in 1965, her owners went bankrupt. The ship was then towed to Cape Haiti for use as a hotel and floating entertainments centre. Unconfirmed sightings in the early 1980s indicated that she was a wreck and had by 1982 disappeared from Lloyds Register.

The *Saltdal* made her first appearance on the Hurtigruten in July 1946, as replacement for *Skjerstad* which was being repaired following her grounding in fog near the lighthouse on Grinna Folla. The ship was to see

The *Saltdal* dated from 1884 and made her debut on the Hurtigruten in 1946 to cover a major tonnage shortage. She is seen here at Trondheim in 1954 (Uwe Jakob Collection)

further relief appearances substituting for the *Skjerstad* throughout the whole of 1947 and more sporadically through into the early 1950s, but was normally on the NDS services from Saltdal and Bodø to Trondheim. The ship dated from 1884, built as *Transit No. 6* for Ångfartygs A/B Transito of Stockholm. Two years later she was sold to Ångfartygs A/B Södra Sverige and renamed *Rhea*. A more powerful 480 ihp Bergsunds M/V triple expansion engine was installed in 1904, giving a service speed of 10.5 knots. The *Rhea* was sold again in 1909 to Stockholms

BDS coastal ship *Lyra* at Svolvær. Used on the Hurtigruten in a relief capacity between 1945 and 1953 (unknown)

Rederi-A/B Svea. In November 1945 the ship was purchased by NDS for 600,000 kroner and renamed *Saltdal*. In 1948, NDS had her rebuilt and modernised, including alterations to her superstructure, a new funnel and conversion to oil firing. She now measured 660 gross tons with a length of 179.5 feet. In February 1957 the ship was purchased by Høvding Skipsopphugging of Sandnessjøen, who renamed her *Meisfjord* for use as a mother ship for diving operations. She is reported as having been scrapped in July 1976.

The *Lyra* dating from 1912 was another BDS ship to make various appearances on the Hurtigruten in a relief capacity. Built by Vulcan Werke of Stettin, Germany for Neue Damfer Compagnies' Baltic routes, she measured 1,474 grt, with a very useful 1,612 dwt and an overall length of 241.5 feet. Her achilles heel was the lack of speed, a mere 11 knots from her 1,180 ihp, Vulcan triple expansion engine. During the First World War, in August 1914, the ship had been captured by the Russian Navy and held at Reval (the old name for Tallinn). She was taken to St Petersburg, renamed *Fert* and used as a troop transport, being converted to a minelayer in 1915. The *Lyra* was then returned to her original owners and in late 1918 assumed her original name before being again renamed *Schlesien* in 1922.

Surplus to requirements in 1925, she was sold to BDS, resuming the name *Lyra* for service between Bergen, Tórshavn and Reykjavik. Requisitioned by the Norwegian Royal Navy in September 1939, for troop transport work, she escaped to Britain in June 1940 to become part of the Nortraship fleet (Norwegian Shipping and Trade Mission). She returned to Norway until the spring of 1945 mainly on the BDS Bergen to Newcastle route but also in a relief capacity on the Hurtigruten between 1945 and 1953. In February 1954 she was sold to Sivert Bakke, a Bergen shipbroker, who renamed her *Nora*. Three months later in May 1954 he sold her on to to

Adel Abdul-Wahib, of Beirut, once more becoming the *Lyra*, for use on pilgrim services linking Lebanon, Egypt and Jeddah (for Mecca). On 9th July 1958 she ran aground off Tor in the Red Sea and sank.

NFDS were in a similar position to their working partner BDS over post war tonnage. Whilst they had the *Kong Harald*, *Sigurd Jarl* and *Ragnvald Jarl* they still needed a fourth ship.

They turned to their *Tordenskjold* which, dating from 1906, was no spring chicken! Built at the Trondheim Mek Shipyard she was a combined passenger and cargo ship for service on their Hamburg link. Primarily built for cargo services she was 921 gross tons (550 dwt) with a hull length of 196 feet. Typical of ships of the time she had most of her cabins and passenger accommodation on the main deck with a passenger certificate of 200 for coastal services. Her triple expansion engine could only develop 800 ihp, so she was slow at 11 knots service speed.

The *Tordenskjold* had first appeared on the Hurtigruten itself in a relief capacity in 1920 and again the following year. The ship's next recorded appearance on the route was in February 1929. In the late 1920s and early 1930s the *Tordenskjold* pioneered the new Trondheim – Hammerfest freight service, which in the summer months was extended to Honningsvåg for the Nordkapp. This became very popular with freelance tourists as a cheap cruise (ilgodsruten).

In 1940 the ship found itself in northern Norway working with the Norwegian armed forces. Shortly before the capitulation in the June the *Tordenskjold*, her bunkers too low to reach Britain safely, sailed to Longyearbyen on Svalbard to refuel and then on to Iceland and freedom. Requsitioned by Nortraship (see *Lyra II*), she sailed with troops

Two A B Wilse photographs of the 1906 NFDS steamer *Tordenskjold*, (above) departing Svolvær in April 1917 and (right) a stern view, location unknown, in 1928 (Norsk Folkemuseum)

and supplies from the United Kingdom to Shetland, the Faroe Islands and
Iceland. In June 1944 she became a depot ship for the Normandy invasion.
At the end of the war she returned home to Norway for a total refurbishment
at the Trondheim Mek Shipyard before entering permanent Hurtigruten
service in May 1946. It is debatable whether it was money well spent as the
Tordenskjold was withdrawn in the spring of 1950 and then sold to Ostende
Remorquage Letzer S/A of Antwerp. As the *Wenduyne* she sailed for a couple
of years as an excursion boat before being scrapped at Bruges in June 1954.

The *Dronningen* was already over 50 years old when VDS chartered her
in 1945 to replace the *Finmarken* (which was undergoing a major refit) on
the Hurtigruten, such was the shortage of suitable post war tonnage.

She had been completed in June 1894 for Det Arendals
Dampskibsselskab (from whom VDS had bought their first *Vesteraalen*) and
was designed for the coastal route between Oslo and Bergen. Her 750 ihp
BMV triple expansion engine produced a service speed of 12 knots. Painted
white with a clipper bow, tall masts and funnel she represented an age of

The *Dronningen* was 50 years
old when she entered
Hurtigruten service, from top
to bottom; at Bergen in earlier
times, note the flared bow; off
Kragerø in 1919; as the *Ionian*
in Greece in 1948
(unknown/A B Wilse, Norsk
Folkemuseum/ Capt Dimitris
Theodoropolous)

long since gone. In November 1940 the ship was sold to Det Helgelandske Dampskibsselskab (HDS) for 467,000 kroner and underwent modernization at Pusnes Mek workshop in Arendal, which slightly raised her gross tonnage to 672 grt. She served on the Trondheim to Harstad route, later extended to Tromsø, effectively forming part of the Hurtigruten.

In October 1944, as a Red Cross ship, she made to trips to assist casualties in the Finnmark region. It was a rather blackened, battered and war weary *Dronningen* that on 25th November 1945 began her charter to VDS at Trondheim. She kept going for a year until in mid-December 1946, when the *Finmarken* returned, she was laid up. Sold to Ole T. Flakk of Kristiansund, in January 1948 she was then resold to Greek shipowner, Haralambos Typaldos for £12,000 as the *Ionian* for services out of Piraeus. She was recorded as being laid up in 1962, and other sources suggest she was not scrapped until 1985.

The *Lyngen* was built in 1931 for Troms Fylkes Dampskibsselskap by the Trondheim Mek Shipyard for their longer routes around Northern Norway. Very much the TFDS 'flagship' she measured 489 gross tons and was 150 feet long. Her triple expansion engine developed about 450 ihp giving a service speed of 12.5 knots.

In 1934, she started a regular passenger, mail and cargo summer service from Tromsø to Bear Island, Longyearbyen and Ny-Ålesund in Svalbard. Backed by an annual subsidy from the Norwegian Parliament the route was widely used both by people who worked in Svalbard as well as tourists. The following year the service was extended to commence from Narvik, with a round trip taking around 14 days. In winter, the ship was often leased for periods of fisheries surveillance.

The Norwegian Navy took over the ship in the autumn of 1939 and equipped it as a submarine tender in Øfotfjord. The ship was seized at Harstad in June 1940 by the Germans and requisitioned for the rest of the war.

At the end of hostilities, between August and November 1945 the *Lyngen*

A TFDS company postcard of their 1932 built *Lyngen* which initially saw service on the summer service to Svalbard - (Bjørn Andersen Collection)

was drafted onto the Hurtigruten. In 1947 after a thorough overhaul and repair at her home shipyard in Trondheim, the *Lyngen* resumed service on the Tromsø – Kirkenes link, which was timetabled to dovetail at Tromsø with the previous Monday's Hurtigruten service from Bergen. In February 1948, the ship was chartered by VDS for thirteen months as a replacement for their *Lofoten* which was under repair.

Her voyages to Svalbard were resumed in the summer of 1951, and this went on until her final season in the summer of 1965. In November of that year she was laid up in Tromsø, the Hurtigruten's last coal-fired steamer. In January 1966, the ship was sold for 150,000 kroner to fishing boat owner Alfred Jensen of Harstad who renamed her *Alfred Jensen* and rebuilt the ship into a cargo ship cum purse seiner including the installation a 1,000 bhp Munktel diesel engine aft. In 1973 she was acquired by Ottar Jensen of Senja who, eight years later, sold her back to Alfred Jensen. She remained active until 1984 but was finally condemned and scuttled off Harstad on 2nd July 1987.

In 1948 NFDS chartered Det Arendal Dampskibsselskab's *Oslo* as a temporary six month replacement for their *Kong Harald* which had gone for a major refit. She joined her predecessor *Christiania* (now owned by DSD) on the Hurtigruten.

The *Oslo* (881 gross tons; 188 feet; 14 knots) was an elegant ship built in 1929 by the Nylands Verksted in Oslo for the coastal service from there to Bergen with a sizeable passenger certificate for 600. The *Oslo* would serve on the Coastal Express until June 1948 when the *Kong Harald* returned and she returned to her old route.

In the winter of 1949-1950, she was modernized at the Drammen Slip and Verksted Shipyard and converted to oil burning. Increasing competition from both road and rail traffic between Bergen and Oslo led to her withdrawal in 1958.

In May 1959, the ship was sold to Epirotiki Steamship Navigation Co for £21,000 and renamed *Aegeus* for services between Piraeus and the Greek

The *Oslo* (Arendals Dampskibsselskab), chartered to NFDS for a six month stint on the Hurtigruten in 1948 (ADS archive)

The *Ottar Jarl* served on the Hurtigruten as a temporary replacement for NFDS' *Sigurd Jarl* in 1947/8. Designed as a reefer ship she had limited passenger accommodation, though the upper lounge was a comfortable area in which to relax (STFM)

islands. She was sold on again in 1961 to the Ionian Steamship Company and in 1965 took the name *Kefaelinia*. On 15th May 1968, whilst being prepared for her summer season at Ambelakia, near Piraeus, fire broke out on board. The ship sank in shallow water and was later scrapped.

The *Ottar Jarl* was quite unlike anything else seen before on the Hurtigruten, built by the Lake Washington Shipyards Inc. in 1929 for the W B Foshay Northland Transportation Co, Seattle and named *W B Foshay*. She was a cargo-passenger ship designed for regular service between Seattle and Alaska and in today's language would have been known as a reefer, albeit with some passenger accommodation. As built she was of 1,262 gross tons and 186 feet in length, with her engine room and bridge amidships and cargo holds fore and aft. A long promenade deck was built over the shelter deck and there was accommodation for 75 passengers. The ship had two American diesel engines totalling 1,120 bhp, giving the ship an 11 knot service speed.

She was sold several times early in her career, firstly in 1929 to Northland Ltd. (Kaye, Son & Co.) of London, UK, who renamed her *Northland* and then two years later she was sold on to the Northland Transportation Co. of Ketchikan, USA. In January 1934 ownership transferred to Gilbert W. Skinner of Seattle as she continued to be employed on Alaskan coastal services.

In 1941 she was requisitioned by the US Army and registered as PR.803 *Northland*. Surplus to Army requirements, NFDS purchased her in 1946 for $325,000 and renamed her *Ottar Jarl*.

Entering service in July 1947, initially on the coastal 'kombinerte' routes, she replaced the *Sigurd Jarl* on Hurtigruten from December 1947 until February 1948, while the latter was under repair. The ship then inaugurated NFDS's new fish cargo service from Kirkenes to Grimsby, her fridge/freezer capacity being of great advantage.

She lasted just over nine years with NFDS before being sold in October 1955 to the Refrigerated Shipping Co. of Puerto Limón (Costa Rica) and renamed *Titika*. She never made it as on 1st November 1955 she grounded off Keflavik, Iceland. It was nearly six months before she was refloated on 24th April 1956 for towing to Dordrecht (Netherlands) to be broken up.

Standardisation
1949–1960

One of the issues that had dogged the Hurtigruten companies since its inception was the lack of standardisation. Ships on the route possessed an incredible range of ages, speeds, dimensions and capacities making the whole service quite inefficient.

Schedules had to be drawn up to match the performance of the slowest ship, while the job of the companies' local agents, who handled most aspects of bookings and reservations for passengers and freight consignments, was made far more complicated than it would have been had a fleet of ships of standard design and capacity been used.

Standardisation was first promoted in 1943 and whilst BDS had shown great interest the other companies were more cautious. Finally on 14th June 1945, all the four main Hurtigruten companies agreed to work together on the project with BDS having the responsibility for plan preparation.

Over the next few months their technical office churned out many variants, all of which would have one engine driving a single screw. They would be one class ships on which the cost of travel would be according to grade of cabin. Public rooms, lounges, a self-service cafeteria and a restaurant would all be located amidships on the promenade deck.

In April 1946 the technical department turned out a final proposal; within an overall length of 264 feet and a beam of 40 feet, the superstructure to be one continuous unit, extending almost to the stern, with all cargo space situated forward, maximising the area of passenger accommodation. This became known as Project 94.

At that time passengers rather than freight were still the main consideration. Whilst the Nordlandsbanen (Nordland Railway) had reached Mosjøen in 1940 and Mo i Rana in 1942, it would be another 16 years before it reached Bodø. Further north, the road network was still very inadequate, private car ownership had yet to take off and short-haul airline services in Norway were still in their infancy.

Of the thirteen shipyards from which estimates for the new ships were requested, the choice was whittled down to two, Aalborg Verft of Aalborg, Denmark, and Cantieri Navale Riuniti dell'Adriatico of Ancona, Italy, the latter being awarded the contract on 27th September 1946 as they had not only submitted the cheapest bid (six million kroner per ship) but had also promised delivery in 1948. Four ships, one per company, were to be ordered. Neither BDS nor NFDS were happy with this arrangement as their greater war losses meant that they needed more than one ship. There were also issues over how the ships were to be financed. In the end agreement was reached and a second ship each for BDS and NFDS would instead be built at Aalborg Verft, Denmark. Soon after, BDS ordered a further ship from the same Danish shipyard.

The Italia-Båtene

The first of the four identical 'Italia-Båtene' to be completed at the Cantieri Riuniti dell'Adriatico Shipyard, Ancona was the *Erling Jarl* for Det Nordenfjeldske Dampskibsselskab. She was handed over at Ancona on 15th August 1949 and sailed for Norway the following day with the company's directors and guests on board. The ship made a brief call at Palermo before proceeding to Gibraltar for bunkers, reaching Trondheim on 28th August, having averaged 15.25 knots on the voyage. The maiden departure on 5th September 1949 marked a significant milestone for the Hurtigruten as from now on all new builds would be motorships.

In terms of outward appearance, the *Erling Jarl* incorporated elements from BDS's earlier proposals. A two-class ship, it measured 2,098 gross tons and 286 feet in length with berths for 77 first and 108 second class passengers and a certificate for 575 when on the Coastal Express. The refrigerated holds had a total capacity of 560 deadweight tonnes or 23,000 cubic feet. Accommodation for both passengers and crew was of a high standard, whilst the navigational equipment reflected the massive technological advances made during (and on account of) the war, i.e. gyro-compass, radar, direction-

The first of the 'Italia-Båtene' completed at Cantieri Riuniti dell'Adriatico, Ancona was the *Erling Jarl* for NFDS in 1949. The new *Midnatsol* is taking shape to her right
(Author's Collection)

finder, echo-sounder and electric log; all a far cry from the course book, compass and chronometer that sufficed on the spartan bridge of the ship's predecessor some 53 years earlier. The prime mover was an 8-cylinder 2,500 bhp Fiat diesel, driving a four-bladed Ka-Me-Wa variable pitch propeller and giving a service speed of 16.5 knots. The great advantage of such propellers is that the angle of pitch can be adjusted to control both speed and movement ahead and astern, without the need to vary engine revolutions or direction, saving a great deal of wear and tear when executing complicated manoeuvres such as approaching and leaving quays. Movements could be controlled directly from the bridge or from the engine room. The *Erling Jarl* cost 9.5 million kroner, this, a significant increase over the original estimate reflecting the substantial devaluation that the Norwegian currency had suffered since the end of the war.

On its first trip, under the command of Captain Paul Holm, the *Erling Jarl* broke the record for the fastest crossing between Bodø and Svolvaer, lowering it to 3 hours and 35 minutes, so claiming the unofficial "Vestfjord Blue Riband".

The *Erling Jarl* is seen northbound off Ørnes in July 1975, (inset) cabin plan of the ship (Mike Bent/David Parsons Collection)

The ship immediately showed its worth on the route but on 8th January 1958, whilst the ship was docked at Bodø, fire broke out aft in the second class accommodation. Thick acrid smoke and heavy fumes filled the corridors and cabins and 14 people lost their lives. Although the damage was relatively light, the subsequent enquiry ordered that the main deck accommodation be refurbished using improved fire

resistant materials. At the same time new and improved emergency exits were to be provided. Subsequently similar precautions were later taken on her three Italian consorts. The *Erling Jarl* emerged from the Trondheim Mek Shipyard ready for renewed service on 12th March. Such was the pace of change that by 1964 the *Erling Jarl* had become the oldest ship in Hurtigruten service at the age of 15 years.

In 1971 the ship was involved in two incidents: on 8th February the *Erling Jarl* grounded in the Risøyrenna and had to go to Harstad for repairs. At the end of the year on 20th November, she again grounded, this time in shallows in the Ørlandet (near Trondheim) and being holed was towed back to Trondheim for repairs. Bad luck tends to come in three's as nine months later on 17th August 1972 there was another grounding, this time in the Raftsundet. Passengers were safely evacuated to Svolvaer and the trawler *Sterkoder* escorted the ship to Harstad for repairs.

Despite all this the *Erling Jarl* was a well-maintained and graceful ship and celebrated its 30th birthday on 11th August 1979. Sailing that day from Bergen, dressed overall, the ship was received by large crowds in festive mood at each port of call along the coast.

The *Erling Jarl's* career was to be cut short less than a year later. At around 02.30 on 13th March 1980, en route from Bergen to Florø, she ran aground in the Steinsundet, near Solund. Although sustaining a considerable amount of damage to one side of her hull, the ship managed to return to Bergen for drydocking at the Laksevåg Shipyard. Following an inspection, she was declared a constructive total loss, no doubt on account of her age.

Reluctant to sell the ship immediately, NFDS had the *Erling Jarl* patched up and moored in Trondheim as a hotel ship during the summer of 1980. In the September, it was announced that the vessel had been sold for use as a floating nightclub in Haiti, but the scheme fell through. On 23rd October 1981 the ship was again sold, this time to Oslo Carriers of Høvik and renamed *Balder Earl,* again with the intention of using it as a hotel ship. Nothing came of the project and the ship was laid up in Grimstad, near Bergen, finally being scrapped at Belgian shipbreakers in January 1985.

A new *Midnatsol* for BDS was the second of the 'Italia-Båtene' ships to be built at Ancona. constructed concurrently with the *Erling Jarl* on an adjacent slipway. Ready on 9th November 1949 barely three months later, the ship other than her funnel colours was an identical sister, including the 9.5m kroner price tag. Externally, in her black and white funnel colours, she could easily be mistaken for a more solid version of Det Bergenske Dampskibsselskab's 1937 built *Nordstjernen*. Her entry into service was more than timely for BDS as the previous *Midnatsol* (now renamed *Sylvia*) was almost 40 years old.

On 3rd December 1949, under the command of Captain Njål Kolbenstvedt, the *Midnatsol* departed from the Festningskaien (Fortress Quay), Bergen on her maiden Hurtigruten voyage. It was reported that when she left Bergen the Ka-Me-Wa variable pitch propeller had inadvertently been left in the 'going astern' position and the *Midnatsol* had to drop both anchors very quickly in order to avoid ramming the quay behind her!

A 1972 view of the *Midnatsol* (1949) arriving at Bergen (Ivor Ireland/Mike Bent Collection)

The new motorships were considerably cheaper to operate than the ageing steamers. In 1950, the total fuel bill for the coal fired *Polarlys* (1912) came to 666,000 kroner whilst the new *Midnatsol's* diesel fuel cost 411,000 kroner, a saving of over 37%. Of course there were the usual teething problems with the new Fiat diesel engine, but eventually it proved to be very reliable. The *Midnatsol* and her three sister vessels did, however, gain a reputation for being notorious 'rollers' and many a journey could become rather too lively for passenger comfort. The ship was relatively easy to keep in good condition but following the fire on the *Erling Jarl* in 1958, as a precaution, new and improved fire retardant materials replaced much of the original throughout

The cosy boat deck of the *Midnatsol* is evident here as she travels southbound from Trondheim in August 1974 (Mike Bent)

the accommodation. In addition, her second class lounge became full width and the second class dining room was turned into a cafeteria.

The *Midnatsol* occasionally found herself in the newspaper headlines, as when early in her career on 11th April 1950 she collided with the freighter *Naddodd* in the Steinsundet, on her way to Bergen. Much later, on 27th February 1965, when northbound near Brønnøysund she went aground and had to return to Bergen for urgent repairs.

Captain Njål Kolbenstvedt left the *Midnatsol* in 1951 to take over the new *Nordlys* and was replaced by Captain Frithjof Quigstad who had previously been in command of the now withdrawn *Polarlys*. Captains B H Brynhildsen and J. Rambo Flem then had command of the *Midnatsol* for a few years each before Captain Nils R. Molstad took over in 1961 and served on her for the next 14 years until 1975.

The 1970s were difficult times for BDS, which culminated in January 1979 when its' President, Torstein Hagen, signed the document to sell the company's four coastal vessels to Troms Fylkes Dampskibsselskap for 32 million kroner. Two months before the *Midnatsol's* 30th birthday on September 4th 1979 she hoisted the TFDS flag and changed her registry to Tromsø. Gradually her old Bergen crew were replaced by those from TFDS and the ship's operational responsibility became based at Tromsø. In October 1982 with the 'new generation' ships now ready, she was renamed *Midnatsol II.*

By the time she retired on 2nd January 1983 she had been in Hurtigruten service for thirty three years, made 900 round trips, travelling over 2.25 million nautical miles between Bergen and Kirkenes.

The *Midnatsol II* was quickly purchased the same month by Drangsholt, Forsberg, & Hoddevik Kjendal, Flekkefjord, for 1.1m kroner for use as a hotel ship at Kragerø, southern Norway and renamed *Midnatsol Norge*, later being moored at Hankø. In the summer of 1984 she was bought by Coast Hotels & Restaurant Ltd in order to be converted to a hotel ship and restaurant at Pipervika, Oslo.

Whilst being refitted at the Sarpsborg Mek Shipyard on Greåker on 8th February 1987 water poured in through an open valve, causing the ship to capsize. The floating crane *Taklift 4* raised her on 1st March, but she was condemned for scrapping, being towed away to Belgium two months later in May 1987.

The *Vesterålen* (note the spelling) was the third of the quartet of vessels ordered from Cantieri Riuniti dell'Adriatico and delivered on 27th March 1950. She was the first Hurtigruten 'new build' for VDS since their *Lofoten* in 1931. Although generally identical to *Erling Jarl* and *Midnatsol,* her décor reflected VDS's own special character and atmosphere.

The company's senior captain Arnleif Hansteen Jorgensen had overseen her construction in Ancona, but for her first Hurtigruten departure from the Festningskaien, Bergen, Captain Oscar Carlson (former master of the *Lofoten*) took over. He would be her master until the new *Finnmarken* came into service in 1956.

As a result of the serious fire on board the *Erling Jarl* in 1958, during the

The *Vesterålen* loading at Ålesund in the 1950s (Bård Kolltveit Collection)

autumn of 1962 the *Vesterålen* too had a major renovation, including the use of improved fire retardant materials, at the Trondheim Mek Shipyard, her second class lounge now full width and the second class dining room turned into a cafeteria.

The *Vesterålen* was in Hurtigruten service for over thirty years and so it is not surprising she was involved in a few incidents; for example, on 18th November 1963, when crossing the Folla, she was holed and had to dry dock at Trondheim, being out of service for nearly a month whilst repairs were completed. Southbound, on 26th March 1970 the ship was in collision with the Paal Wilson ship *Venlo* in the Valderhaugfjorden, off Alesund, which

A 1972 image of the *Vesterålen* at the Festningskaien (Fortress Quay), Bergen, the original terminus for the Hurtigruten (Ivor Ireland/Mike Bent Collection)

sank but was later raised for further service. On 19th January 1972, the *Vesterålen* was in another collision, this time in Hjeltefjord involving the cellulose-carrying vessel *Hystein*; sadly two lives were lost.

Northbound, off the Hornelen, south of Måløy on 16th November 1978 the *Vesterålen* holed herself badly and was almost lost. When she was refloated, it was found that her pumps were unable to cope, so it was decided to beach her nearby at Hamnen. Despite having considerable damage to her hull as well as her engine being forced upwards by the impact, it was decided to repair her and to renew all her electrical wiring. After this costly repair at the BMV Laksevåg Shipyard, she returned to service on 20th January 1979, though with her engine still out of alignment it might have seemed that her Hurtigruten days were numbered, but not for another four years!

In January 1983 with a new ship nearing completion at Harstad, the *Vesterålen* was renamed *Vesterålen II*. She was, by then, the last of the 'Italia-Båtene' still in service.

The following month she was laid up to be sold four months later to Northern Shipping AS of Oslo, with her name shortened to *Rålen*. Several offers came to nothing but in April 1984 Fekete & Co. AS, Tønsberg bought her, renaming her *Annexet* for use as a hotel ship in Tønsberg. In 1986 she was moored at Drammen and for several years became a reception centre for asylum seekers and refugees. In the spring of 1990, Fekete resold the ship for 3.15m SEK to Sundsvall, where the ship was promoted as the hotel boat *Nordstjernen af Sundsvall*. Within a year, in September 1991, she had been sold on for 1.0m SEK to Etoile Marine of Cyprus, again for use as a hotel ship, but the tow to the Mediterranean didn't get any further than Rotterdam. After lying there for four years, becoming more and more derelict, the old *Vesterålen* was sold in October 1995 to Spanish breakers for demolition at Vigo.

Det Stavangerske Dampskibsselskab would be the last of the Hurtigruten companies to receive one of the 'Italia-Båtene'. Named *Sanct Svithun* after the city's patron saint the ship was launched at the Cantieri Riuniti dell'Adriatico Shipyard, Ancona on 18th May 1950. So complete that, having been launched, the first test run was only two hours later, immediately achieving the full specification speed of 17 knots!

The *Sanct Svithun* was handed over on 25th May and arrived at the ship's home port of Stavanger on 7th June, receiving a tremendous welcome. Commanded by Captain Samuel Alshager, she was soon as popular as its predecessor (lost in 1943) had been. The new *Sanct Svithun* replaced the old *Kong Haakon* which dated from 1904.

Known as the 'ambassador ship', the *Sanct Svithun's* maiden voyage was from the Festningskaien, Bergen on 8th June 1950. Although identical in layout to its three sisters the décor, detailing and atmosphere very much reflected her Stavanger roots, the red funnel rings and the DSD motif on the bow being quite distinctive.

As with all ships on the Coastal Express the *Sanct Svithun* experienced accidents and breakdowns. In early January 1952, the ship lightly touched the bottom whilst traversing the Risøyrenna, but was able to continue in service. On the return southbound voyage there were still issues to be resolved so the ship sailed directly to the shipyard in Bergen for remedial work. On 1st May that same year the *Sanct Svithun* again grounded, this time on the Rødskjærsnaget, near Brønnøysund, and had to go to Sandnessjøen for an underwater survey. The passengers were transferred to the *Midnatsol* and once again the ship returned to Bergen for repairs. In 1956 Captain Alshager relinquished command and Captain John A. Klevland became its new master.

In February 1961, the *Sanct Svithun* had a thorough refurbishment at the Rosenberg Mek Shipyard in Stavanger in order to bring her into line with the new classification requirements in the light of the fire aboard the *Erling Jarl*, her gross tonnage increasing slightly to 2,172 grt.

The *Sanct Svithun* is mainly remembered for the greatest tragedy ever to hit the Hurtigruten in peacetime. The ship was northbound from Trondheim to Rørvik on Sunday 21st October 1962. On board were the crew of 47, two postal clerks and 40 passengers. The ship followed the normal shipping lanes out to Buholmråsa and into the Folla (Folda), but after this something became amiss. The *Sanct Svithun* never reached Rørvik, where it was due to arrive at 21.30.

At 22.00, a distress signal was received at Rørvik to the effect that the *Sanct Svithun* was sinking. For reasons still not totally clear, the ship had gone off course and grounded on rocks at Nordøyan, in the Folla. The grounding had ripped open the bottom and the ship had begun to sink. As a result, her position was incorrectly reported and so search operations were concentrated in the wrong place. 48 people survived but 42 died that night.

Many questions were raised, how could such an accident happen, with modern navigational aids and under normal weather conditions? How could experienced people not notice that the ship was on the wrong course? Sadly, the only people who could answer the questions, the duty pilot, mate and helmsman, all perished in the incident. *(see separate article)*

A Schrøder postcard of the ill-fated *Sanct Svithun* (1950) off Trondheim
(Uwe Jakob Collection)

The Aalborg Trio

The need for BDS to have more than one ship to replace their war losses meant that out of expediency they turned to Aalborg Værft, Denmark, for their second and third ships.

The first of the Danish vessels to be completed was the *Nordlys*, handing over taking place at Aalborg on 12th May 1951. Under Captain Njål Kolbenstvedt she sailed for Oslo with 150 guests on board, where a reception was held on board for King Haakon, members of the Storting (Norwegian Parliament) and journalists. She reached Bergen on the morning of 17th May, making her maiden Hurtigruten sailing three days later. 1951 was an important year for Norway's oldest shipping company, Det Bergenske Dampskibsselskab, as it would celebrate its centenary on 12th December.

The *Nordlys* measured 2,162 gross tons (550 dwt) and was 262.5 feet in length, slightly greater but also marginally shorter than the 'Italia-Båtene' quartet. Her design owed much to the 'Project 94' proposals of the late 1940s (see *Standardisation 1949-1960*) with a compact superstructure and all public saloons at promenade deck level. The *Nordlys* was another step forward in the development of coastal vessels as the distinction between first and second class was abolished, a restaurant and a cafeteria replaced the previous first and second class dining saloons. Cabins with one, two and four berths were provided for 186 passengers; for the first time the price you paid for your voyage reflected the accommodation you chose. A passenger certificate was granted for 450 persons on coastal voyages. Costing 8.5 million kroner, the *Nordlys* was cheaper than her four predecessors.

The ship's power plant was an 8-cylinder Burmeister & Wain diesel of 2,950 bhp, giving a service speed of 15 knots. As with the Italian built ships, the *Nordlys* had a variable pitch propeller. Aluminium was used for all structures above boat deck level and with the bridge deck only half a deck higher than the boat deck, it offered greater stability. Her two holds were situated forward and worked by electric cranes instead of the old mast and boom arrangement.

Elegance on board the *Nordlys* (1951), the café (below left) and the smoking lounge (below right) (Bård Kolltveit Collection)

The southbound *Nordlys* departing Hammerfest in July 1975 (Mike Bent)

Overall, the *Nordlys* introduced a new, clean, functional design to the Hurtigruten, with its low profile dominated by the large black funnel with the white BDS rings around it, giving this Aalborg creation a very modern feel. The ship soon gained the reputation of being a good sea boat, in sharp contrast to the notorious rolling of the Ancona quartet which were difficult to manoeuvre in high side-winds. Masters would have long associations with the *Nordlys*; Captain B H Brynhildsen commanded her from 1954 to 1959 to be succeeded by Captain Kjeld Iversen over the next six years.

Throughout the whole of its 32 years in Hurtigruten service the *Nordlys* was rarely in the news, though on a misty 13th June 1968 the ship collided with the freighter *Stjernøy* in Trondheimsfjorden, which subsequently sank, her crew being picked up by the Hurtigruten vessel which escaped major damage.

On 30th August 1979, the *Nordlys* was formally taken over by Troms Fylkes Dampskibsselskap, who had bought BDS's four Coastal Express vessels for 32 million kroner. With the TFDS funnel livery applied and her port of registry changed to Tromsø she still had a few more years of service left in her.

At the end of March 1982 when northbound, the *Nordlys* with 91 passengers on board had her one major incident, going aground on the Vetegjøgraskjæret, Fedje, just north of Bergen, sustaining a gash in her cargo holds which caused severe leakage. She was refloated by the salvage tug *Nordsjøbas* the following day and towed back to the Mjellem & Karlsen shipyard at Bergen for repairs.

With three new ships scheduled to come into service during the winter of 1982/83 the *Nordlys* was laid up from 23rd February 1983. In May, the ship was purchased by John Klovning of Haugesund, for use as an accommodation vessel in conjunction with the Alexander L. Kielland Oil Platform project, her funnel now painted in white with blue rings. Later that year in November 1983 the ship was sold to Torkel Alendal of Haugesund for the same purpose and was towed to the nearby Karmsund Karmøy shipyard. Other potential projects came to nothing and the ship began to

A wet July 1975 day in
Hammerfest as the *Nordlys*
prepares for her southbound
journey, next stop Øksfjord
(Mike Bent)

show signs of external deterioration, though in March 1986 she was in use as an accommodation ship at Lakseväg. In the winter of 1987-1988 the *Nordlys* was going to be turned into a conference centre and restaurant in Oslo and was towed to Greåker for refurbishment. Whilst there, fire broke out on 13th April 1988. The ship was condemned, then purchased by Teens A / S of Tønsberg who sold her on for scrapping at Bilbao, Spain. On 31st May 1988 under tow, the ship grounded off Farsund and then later sank about 100 km northwest of Texel.

Det Nordenfjeldske Dampskibsselskab's *Håkon Jarl* was the second of the Aalborg ships to be built, being ready on 15th February 1952, some nine months after the *Nordlys*. The NFDS ship measured 2,173 gross tons (674 dwt) and was 265.1 feet in length. In external appearance, the *Håkon Jarl* differed slightly from *Nordlys* in having a mast with derricks on the foredeck rather than electric cranes and also had a tripod mast on her wheelhouse. The bridge deck was a full deck higher than the boat deck, the extra space gained being used for officers' accommodation. The ship's coastal certificate was for 508 passengers and it had a cargo capacity of 24,000 cubic feet. Unlike the other vessels in the series the ship had two main engines, 8-cylinder Atlas diesels geared to a single propeller, developing 3,040 bhp and giving a service speed of 16 knots (17 knots was achieved on trials). Curiously, the two smaller diesel engines actually took up less space than one large one. Overall, the *Håkon Jarl* had the same internal configuration as the *Nordlys,* a one class ship with berths for 189 passengers, though the décor reflected the NFDS distinctive image.

A Normann postcard of the *Håkon Jarl* (1952) near Bodø in 1961 (David Parsons Collection)

An NFDS postcard of the *Håkon Jarl* showing her upper decks to good effect (David Parsons Collection)

The *Håkon Jarl* left Trondheim on its first Hurtigruten sailing on 26th February 1952 with Captain Paul Holm as master replacing FFR's (Finnmark Fylkesrederi og Rutelskap) *Alta*, which had been chartered by both NFDS and BDS as a 'stand in' until the new builds came into service.

The *Håkon Jarl* sailed on the Hurtigruten for 31 years, virtually without incident. One of the few incidents happened on 25th January 1959 when, northbound, the ship ran aground near Rørvik and had to return to Trondheim for repairs. Seven years later at Svolvaer, on 23rd February 1976, the *Håkon Jarl* touched the bottom and lost its propeller, having to be towed all the way back to Bergen.

NFDS received permission in 1980 to build two new ships for the Hurtigruten to replace both the *Erling Jarl* and *Håkon Jarl,* but it came as a surprise when in October 1980 it became known that the *Håkon Jarl* would now be sold to Det Ofotens Dampskibsselskab (ODS) for 8 million kroner

Another Normann postcard, this time of the *Håkon Jarl* about to enter Trollfjord (Author's Collection)

and that ODS would now also take over the new build. In January 1981 the *Håkon Jarl* was re-registered at Narvik and carried the Ofotens livery.

On 18th December 1982, when the new ODS ship *Narvik* took over the *Håkon Jarl*'s schedule, the ship was laid up at Narvik, with most of her crew being transferred to the *Nordnorge*. In order to prevent her on-board systems from malfunctioning in the cold weather, a crew of six had to stay on board, at a cost to the company of 6,500 kroner per day.

In January 1983, the ship was bought for 500,000 kroner by Fekete & Co. AS, Tønsberg, where she was renamed *Håkon Gamle*. Shortly afterwards the ship was resold for 1.35 million kroner to a consortium headed by Per Bjørung and Peter Wesel for use as a restaurant and hotel ship based at Pipervika, Oslo. At the same time her original name of *Håkon Jarl* was restored. The ship led a rather precarious existence after her owners went bankrupt in 1988. Taken over by its main creditor, the Tromsø Savings Bank, the *Håkon Jarl* was sold on in 1990 to A/S Akershus Strand, then yet again in 1991 to Preço AS, Oslo (who had also owned the *Nordlys*). In the November, the ship was towed to Antwerp where in May 1992, after renovation (and with her funnel back in NFDS colours), it opened as a hotel ship at the Bonaparte Dock, Antwerp, taking the name *Christian V*. In 1996 the ship was rather disfigured by the addition of a large structure aft of the funnel, remarketed as the *Diamond Princess*, though her bow and stern still clearly state *Håkon Jarl*. In March 2012, the ship's website was reporting that 'the *Diamond Princess* will be closed for reconstruction for an undetermined period'. The following month she was towed from the Bonaparte Dock, the area around which is to be redeveloped, and moored upstream. On 11th August 2012 she was towed to Sluiskil, near Terneuzen (Netherlands) reportedly to be prepared for towing to Morocco, though asbestos issues may preclude this.

The last of seven ships to be ordered in the aftermath of the Second World War, the *Polarlys* was launched on 15th March 1952, finally being handed over to BDS on 27th September, some six months behind schedule. Measuring 2,163 gross tons (600 dwt) and 262.5 feet in length, she was an identical twin sister of the *Nordlys* and it was virtually impossible to tell one from the other. Though excellent sea boats, the arrangement of two holds forward and machinery amidships meant that when fully laden the three

The *Håkon Jarl* was still recognizable in 2004 in her role as a hotel and restaurant ship based at Antwerp (Henk Jungerius)

Aalborg vessels were bow heavy and consequently more difficult to manoeuvre at speed.

The maiden voyage of the *Polarlys* on 3rd of October 1952 marked the end of the first phase in the post war rejuvenation of the Hurtigruten. It was now possible to have daily departures north of Trondheim and five times a week from Bergen.

Four phases in the career of the *Polarlys* (1952)
Left: In BDS funnel colours at Honningsvåg, July 1974.

Below left: At Bergen in TFDS livery.

Bottom left: As the *Caribbean Mercy*.

Bottom right: Today as a hulk at Christobel, Panama
(Mike Bent/Bruce Peter/ Author's Collection)

Being operated by the same company the décor was almost identical to the *Nordlys,* a one class ship, with all lounges and facilities on the main promenade deck and the majority of the 186 cabin berths on decks B and C. Her passenger certificate for coastal waters was set at 450 persons. Power from a single 8-cylinder Burmeister & Wain diesel of 2,950 bhp gave the ship a 15.5 knots service speed.

As with the *Nordlys,* the *Polarlys* had a clean and functional profile, recognisable by its low wheelhouse. Captain Frithjof Quigstad was her first master until 1954 when several other masters then had command of her. Captain Thoralf Tønseth took over in 1960 and stayed with the *Polarlys* until 1973.

The *Polarlys* generally kept a low profile during her Hurtigruten career, though on the night of 13th June 1968 at Kjeungskjær, having just left the confines of Trondheimsfjorden she collided with the cargo ship *Stjernøy,* which sank within ten minutes; fortunately her crew of 11 were able to be quickly rescued by the Hurtigruten ship.

In January 1979, together with the three other BDS ships (*Midnatsol, Nordlys* and *Nordstjernen*), the *Polarlys* was sold to Troms Fylkes Dampskibsselskap receiving the TFDS funnel livery and port of registry changed to Tromsø.

The *Polarlys* suffered a further grounding on 19th November 1981 in the Øyskjæret just off Sandnessjøen, which caused a great deal of damage. She was repaired by Mjellem & Karlsen at Bergen, where a decision was taken to install a new MaK engine of 3,670 bhp. With no further new tonnage planned for the immediate future it made good sense. Returning to service in March 1982, the *Polarlys* was now the fastest ship in the fleet with a top speed in excess of 18 knots! Two years later, she was further upgraded to bring her into line with the new fire protection regulations and many of her cabins were rebuilt as en suite. This slightly reduced the cabin capacity to 172 berths.

Her 40th anniversary on the Coastal Express was celebrated on 27th September 1992 at Bergen. By then she had travelled the equivalent of 130 times around the world – not bad for a 40 year old. The writing was on the wall for her as the new *Kong Harald* was scheduled to be delivered in late June 1993. The *Polarlys* started her last round trip from Bergen on 6th June before going to lay up near Ålesund.

A summer 1957 BDS poster advertising the delights of the Norwegian Coastal Voyage (Bård Kolltveit Collection)

In late April 1994, the ship was sold to Mercy Ships based at Lindale, Texas, in conjunction with the inter-church organization Youth with a Mission. Under the Panamanian flag she was renamed *Caribbean Mercy* and on 16th May she set off on a cruise via Alaska, Kamchatka (Russia), Korea and the Philippines before returning via Guam and Hawaii. The ship was then converted for its new role as a floating medical centre and eye clinic. For almost a decade the *Caribbean Mercy* worked in the Caribbean Basin, Central and South America regions. On 3rd May 2005 the announcement came that she would cease service and one month later her crew transferred to other Mercy Ship locations. Her last resting place (2012) appears to be at Christobel, Panama, now just a derelict hulk.

Vital Relief

The post war renewal of the Coastal Express fleet took far longer than anticipated and it was over four years before the first phase of new vessels was completed. By 1949, the Hurtigruten companies had an acute lack of ships, most of those still in traffic were worn down by war and to bring them into line with the new regulations would be costly, given the short time that remained before their replacement. Equally, the remaining coal fired ships had become both costly and uneconomic to operate.

As the next trio of new builds from Aalborg Værft were not expected before 1951/52, both NFDS and BDS turned to Finnmark Fylkesrederi og Rutelskap (FFR) for help. In the late 1940s FFR, based in Hammerfest, having looked at the possibility of introducing their own express coastal service from Finnmark to southern Norway, had, in 1946, ordered two relatively large ships with good cabin space from Trosvik Verksted, Brevik. They were designed to serve between Hammerfest and Mosjøen, which at that time was the northern terminus of the Nordlandsbanen (Nordland Railway). The railway was not to reach Bodø until 1962.

The *Sørøy* was the first to be delivered on 1st September 1949, followed by her sister, *Alta,* in the July of the following year. Both ships were representative of a new generation of Norwegian coastal steamer ships, good looking, compact and sturdy, their grey hulls set off by FFR's yellow, white and blue funnel colours. In appearance, they resembled a smaller version of the 'Italia-Båtene' which were then under construction at Ancona.

Both ships were of 686 gross tons (588 dwt), with a hull length of 167 feet and two continuous decks. Each ship had a crew of 27 and a passenger certificate for 175 persons in two classes, with 30 berths amidships in first class, another 28 aft in second class and a further 26 reclining seats in the

FFR's diminutive *Alta* (1950) was to do sterling work on the Hurtigruten until more new builds were available
(Bård Kolltveit Collection)

The *Alta's* sister ship *Sørøy* was also used for relief work by each of the Hurtigruten companies in the 1950s (Bård Kolltveit Collection)

lounges. There was also a dining room and a cafeteria. Each ship had a 5 cylinder Swedish Atlas Polar diesel of 690 bhp, which provided a service speed of 12.5 knots, and a controllable pitch propeller which could be operated from the bridge.

In October 1950, only three months after coming into service, the *Alta* was chartered to NFDS as a replacement for their *Kong Harald* on the Hurtigruten service. Fifteen months later on 10th February 1952, with the Aalborg new build *Håkon Jarl* ready to come into service, she was returned to FFR only to be chartered again in the October of the following year by BDS in October to cover the absence of the *Nordstjernen*. Just to even things up, in 1958 the *Alta* was chartered by VDS, the third main Hurtigruten operator, whilst their *Lofoten* was out of service.

The *Sørøy* was also used for more short term charters on several occasions to both NFDS and BDS, and in 1951 the ship was chartered by the Kings Bay Kull Compani as a replacement for the *Lyngen* on cruises between Tromsø and Svalbard.

In 1962, with the Nordlandsbanen to Bodø completed, the *Sørøy's* regular service between Hammerfest and Mosjøen was truncated at Bodø. After the tragic sinking of Det Stavangerske Dampskibsselskab's *Sanct Svithun* in October 1962, the *Sørøy* became one of the temporary replacements. She continued to work regularly on the Hurtigruten until DSD's new vessel, the *Kong Olav,* was delivered in 1964.

These versatile sisters became the victims of the vast improvements in the road network and the growth of air travel that the 1960s brought to the Nordland and Troms regions. In December 1965, the *Sørøy* was sold to become a government floating training ship, based in Trondheim, being renamed *Skule*. The *Alta* continued in service until 1967 when she was sold to the Maritime Co-Operative Shipping Association Ltd, Suva, Fiji for $800,000. After rebuilding and the installation of air conditioning at the Kaarbøs Mek Shipyard in Harstad, she was renamed *Tui Lau* and put into service around the Fiji Islands. It would not be a long career as on 25th

The *Sørøy* today, now the *RTS Sindbad,* a training ship based at Port Rashid, Dubai and in immaculate condition (Uwe Jakob)

October 1968 the *Tui Lau* grounded on a reef about 120 nautical miles from her home port of Suva and sank.

In 1981 the *Skule* (ex *Sørøy*) was transferred to the Østfold Fylkeskommune and renamed *Østfold*. In 1991 she became the *Glommen* only to be sold on in July 2003 with the intention of becoming a private residence moored at Oanes, near Stavanger. Resold again in May 2004 to Reef Line/Zambesi Shipping of Dubai, she was renamed *RTS Sindbad*. In partnership with the Australian Institute of Marine Education, she was totally refurbished for use as a training ship and based at Port Rashid, Dubai. Kept in immaculate condition she continues to serve today.

After the war the Narvik based Det Ofotens Dampskibsselskab (ODS) was forced to withdraw from the Hurtigruten because it no longer had a vessel suitable for the service. With the Nordlandsbanen being completed in 1940 to Mosjøen, the three main coastal shipping companies based in Northern Norway, ODS, FFR, and Det Saltens Dampskibsselskab (SDS) agreed to create a regional coastal service from Mosjøen to Hammerfest and as a result *Sørøy, Alta* and *Salten* were built. In June 1951, ODS ordered their ship from the Drammen Shipyard, Trondheim which became their *Barøy*.

Delivered on 21st February 1952, the ship was very similar to the *Sørøy* and *Alta*, being of 700 gross tons, 178 feet in length with two continuous decks and superstructure amidships and aft. She had a passenger certificate for 250 persons and cabin accommodation for 26 in first class and 24 in second class. Her engine was a standard 6-cylinder Atlas Diesel which generated 870 bhp and gave a 13.5 knots service speed. The *Barøy* was equipped with radar, echo-sounder, electric log and radio telephone, while part of her forward hold was refrigerated. In all the ship cost 4.3m kroner, twice the original price quoted!

She had only completed a couple of round trips on the Mosjøen to Hammerfest route when BDS chartered her for Hurtigruten service until their new *Polarlys* was ready. In spite of her small size, she acquitted herself

well, being highly manoeuvrable when berthing. In the summer of 1953
ODS were given a contract for the service and from 4th September the
Barøy became the permanent fourteenth member of the fleet. For the first
time in its history the Hurtigruten became a daily service between Bergen
and Kirkenes.

Such was her success that in December 1955 the ship was sent to
Laksevåg M/V, Bergen for lengthening by 30 feet, increasing her gross
tonnage to 860, her forward hold capacity by 25% and providing additional
berths for another 28 passengers. She returned to service on 29th April 1956,
her place, in the meantime, on the Coastal Express having been taken by
SDS's *Salten.*

When Det Nordlandske Dampskipsselskap (NDS) withdrew from the
Hurtigruten unable to provide a replacement for their *Skjerstad*, ODS were
awarded a permanent place on the Hurtigruten under the terms of the new
contract which began in January 1963. With the new *Nordnorge* now
completed, the *Barøy* stepped down from the Coastal Express after eleven
years of exemplary service.

A posed picture of the *Barøy*
in her original form at a rainy
Narvik (unknown)

The *Barøy* was sold on to Birger Svendsen & Sons, Fredrikstad for 2m kroner for ferry services across the Skagerrak between Arendal, Lysekil and Marstrand, tapping into the tax free market. By October 1966, with car ferries taking over, the *Barøy* was sold to the Government of the Gilbert and Ellice Islands, Pacific Ocean for £92,000 (1.85m kroner). At Smith's Dock Co, Middlesbrough she was converted into a training ship and renamed *Teraka*. Sadly, her new career was short as, after suffering major engine and mechanical problems, she was condemned and scuttled near the Betio lighthouse, Tawara on 19th June 1973.

Up to the outbreak of the Second World War, the Hurtigruten companies had always been in a position to draw on their own tonnage reserves for relief ships whenever needed. Post war, the situation had changed dramatically and chartering became the most viable option.

In 1951, Saltens Dampskipsselskap (SDS) ordered a new motor ship from Trosvik M/V of Brevik for service between Mosjøen and Finnmark in conjunction with ODS and FFR. Of 677 gross tons (350 dwt) and 173.9 feet in length, the *Salten* was delivered in March 1953. Similar in appearance to the *Barøy*, she had a certificate for 290 passengers and her standard six-cylinder, 870 bhp Atlas diesel enabling a service speed of 13.5 knots.

SDS were advised not to become too heavily committed to the Mosjøen service as once the Nordlandbanen (Nordland Railway) reached Bodø, that part of the route would be truncated. However, the *Salten* was deemed to be an ideal permanent relief ship for the Hurtigruten, particularly during the off peak and winter months. It was in this role that she served the Hurtigruten until 1964. NFDS, with whom Saltens had close ties, immediately chartered her for two months for the spring of 1953, before she returned to her Mosjøen service, extended to Nordkapp and Honningsvåg for the summer months. When Det Nordlandske Dampskipsselskap's (NDS) *Skjerstad* was retired in September 1958, the *Salten* took over her role until the May of the following year. The disaster which befell the *Sanct Svithun,* wrecked in October 1962, saw the *Salten* almost permanently on the Hurtigruten until 1964, after which she was placed on the summer service to Svalbard.

In the spring of 1967, the *Salten* was sold back to the Government for 1.4m kroner to become an adult education training ship based at Grimstad.

The SDS coastal ship *Salten*, seen off Bodø, saw almost permanent service on the Hurtigruten during the late 1950s and early 1960s (unknown)

Today the *Salten* is now the *Gamle Salten*, a Cultural heritage ship, owned by Saltens A/S based at Bodø and is as good as ever! (John Bryant)

She was renamed *Sjøkurs* and later in 1973 was based at the Sørlandets Seilande Skoleskib Institution in Kristiansand. Twenty two years later in 1995, the ship was temporarily renamed *Sjøskole* for sale to the Ryfylke Steamship Company of Stavanger and renamed *Gamle Salten*. Veteran Ship enthusiasts in Stavanger restored the ship to her former glory and she was officially granted 'Cultural Heritage' status.

In 2008, when it became known that the Ryfylke Steamship Company were going to sell the *Gamle Salten* as they were taking on another veteran ship, local enthusiasts based in Bodø formed Saltens A/S in order to purchase the ship for 8.9m kroner. Today, in addition to her Cultural Heritage work, she has regular charter work, runs her own cruise programme and in between serves as a restaurant and hotel ship. Sixty years old in 2013 the *Gamle Salten* is as good as ever!

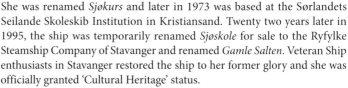

When, in September 1954, the *Nordstjernen* foundered in the Raftsundet, Det Bergenske Dampskibsselskab immediately turned to their elderly North Sea steamer *Jupiter* as a temporary replacement. Built by Lindholmens Verkstads of Gothenburg and delivered in January 1915 for the Stavanger and Bergen to Newcastle service, the *Jupiter* was very large and impressive by the standards of the day. Of 2,511 gross tons (1,830 dwt) and 305 feet in length, her Lindholmen triple expansion engine gave her a service speed of 15.5 knots. In 1931 she transferred to Bergen Line's Rotterdam route running opposite the *Ariadne*. The *Jupiter* was requisitioned by the Germans in the early days of the occupation, being used for a while as an accommodation ship for Norwegian prisoners of war. In 1944 towards the end of the war she was mainly on routes from Oslo to Denmark.

BDS' elderly *Jupiter* (1915) was hastily drafted into Hurtigruten service after the loss of the *Nordstjernen* in 1954, fortunately a modern replacement was soon to hand (BDS/ Hurtigrutemuseet)

After hostilities had ended and following repairs and refurbishment the *Jupiter* again saw service on the North Sea route to Newcastle until 1953, when she began relief work on the Hurtigruten. One of the largest ships to have served on the Coastal Express she was also one of the most comfortable and being a steamer did not suffer from vibration. However, she was extremely costly to operate and BDS sought to replace her at the earliest possible moment.

With the arrival of the *Meteor* in January 1955 the *Jupiter* was withdrawn and on 2nd September sold to the Epirotiki Steamship Navigation Co. Ltd, Piraeus, Greece for rebuilding as a cruise ship, being renamed *Hermes*. On 4th March 1960 whilst refitting at Piraeus she was destroyed by a devastating fire. In the December she was towed to Split (some sources suggest Italy) for breaking up.

Previously in 1952, BDS had ordered a new cruise ship to replace the *Stella Polaris*. Of more modest proportions than her predecessor, at 2,856 gross tons and 296.7 feet in length, the *Meteor* was delivered from Aalborg  Verft on 15th January 1955, painted in the company's new cruising colours of white hull and superstructure and buff funnel with three white hoops. In essence she was a larger and more luxurious version of *Nordlys* and *Polarlys*, but still with the ability to be able to call at many of the smaller ports denied to large cruise liners; in other words, ideal to serve on the Hurtigruten in a relief capacity. The loss of the *Nordstjernen* meant that the *Meteor* was immediately put into Hurtigruten service from 22nd January 1955, though in June, July and August she was replaced by *Jupiter* while she undertook eight cruises, five to Nordkapp, two to the Baltic and one to Svalbard and the ice cap. The ship was designed to carry 157 passengers in a single class when cruising and 200 in two classes when on the Coastal Express. She had a single refrigerated hold (forward), with a capacity of 18,000 cubic feet. Her engine was a nine-cylinder Burmeister & Wain diesel of 5,000 bhp, giving her a maximum speed of 18 knots, though 15.5 knots was her norm for cruising.

Right and bottom: BDS
(Bergen Line) postcards of
their cruise ship *Meteor* in
above Geirangerfjord and
below rounding Nordkapp.
She replaced the *Jupiter* on
the Hurtigruten until the new
Nordstjernen was ready in
1956 (Author's Collection)

Bergen Line Song book, part
of the on board 'do it yourself'
entertainment programme
(David Parsons Collection)

Just over a year later and a month ahead of schedule, on 24th February 1956, BDS took delivery of a new *Nordstjernen* which meant that the *Meteor* was now free to undertake a more extensive and worldwide cruising programme, only appearing rarely on the Hurtigruten. On 22nd May 1971, having just returned to Vancouver from an Alaskan coastal cruise, fire broke out, gutting the crew accommodation where 32 lost their lives. The ship was sold to Epirotiki of Greece where she was completely rebuilt. Renamed the *Neptune*, she operated cruises in the Aegean and Mediterranean, as well as frequently visiting Norway. In 2002 the ship was towed to Aliaga in Turkey to be scrapped.

With the sale of the *Jupiter*, once again BDS was without a suitable relief ship. During *Meteor*'s annual overhaul in the winter

of 1955/6 the company chartered the *Ingøy* from Finnmark Fylkesrederi (FFR) which was a case of going from one extreme to another.

The *Ingøy* had been built by Drammen Mek, Trondheim, and was completed in July 1950, designed as a combined cargo and passenger ship for local services around Finnmark. She measured a mere 433 gross tons and was only 135.3 feet in length. Powered by a NOHAB diesel generating 600 bhp the *Ingøy* had a certificate for 150 passengers and could carry up to 100 tons of cargo.

As far as is known, the winter of 1955/6 was her only spell on the Hurtigruten; a complete 13-day round voyage on board must have been quite a unique experience. From 1957 to 1961 the *Ingøy* was primarily on the summer service between Russenes (halfway down the Porsangerfjord) and Honningsvåg. In 1971 Finnmark Fylkesrederi sold her to Gardline Shipping of Lowestoft, who renamed her *Researcher*. Three years later, the ship was resold to Sidney Sea Search of the Cayman Islands before being acquired in 1983 by the South Carolina Wildlife & Marine Rescue Department who deliberately scuttled her off the coast of South Carolina to form an artificial reef.

At 433 gross tons and 135 feet in length the *Ingøy* was probably the smallest relief ship to serve on the Hurtigruten (unknown)

Hurtigruten Timetable – Summer 1955

Northbound	Day	1	2	3	4	5	6	7
Bergen	1	22.00	22.00	22.00	22.00	22.00	22.00	22.00
Florø	2	05.00	05.00	05.00	05.00	05.00	05.00	05.00
Måløy	2	08.00	08.00	08.00	08.00	08.00	08.00	08.00
Ålesund	2	13.30	13.30	13.30	13.30	13.30	13.30	13.30
Molde	2	17.00	176.00	17.00	17.00	17.00	17.00	17.00
Kristiansund	2	22.00	22.00	22.00	22.00	22.00	22.00	22.00
Trondheim	3	06.00	06.00	06.00	06.00	06.00	06.00	06.00
Trondheim	3	12.00	12.00	12.00	12.00	12.00	12.00	12.00
Bessaker	3		18.00					
Rørvik	3	21.30	21.30	21.30	21.30	21.30	21.30	21.30
Brønnøysund	4	02.00	02.00	02.00	02.00	02.00	02.00	02.00
Sandnessjøen	4	05.30	05.30	05.30	05.30	05.30	05.30	05.30
Nesna	4	07.00			07.00			
Grønøy	4			10.00				
Ørnes	4	10.45	10.45		10.45	10.45	10.45	10.45
Bodø	4	14.00	14.00	14.00	14.00	14.00	14.00	14.00
Bodø	4	16.00	16.00	16.00	16.00	16.00	16.00	16.00
Stamsund	4	20.45	20.45	20.45	20.45	20.45	20.45	20.45
Svolvær	4	22.45	22.45	22.45	22.45	22.45	22.45	22.45
Svolvær	4	23.45	23.45	23.45	23.45	23.45	23.45	23.45
Stokmarknes	5	03.00	03.00		03.00	03.00	03.00	03.00
Melbu	5			02.45				
Sortland	5	04.45	04.45	04.45	04.45	04.45	04.45	04.45
Risøyhamn	5	06.45	06.45	06.45	06.45	06.45	06.45	06.45
Harstad	5	09.00	09.00	09.00	09.00	09.00	09.00	09.00
Harstad	5	10.15	10.15	10.15	10.15	10.15	10.15	10.15
Finnsnes	5	14.00	14.00	14.00	14.00	14.00	14.00	14.00
Tromsø	5	17.00	17.00	17.00	17.00	17.00	17.00	17.00
Tromsø	5	19.00	19.00	19.00	19.00	19.00	19.00	19.00
Skjervøy	5	23.15		23.15		23.15		23.15
Øksfjord	6		01.45		01.45		01.45	
Hammerfest	6	05.30	04.45	05.30	04.45	05.30	04.45	
Hammerfest	6	06.00	05.15	06.00	05.15	06.00	05.15	05.15
Havøysund	6		08.00				09.00	
Honningsvåg	6	14.00	15.30	14.00	15.30	14.00	15.30	15.30
Kjøllefjord	6	16.30			18.00		18.00	
Mehamn	6	19.00		17.45		20.00		
Gamvik	6		19.45		18.30			
Berlevåg	6			21.00				21.00
Båtsfjord	6			23.30		23.30		
Vardø	7	01.30	02.30	01.30	02.30	01.30	02.30	02.30
Vardø	7	02.30	02.30	02.30	02.30	02.30	03.30	03.30
Vadsø	7		07.30		07.30			07.30
Kirkenes	7	06.30	09.30	06.30	09.30	06.30	07.30	09.30

Southbound	Day	1	2	3	4	5	6	7
Kirkenes	7	08.00	11.30	08.00	11.30	08.00	09.30	11.30
Vadsø	7		11.00		11.00		11.00	12.00
Vardø	7	14.30	15.30	14.30	15.30	14.30	15.30	15.30
Vardø	7	15.30	16.30	15.30	16.30	15.30	16.30	16.30
Båtsfjord	7	19.30			19.30	20.30		
Berlevåg	7			20.30	21.45		20.00	20.30
Gamvik	7				23.45		22.00	23.00
Mehamn	7/8	00.30	23.45		01.00		00.30	
Kjøllefjord	8		02.00			01.15	02.45	02.00
Honningsvåg	8	06.00	06.00	06.00	06.00	06.00	06.00	06.00
Havøysund	8		08.30			08.30		
Hammerfest	8	11.30	11.30	11.30	11.30	11.30	11.30	11.30
Hammerfest	8	12.30	12.30	12.30	12.30	12.30	12.30	12.30
Øksfjord	8		15.45			15.45	15.45	15.45
Skjervøy	8	18.30		18.30	19.30	18.30		19.30
Tromsø	8	23.30	23.00	23.00	23.30	23.00	23.00	23.30
Tromsø	9	01.30	01.30	01.30	01.30	01.30	01.30	01.30
Finnsnes	9	04.45	04.45	04.45	04.45	04.45	04.45	04.45
Harstad	9	08.30	08.30	08.30	08.30	08.30	08.30	08.30
Harstad	9	09.30	09.30	09.30	09.30	09.30	09.30	09.30
Risøyhamn	9	12.00	12.00	12.00	12.00	12.00	12.00	12.00
Sortland	9	14.00	14.00	14.00	14.00	14.00	14.00	14.00
Stokmarknes	9	16.00	16.00		16.00	16.00	16.00	16.00
Melbu	9		16.00					
Svolvær	9	19.00	19.00	19.00	19.00	19.00	19.00	19.00
Svolvær	9	20.00	20.00	20.00	20.00	20.00	20.00	20.00
Stamsund	9	22.30	22.30		22.30	22.30	22.30	22.30
Bodø	10	03.00	03.00	01.00	03.00	03.00	03.00	03.00
Bodø	10	04.00	04.00	02.30	04.00	04.00	04.00	04.00
Ørnes	10	07.15	07.15	06.00	07.15	07.15		07.15
Grønøy	10						07.15	
Nesna	10		11.00			11.00		
Sandnessjøen	10	12.30	12.30	12.00	12.30	12.30	12.30	12.30
Brønnøysund	10	15.45	15.45	15.15	15.45	15.45	15.45	15.45
Rørvik	10	19.30	19.30	19.00	19.30	19.30	19.30	19.30
Bessaker	10							23.00
Trondheim	11	06.00	06.00	06.00	06.00	06.00	06.00	06.00
Trondheim	11	20.00	20.00	20.00	20.00	20.00	20.00	20.00
Kristiansund	12	04.30	04.30	04.30	04.30	04.30	04.30	04.30
Molde	12	09.00	09.00	09.00	09.00	09.00	09.00	09.00
Ålesund	12	13.30	13.30	13.30	13.30	13.30	13.30	13.30
Måløy	12	18.30	18.30	18.30	18.30	18.30	18.30	18.30
Florø	12	21.30	21.30	21.30	21.30	21.30	21.30	21.30
Bergen	13	06.00	06.00	06.00	06.00	06.00	06.00	06.00

New Builds on the Block

On 24th February 1956, a month ahead of schedule, Bergenske took delivery of their new *Nordstjernen* ordered from Blohm & Voss of Hamburg in December 1954. The fourth of the company's ships to carry this name, but only the second for Hurtigruten service, she was launched on 26th October 1955 and measured 2,149 gross tons (645 dwt) and 265.0 feet in length. The *Nordstjernen* was a near sister to the earlier *Nordlys* and *Polarlys*; the main changes were in the modified styling of the forward end of her superstructure and only having four lifeboats instead of the five (2 port, 3 starboard) on the earlier ships. Berths were provided for 192 passengers, and her passenger certificate was for 410 persons on coastal services. Her six-cylinder Burmeister & Wain diesel of 3,000 bhp gave her a service speed of 15.5 knots.

She was, initially, under the command of Captain Einar Dragbø, later succeeded by Captain C Lund, before in 1960 Captain Sverre Holck took over for the next 13 years. The flagship of the BDS Hurtigruten fleet, *Nordstjernen* also had a class certificate for international waters which enabled her to sail to Svalbard as well as to undertake spring shopping cruises to Lerwick in the Shetlands, which she did from 1976 to 1979, making no less than 16 North Sea crossings.

In January 1979, BDS sold its Hurtigruten ships to Troms Fylkes Dampskibsselskap, the *Nordstjernen* becoming the TFDS flagship. On 4th September that year, with all the takeover formalities completed, the ship was repainted in her new funnel colours.

Ready for the launching of the *Nordstjernen* on 26th October 1955 at the Blohm and Voss Shipyard, Hamburg (Hurtigruten ASA)

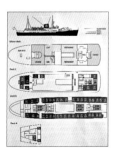

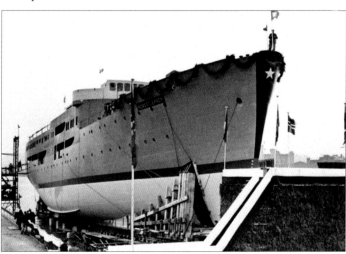

On board and still in immaculate condition, left the bar and right the panorama lounge (Uwe Jakob)

Under the terms of the new 1983 contract for the Coastal Express which was now to be run with only 11 ships (as today), TFDS sent the *Nordstjernen* to the Mjellem & Karlsen Shipyard, Bergen in the winter of 1982-83 for a comprehensive modernization in order to bring her into line with the new safety regulations. Her old B & W engine was replaced by an 8-cylinder MaK of 3,600 bhp which improved both economy and speed. The results were startling as once considered to be the slowest of all the new motorships, the *Nordstjernen* now had a new top speed of over 20 knots! In addition, the cabins on the main deck were gutted and rebuilt, many with en suite facilities. As a result the number of berths was reduced from 192 to 179. On 23rd March 1983 the *Nordstjernen* resumed service on the Hurtigruten.

With a new *Nordlys* arriving in the spring of 1994, the *Nordstjernen* became the relief ship for the Hurtigruten, though from late June to early September she found employment on weekly cruises between Tromsø and Svalbard. In September 1995, she again returned to full Hurtigruten service, replacing the *Ragnvald Jarl* until April 1996 when the new *Polarlys* arrived.

Her busy pattern of summer cruises along the 'long coast' and to Svalbard

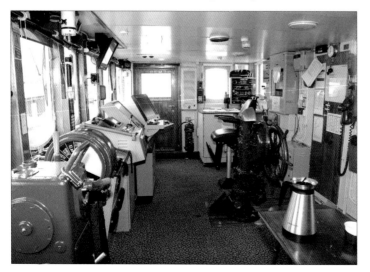

The wheelhouse, a wonderful sense of timeless days gone by! (Uwe Jakob)

A stern view of the
Nordstjernen in her original
BDS funnel livery at
Honningsvåg in July 1974
(Mike Bent)

(later extended to include Greenland), as well as covering for winter absences, were to continue throughout the next decade. Granted Cultural Heritage status by the Riksantvikvaren, Norway's Directorate for Cultural Heritage, the *Nordstjernen* has continued to be a very important niche unit within the fleet. In the winter of 1999/2000 she had a further 10m kroner upgrade at the Ibestad Mek Verksted, South Tromsø. The following year she replaced the *Harald Jarl* until the *Trollfjord* was delivered in May 2002.

On 16th March 2003, the *Nordstjernen* undertook a special cruise to her birthplace, Hamburg, to celebrate the arrival of the new *Midnatsol*. Sailing from Bergen via Hardangerfjorden and Stavanger on 20th March she met up with the *Midnatsol* at the mouth of the River Elbe in order to cruise together up river to Hamburg. Whilst there, she offered a special cruise for locals as far as Cuxhaven. Following the *Midnatsol*'s naming ceremony the next day, she returned home to Bergen.

Below: Now in TFDS livery the
Nordstjernen is pictured off
Stamsund during her 50th
Anniversary Cruise in June
2006 (Bryan Kennedy)

Between 1st and 9th June 2004 the *Nordstjernen* acted as an escort for the Norwegian royal yacht, *Norge*, which was visiting Caen in connection with the 60th anniversary commemorations of the Normandy landings.

Below right: The *Nordstjernen*
is captured speeding away
from Bodø bound for the
Lofotens in June 2010
(Uwe Jakob)

With both the *Nordnorge* and *Nordkapp* on expedition voyages around Antarctica for the winters of 2005-07 *Nordstjernen* returned to Hurtigruten service on a regular basis. In the summers of 2007 and 2008 the ship was used for short Svalbard cruises organised by Spitsbergen Travel, under the *Spitsbergen*

Adventure banner, including sailing as near to the polar ice as possible.

With the arrival of the expedition ship *Fram* in 2007, many thought that this would see her retirement. Not in the least, as for the next few years the *Nordstjernen* continued to be a regular on the Hurtigruten run, most recently covering for the *Finnmarken* whilst she was on charter as an accommodation ship for workers on the Gorgon oil and gas field project, north west Australia (from late 2010 to early 2012).

The *Nordstjernen* is reputed to have a ghost on board called 'Ernst', a German shipyard worker who was unfortunately killed during the ship's construction at Blohm & Voss in Hamburg, reportedly meeting up with both crew and passengers alike. According to the *Nordstjernen's* master, Ole Johan Andreassen, 'Ernst' is very much a friendly ghost. In September 2011 a team of 'ghostbusters' from Norwegian Ghost Hunters showed their interest and wanted to bring in technical equipment to check out some of the mysterious things that people have experienced aboard the *Nordstjernen*. It would be interesting to know what was found, if anything!

Now 56 years old, 2012 was scheduled to be the *Nordstjernen's* swansong as new SOLAS regulations made further upgrading too prohibitive. Her last classic round voyage on the Hurtigruten began on 11th March 2012 and ended at Bergen on 22nd March where she was replaced by the returning *Finnmarken*. The ship sailed to the Fiskerstrand Shipyard near Ålesund for temporary lay up before embarking on a last season of cruises to Svalbard.

Upon arriving at Bergen from her last Svalbard cruise on September 1st 2012, she immediately undertook a 45 day charter for CCB (Coast Centre Base) as a hotel ship at their Ågotnes oil rig maintenance facility, Store Sotra, near Bergen. After this the *Nordstjernen* was sold.

Both Det Vesteraalens Dampskibsselskab and Det Nordenfjeldske Dampskibsselskab ordered new ships in 1954 to replace their oldest Hurtigruten steamers. VDS's *Finnmarken* dated from 1912 and, although still very popular, was by now too costly to operate and her accommodation standards fell well below those of other members of the Hurtigruten fleet. Although both companies would have preferred to order their new ships

The Finnmarken is seen here preparing to sail southbound from Harstad in July 1975; note her rather outmoded cargo handling gear (Mike Bent)

from a Norwegian yard, the prices the latter were asking were far too high, so in the end Blohm & Voss of Hamburg won contracts for two similar ships.

However, this new *Finnmarken* (note the spelling) differed radically from the new BDS ship, *Nordstjernen,* which Blohm & Voss were also building at the same time. The *Finnmarken* had been designed with the engine room located towards the stern, which improved the trim as well as providing space for more cabins with the amidships dining room no longer divided by a funnel casing. The *Finnmarken* was launched on 4th February 1956 and delivered to VDS on 29th May. She measured 2,189 gross tons and was 266.6 feet in length; her holds, both forward, had a total capacity of 21,830 cubic feet. The cargo handling gear on the foredeck was still of the traditional boom and derrick type. With a passenger certificate for no less than 585 on coastal voyages, she had berths for 67 first class and 142 second class travellers. Her engine was a 10-cylinder MAN diesel of 2,960 bhp which gave her a speed of 16.6 knots on trials. In addition, her engine could be reversed which, when combined with her variable pitch propeller, made it possible for her stern to be swung to port or starboard when moving astern.

Her radical appearance took a lot of people by surprise and there was a good deal of adverse comment. She had lighter weight aluminium superstructures above boat deck level to offer greater stability, the bridge deck being one full deck higher than the boat deck. She was an excellent sea boat, a very practical ship, easy to keep clean and functional, but many found it hard to get used to her squat streamlined funnel astern and midships foremast.

On her delivery voyage from Hamburg, with Captain Oscar Carlson as master, the *Finnmarken* called at Oslo on a promotional visit before setting sail on her maiden voyage on 8th June 1956. Captain Carlson was to be succeeded by Captain Rolf Holten for a number of years until Captain Hilmar Stenersen took over in 1971.

On board the *Finnmarken* as she cruises down Trollfjord in July 1975, her VDS blue funnel always suited her best (Mike Bent)

On 30th November 1974, the *Finnmarken* had the honour of being the first Hurtigruten ship to use the new harbour berth at Berlevåg, now protected by two massive breakwaters using the French tetrapod interlocking system; prior to this passengers and cargo were unloaded by tender.

In 1976 the *Finnmarken,* with Captain Hilmer Stenersen in command, made the headlines for all the wrong reasons, when crossing the Folla northbound, she suffered a major engine breakdown, and with the wind blowing off the land drifted westwards out to sea. The salvage vessel *Parat* was summoned and took the *Finnmarken* in tow to safer waters whilst engineers worked flat out to repair the engine. For over three days the *Finnmarken* continued to drift slowly northwestwards, rolling in the Atlantic swell before the engineers succeeded in getting the engine started again and she was able to reach Bodø.

In general, the *Finnmarken* was an extremely reliable ship, though on the evening of 6th February 1981 in a snow storm with very rough seas, she managed to go aground off Moldøra near Svolvær. After an underwater inspection the ship continued in service the next day.

In February 1983, the *Finnmarken* was sent to the Mjellem & Karlsen Shipyard in Bergen for a refurbishment and machinery upgrade, new linings and cylinder heads being fitted. Her midship cabins were rebuilt as en suite resulting in berth capacity being reduced to 131. The formal merging of VDS and ODS into Det Ofotens og Vesteraalens Dampskibsselskab (OVDS) in January 1988 meant new funnel colours. The loss of the attractive VDS livery of blue band with white rings meant that she never quite looked the same again.

After 37 years of excellent service, with the imminent delivery of the new *Richard With* in December 1993, the *Finnmarken* was laid up. In a bold move OVDS agreed to allow the ship to become an integral part of the new Hurtigruten Museum at Stokmarknes. Funding was secured in 1997/98 and after 6 years of inactivity on 3rd May 1999 the *Finnmarken* was sent under her own power to the Kaarbø shipyard at Harstad, where her hull was sandblasted and repainted. On 14th June, with Captain Sten Magne Engen in command, she sailed for Stokmarknes where he was able to order 'finished with engines' for the very last time. Two days later the ship was lifted ashore and placed close to the Hurtigruten Museum in time for its opening on 4th July 1999.

The *Finnmarken* is the largest land based museum exhibit in Norway, preserved in a unique environment for all to enjoy for many years to come *(see also article on the Hurtigruten Museum)*

Det Nordenfjeldske Dampskibsselskab's new ship ordered from Blohm & Voss of Hamburg in 1954 was to be a replacement for their *Ragnvald Jarl* of 1942 which was by now too slow for the Coastal Express service.

The new *Ragnvald Jarl* was launched on 19th April 1956, its predecessor being temporarily renamed *Harald Jarl,* and delivered to NFDS on 24th July with Captain Paul Holm as her first master. Of 2,196 gross tons and with a length of 266 feet, NFDS and VDS had cooperated in the design of the *Ragnvald Jarl* and *Finnmarken* in having the engine room towards the stern,

NFDS postcard depicting on
board facilities on their
Ragnvald Jarl (1956)
(Bård Kolltveit Collection)

The location is unknown but
it looks like a bumpy ride as
the *Ragnvald Jarl* heads out
for her next port of call
(Bruce Peter Collection)

a low, streamlined funnel aft and foremast amidships. The *Ragnvald Jarl* was not an identical twin to *Finnmarken*, since the dining room on the promenade deck, occupying the full width of the superstructure, was without alleyways on either side. There were also differences in interior decoration and furnishings. The ship had an aluminium superstructure above boat deck level to improve stability and the bridge deck was one full deck higher than the boat deck. It was an exceptionally good sea boat, though as with the *Finnmarken* the overall profile promoted a good deal of adverse comment.

The *Ragnvald Jarl* had furnished cabins for 205 passengers and could carry 585 on coastal services. Her holds, both forward, had a total capacity of 21,830 cubic feet. The propulsion unit, a 10-cylinder MAN diesel of 2,960 bhp, produced a maximum speed of 16.6 knots, and being reversible, when combined with the variable pitch propeller, made manoeuvring at slow speeds very much easier.

After eleven years of excellent service, the *Ragnvald Jarl* returned to Hamburg in Autumn 1967 for a thorough overhaul. The interior was refurbished in line with the new regulations and the engine converted to use heavy fuel oil. The ship had the reputation of being the most economical on the route.

Sixteen years later, this time in Autumn 1983, the ship received another major refurbishment at the Mjellem & Karlsen Shipyard in Bergen, costing 12m kroner in which the hull was sandblasted and the engine totally rebuilt with a new cylinder block and liners. The two lounges were merged, 12 new

cabins built and others rebuilt with private shower and toilet. Overall this greatly reduced cabin capacity from 205 to 144.

In the spring of 1984 the *Ragnvald Jarl* was chosen for an unusual experiment with the European Space Agency in partnership with Norsk Elektrisk Bureau. The ship was fitted with experimental lightweight satellite communication terminals and data recording equipment as part of the Prosat project to improve satellite communication technology for use with all forms of transport. The terminals were linked to the Villafranca satellite tracking station near Madrid, via the Space Agency's Marecs satellite. In the higher latitudes the elevation of Marecs satellite was very low, only 14 degrees above the horizon in Trondheim and close to zero degrees at Nordkapp, so a Hurtigruten ship was ideal for this purpose in which the technology could be tested under extreme conditions.

In August 1995 the *Ragnvald Jarl* was sold to Rogaland Sjøaspirantskole, Stavanger to become a training and cruise ship for young people. Renamed *Gann* she is seen here at Bergen in June 2006 (Uwe Jakob)

In March 2007 the ship was sold on to Sørlandets Seilende Skoleskibs Institution, based at Kristiansand for a similar role. Renamed *Sjøkurs*, the ship is seen entering Portsmouth Harbour in July 2012 (Neil Watkin)

1984 was also the year in which Norcem acquired a majority share in NFDS and within a year the company had been sold on to AS Kosmos who had also acquired BDS. The Hurtigruten part of the business was then sold in December 1988 to RoNoTro AS, a consortium of the DSD, SDS and TFDS shipping companies. Eight months later in August 1989 all were transferred to TFDS at which point the *Ragnvald Jarl* had its funnel colours changed again and the distinctive NFDS red band disappeared forever.

It came as a surprise when in August 1995 TFDS sold the *Ragnvald Jarl* to Rogaland Sjøaspirantskole, Stavanger. She was renamed *Gann*, replacing the previous ship of that name, the old *Finmarken* of 1912. Based at Hundvåg near Stavanger, the vessel combines the role of training and cruise ship, operating in summer between Stavanger and Nordkapp, and occasionally venturing to Svalbard as well. In March 2007, the *Gann* was replaced by another Hurtigruten ship, the *Narvik* of 1982 (which also took on the same name), but was sold on for a similar role to Sørlandets Seilende Skoleskibs Institution, based at Kristiansand. Renamed *Sjøkurs*, the ship is still in active service today.

Det Nordenfjeldske Dampskibsselskab too placed a further order for new tonnage, this time with Trondheim Mek Shipyard in 1959, the *Harald Jarl* being launched on 29th January 1960 and delivered some five months later. Whilst basically of similar design to the *Finnmarken* and the *Ragnvald Jarl,* the architects had responded to the criticisms and produced a beautifully well proportioned ship with a combined mast and funnel positioned just aft of amidships. In addition, the placing of the lifeboat davits above and clear of the boat deck was much more pleasing aesthetically. These improvements were to be further developed in the next three Coastal Express ships to be delivered in 1964.

The ship was much bigger than the previous two vessels measuring 2,568 gross tons and 20 feet longer at 286.8 feet. There were two holds forward with a total capacity of 25,940 cubic feet, together with a 4,900 cubic foot freezer room. The *Harald Jarl* had a certificate for 652 passengers with 55 first class and 170 second class berths, and both first and second class dining rooms

A Coastal Express 'welcome on board' booklet cover dating from the 1960's (Bård Kolltveit Collection)

Cabin and Deck Plan information for travellers on aboard the *Harald Jarl* (1960) during the 1992 season (David Parsons Collection)

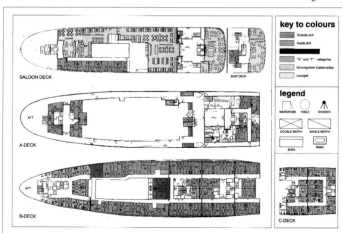

A postcard showing the
Harald Jarl southbound
passing the Seven Sisters
between Sandnessjøen and
Brønnøysund
(David Parsons Collection)

were provided, together with a cafeteria. The first class lounge was forward, overlooking the foredeck, situated just below the bridge. The décor was of a high standard with Arnstein Arneberg's architect Find Nilson responsible for the interior, while artist Kaare Espolin Johnson co-ordinated the art work. The ship's navigation equipment for the first time included an auto-pilot. The *Harald Jarl's* prime mover was a 5-cylinder Burmeister & Wain diesel of 3,450 bhp, built under license by Akers M/V, which on trials achieved 18.3 knots. The total cost of building the ship came to 14.5 million kroner.

On 23rd June 1960 the *Harald Jarl,* now the NFDS's flagship, under the command of Captain Christian O. Odegaard, departed from the Festningskaien, Bergen on her maiden voyage to Kirkenes. The ship had replaced the *Sigurd Jarl,* which was the last of their steamships in Hurtigruten service. In 1962, 569,579 passengers were carried on the Hurtigruten, the highest number ever and a record still unbroken some 60 years later.

The *Harald Jarl* was to serve the Hurtigruten well. In June 1968 the ship reopened the service to Svalbard as well as undertaking various spring shopping cruises from Bergen and Trondheim (prices in the UK being significantly less than those in Norway) to Lerwick and Aberdeen between 1970 and 1979.

In 1983, the *Harald Jarl* was further upgraded to comply with the new safety regulations, the engine thoroughly overhauled, cabins torn out and rebuilt with en suite facilities, reducing the berth capacity to 169.

The *Harald Jarl* served without any major incident until 6th August 1987 when the ship ran aground just north of Rørvik. No less than 30 tons of steel were required to repair the extensive damage to the keel which was carried out at the Myklebust Mek Shipyard, Sandøy, near Molde. In August 1989 with a final transfer of ownership to TFDS, the *Harald Jarl* lost her funnel colours and the distinctive NFDS red band was to be no more.

On 22nd February 2001, again near Rørvik, in very rough weather, the ship once more ran aground. Although she appeared to be undamaged, it

This August 1975 image shows the *Harald Jarl* and *Midnatsol* at the Festningskaien, Bergen preparing for their next voyages (Mike Bent)

was deemed wise to get the rescue vessel *Kaptein Skaugen* to take the 67 passengers to Rørvik until the *Harald Jarl* had been thoroughly checked over.

After 41 years of service with new ships about to come into service, the *Harald Jarl* set out on its last round trip on the Coastal Express from the Frieleneskaien Terminal, Bergen on 9th October 2001. Her temporary replacement was to be the *Nordstjernen*. Upon her return she continued from Bergen to Oslo, where she remained for a week while the paintings and murals by Kaare Espolin Johnson were carefully removed for transfer to the new *Trollfjord*, which was fitting out at the Fosen Mek Shipyard at Rissa, near Trondheim. Apparently the paintings were valued at NOK 15 million, while the ship was advertised for sale at just NOK 10 million! The *Harald Jarl* was in fact to spend the winter at the Fosen shipyard, serving as an accommodation ship.

A number of schemes to purchase the ship for further work were promoted but it was not until July 2002 that the *Harold Jarl* was sold to Elegant Cruises Inc, who renamed the ship *Andrea*. The following month the ship sailed to Uddevalla in Sweden, where large areas of the lounges including furniture were renewed and cabins upgraded. The *Andrea* was marketed as a 4-star cruise ship, with a capacity for just 106 passengers, advertising a series of cruises around the Baltic Sea and Norwegian coast. Generally, the *Andrea* was used on cruises mainly around the Adriatic, though she has also visited Antarctica. Laid up at Vranjic, Split in Croatia, in April 2012 she was sold to the Moscow based Volga Dream Cruises for further service. Now renamed *Serenissima* and under the Premier Cruises banner, for 2013 she was chartered to several operators (including Noble Caledonia) for cruises around the Mediterranean, Black Sea, British Isles and Norway.

The *Harald Jarl* as *Andrea* (Elegant Cruises) at Korpo, Finland, 2008. In 2013 she will operate as Premier Cruises' *Serenissima* (Folke Österman)

Disaster 1962
SANCT SVITHUN

Given the length of time that ships are in service, the distances they travel and the extreme conditions under which they sometimes operate, mishaps on the Hurtigruten are fortunately relatively few and far between, generally involving minor groundings resulting in no more than a few damaged plates below the waterline and, if necessary, a drydocking. Tragedies involving the loss of vessels and lives are rare. The Hurtigruten has an outstanding safety record; the standard of seamanship and maintenance of the vessels that operate is of a high order.

The events of the night of Sunday 21st October 1962 have not been forgotten in Norway, as even today some 50 years later an element of mystery still surrounds what happened out on the Folla on board DSD's flagship, the *Sanct Svithun*.

At lunchtime the *Sanct Svithun* had sailed from Trondheim for Rørvik where she was scheduled to call around 21.00. The wind was in the southwest with a swell rolling in from the Atlantic. A total of 89 persons were on board; 40 passengers, 2 postal workers and 47 crew.

The course steered by the *Sanct Svithun* on that fateful night (Mike Bent)

At 21.55 the Rørvik harbourmaster received a radio message from the *Sanct Svithun,* that the ship was aground between Allgarden and Gjæslingen, in the main shipping channel, some 12 nautical miles southwest of Rørvik. The *Ragnvald Jarl,* which the *Sanct Svithun* would normally meet at Rørvik, immediately set out for the reported position,

Idyllic times, the *Sanct Svithun* at Svolvær with an admiring audience
(Bård Kolltveit Collection)

and on reaching it sent up a series of distress flares. With all her lights on, the ship should have been visible to any other ship in the vicinity. In radio contact, both ships' masters were rather puzzled as neither of them could see the flares from each other's vessel.

At 22.45 all radio contact with *Sanct Svithun* was suddenly lost. The final message from Captain Klevland was to the effect that the ship was afloat again, but taking in water. At 02.00 the mystery deepened further when a ship's lifeboat came ashore at the Nordøyan lighthouse, some 15 miles west of *Sanct Svithun*'s reported position, its occupants convinced that they had landed at Grinna lighthouse, near Gjæslingen. A second lifeboat then came ashore at Nordøyan, making a total of thirty survivors on the islet. The local steamer, *Vikna*, was sent from Rørvik to collect them.

As soon as it was light small boats, helicopters and light aircraft joined in the search for any survivors; 17 more were rescued, but sadly 35 bodies were recovered. The total of dead was later to rise to 42. Among those missing or dead were Captain Klevland, Karl Tysnes, (pilot/navigator) and Ole Solheim who was one of the helmsmen. The following day, Tuesday 23rd October, the local priest, Hilmar Romsøy, held a memorial service at the local church in Rørvik.

It was not until some 38 hours after the first distress call, around noon on the 23rd, that the *Sanct Svithun* was eventually located, lying in 35 fathoms of water, 3.2 nautical miles from Nordøyan lighthouse, about 200 metres from the Osken reef. This was no less than fifteen nautical miles from the reported position of her grounding and a very long way from the shipping lane used by the Hurtigruten ships.

An inquest into the tragedy was opened in Rørvik on 3rd October attended by survivors from the passengers and crew as well as officials from Det Stavangerske Dampskibsselskab.

From the survivors' accounts it would appear that up to 20.00 on that fateful evening the voyage had been totally uneventful as the ship set off down Trondheimsfjorden, later winding its way through the Stokksundet and out into the less sheltered waters off the Buholmråsa lighthouse. Here the *Sanct Svithun* followed a course of 350° into the Folla, at which time Karl Tysnes took over as duty pilot and 17 year old John Karlsen relieved the helmsman.

Between 20.00 and 20.30 the course steered was 342°, taking *Sanct Svithun* well clear of the Nord-Trøndelag coast. As the *Sanct Svithun* neared the group of rocks known as the Grunnan, the order was given to 'steer '35°'. The helmsman repeated the command, and altered course from 342° to 335°. At 20.45 the course was altered to 333° so as to to give way to an approaching ship, before resuming on 335°. It was customary at that time for pilots to give only the final two numbers of a course alteration unless it involved a change of the 'hundreds' digit.

The ship's navigation systems were in good order. There were two compasses in the wheelhouse and whilst both would tend to err by a couple of degrees after a spell of rolling (the Italian built ship *Sanct Svithun* had a reputation as a lively sea-boat), conditions that night were not so adverse as to be of any consequence.

Shortly before 21.00 Captain Klevland came up to the bridge and was informed by the pilot that according to the reading on the electronic log there should be a lighthouse up ahead. Visibility was now poor so he asked the pilot to switch to a larger range on the radar screen.

At the same time Ole Solheim relieved John Karlsen as helmsman, the latter informing him that the course was '35°'.

At 21.55 the ship ran aground. Down in the engine room the main engine was forced upwards by the impact and the two auxiliary diesels almost immediately seized up. Captain Klevland ordered the evacuation of the ship and No. 2 lifeboat was launched and held alongside so that people could board. A number of passengers standing near the deck rail were reluctant to take to the lifeboat.

A large breaker then pushed *Sanct Svithun* off the reef and Captain Klevland gave the order for the port anchor to be lowered so as to prevent the ship from being driven ashore again. Distress flares were again launched and a further radio message transmitted, indicating that the *Sanct Svithun* was afloat again but taking in water.

On deck, the two helmsmen, Karlsen and Solheim, bumped into one another, the latter shouting, 'You gave me the wrong course! It should have been 035°, not 335°!'

The *Sanct Svithun* was now rapidly sinking, listing 35° to starboard with her foredeck almost submerged. At 22.45 the lights went out and the radio became dead. One of the lifeboats was smashed against the side of the ship, tipping its occupants into the water. Among the very last to leave the sinking ship was deckhand John Karlsen; caught in the undertow he managed to resurface underneath a life raft and was able to save himself.

As far as the causes of the tragedy are concerned it would appear that the answers lie in the orders given, the actual courses steered and whether these were physically checked by all concerned, particularly at a time when three bridge personnel were being relieved. Nobody, therefore on the bridge was aware how far off course the ship was. The possible misunderstanding between '035°' and '335°' should have been spotted quickly as any decisions after this compounded the situation. Sadly, three of the bridge personnel who could have thrown light on this lost their lives in this tragedy.

Surprisingly, after Tysnes ordered Karlsen to 'Steer '35°, he failed to notice that the nature of the ship's motion had not altered, something which, had he given a course alteration as much as 53° would have been obvious. The sea, which would previously have been on the port beam, would then have been on her quarter.

Likewise, the lights at Gjæslingen and Nordøyan were not properly checked out, as the former had a continuous white beam whilst the light on the latter shone once every four minutes. Those on the bridge had become somewhat disorientated.

There was also an issue with charts. The *Ragnvald Jarl*, which had set out to search for the *Sanct Svithun*, needed to return to Rørvik for a large scale chart of that area, mainly because Nordøyan was such a long way from the main shipping channel. It was therefore unlikely that the *Sanct Svithun* would have such a chart. If it had, then those on her bridge might have become aware of the differing characteristics of Gjæslingen and Nordøyan lights.

Afterwards, with all the benefit of hindsight, it was suggested that if the Decca direction-finding system been in place along the Norwegian coast (as it was in neighbouring countries), the tragedy could probably have been averted. A Decca system for the Helgeland coast would have cost at that time 1.5 million kroner, a totally insignificant amount when compared with the loss of 42 lives and of a relatively new Hurtigruten ship.

One of a number of ships hastily called in to fill the gap on the Hurtigruten after the loss of the *Sanct Svithun* was the *Kronprinsesse Märtha*. The ship is still in existence today and has had an interesting career, built for Det Stavangerske Dampskibsselskab by the International Shipbuilding & Engineering Company, Danzig, as long ago as 1929. Of 898 gross tons she

The *Kronprinsesse Märtha* (1929) was one of a number of ships which was drafted in to fill the gap after the loss of the *Sanct Svithun*. She is still in existence today as a floating hotel/restaurant ship in Stockholm (LogInn Hotels)

had a registered length of 176.8 feet and her 900 ihp Lenz double-compound engine gave a service speed of 13 knots. Designed for the Bergen and Stavanger to Oslo route she managed to run aground near Bru, north of Stavanger, on 19th December 1939 and sank. Raised and repaired, on the orders of the occupying forces, the ship was renamed *Ryfylke*, not resuming her original name until 1945. In 1948, the *Kronprinsesse Märtha* was fitted with a new 1,200 bhp 16-cylinder 2T EV DM General Motors diesel engine. On 26th June 1956 she ran aground on Grønholmskjær, east of Risør and sank yet again. The ship was raised and towed to the Pusnes Mek Shipyard, Arendal, where her superstructure was rebuilt and a new bow fitted, before being sent to DSD's own shipyard at Stavanger for her interior to be gutted and refurbished. The *Kronprinsesse Märtha* now measured 996 gross tons with a registered length of 182.2 feet and returned to the Bergen to Stavanger Nattrute (night) service.

The *Kronprinsesse Märtha* was withdrawn and sold in October 1974 to Nika Investments of of Sandefjord, who renamed her *Koster* for use as an accommodation ship. The ship was sold again in March 1979 to Sport Rover Shipping Corporation, renamed *Sport Rover* and rebuilt to serve as a mother ship for diving operations. In the 1990s under the name of *Emerald Sea*, she spent some time laid up in the River Fal, between Truro and Falmouth. In April 2000, the ship was towed to Sweden for conversion into a floating restaurant and hotel ship. Today she is to be found at Södermälarstrand in central Stockholm, serving as the 'LogInn Hotel *m/s Kronprinsesse Märtha*'.

In her original VDS funnel livery the *Lofoten* (1964) approaches Svolvaer with a northbound service in July 1975 (Mike Bent)

More Additions to the Fleet 1964

A rare image of the *Lofoten* in her FFR colours which she wore from 1988 until 1996 (Bruce Peter Collection)

In 1962, Det Vesteraalens Dampskibsselskab decided that despite still being in good condition and continuing to be extremely popular amongst the travelling public, it was now time for their 1932 built *Lofoten* to be replaced. In February 1962, together with sister companies ODS and SDS they signed a contract with the Aker group for three ships, all to be built to the same basic design based on the *Harald Jarl*. The Vesteraalen and Ofotens ships were to be constructed simultaneously at Aker's Oslo shipyard, whilst the contract for the Stavanger vessel was given to their Bergen shipyard.

On 7th September 1963, the new *Lofoten* was named and launched by Asbjørg Bergsmo of Stokmarknes, with the traditional breaking of the champagne bottle over the bows. Her predecessor had been renamed *Vågan* the previous autumn. The *Lofoten* measured 2,597 gross tons and was 286.8 feet in length. Powered by a 7-cylinder Aker built 3,325 bhp Burmeister & Wain diesel, she attained a speed of 17.49 knots on trials. Her lounges were located on the promenade deck, with an observation saloon forward. The ship had berths for 53 first class and 180 second class passengers, with several of the cabins being interchangeable between classes. Relatively few however, were en-suite.

Following a final four-hour trial on the morning of 27th February 1964, she made a short cruise down Oslofjorden for around a hundred of the company's guests. The following day the ship was formally handed over to VDS and sailed immediately for Bergen.

Late in the evening on 5th March 1964, under the command of Captain Svein Eriksen, the *Lofoten* slipped out from the Festningskaien, Bergen, on her maiden voyage. By mid June her two near sister ships *Kong Olav* and *Nordnorge* would also enter service. Whilst built to the same specification, each company would mark their individuality particularly in the design and placement of the funnel, the *Lofoten* having a very squat funnel, not dissimilar to the *Harald Jarl* in profile.

During her long and varied career (including a spring cruise to Lerwick in April 1977) the *Lofoten* has rarely been involved in any dramatic incidents. She was regularly on the 'Svalbard Express' from the summer of 1968 until 1982. On one of these Svalbard sailings, on 19th July 1977, she grounded at Nordøy in Tjeldsundet and sustained significant damage to the keel. Temporary repairs were carried out at Harstad before the ship went to the Nyland Shipyard at Oslo for further attention.

In October 1980, the *Lofoten* was sent to Aalborg Værft, Denmark for reconfiguration into a one class ship, the former second class dining room being converted into four large cabins. At the same time her engines were thoroughly overhauled. Only five years later, the ship was again back at Aalborg for further upgrading with many of the cabins on B deck being rebuilt with en suite facilities, reducing her berth capacity to 223. She even received a blue hull, but this was to be a short-lived experiment.

In the mid 1980s Det Vesteraalens Dampskibsselskab sold a substantial number of its shares to Det Ofotens Dampskibsselskab, eventually the latter gaining a majority shareholding. In January 1988 the companies formally merged into Det Ofotens og Vesteraalens Dampskibsselskab (OVDS), with all VDS ships now registered in Narvik and sporting the Ofotens funnel logo.

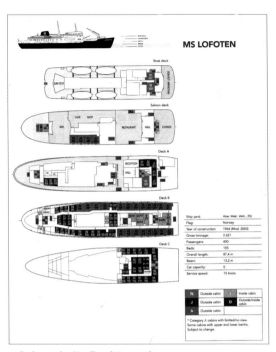

Deck Plan of *Lofoten* in present day configuration

The *Lofoten* was sold back to OVDS in January 1996 and she is seen here at Trondheim in her 'new' funnel colours (Bruce Peter Collection)

The *Lofoten* is a comfortable and beautifully maintained ship; from top to bottom, the bar, lounge, panorama lounge (Ove Jakob)

The *Lofoten* was not to remain long under this new ownership as on 1st September 1988 the ship was sold for NOK 20m to Finnmark Fylkesrederi og Rutelskap, based in Hammerfest. FFR had been invited to join the Hurtigruten consortium and the *Lofoten* was to be their contribution, and as a consequence it meant another funnel livery change. The company had big plans for the future but in late 1991 with first of the 'new generation' ships being built at Stralsund in Germany, they were not able to secure the necessary funding for a further new build for the route. As a result on 1st January 1996, the *Lofoten* was sold back to OVDS for NOK 35m (that's inflation for you!) and formally handed back a month later.

In the meantime the *Lofoten* had made four very interesting cruises to Murmansk in 1993, and the following March celebrated its 30th birthday with a special anniversary cruise. More upgrading to the cabin accommodation followed in January 1996 at the Mjellem & Karlsen Shipyard, Bergen, which again further reduced cabin capacity now at 184 berths.

In January 2001, the *Lofoten* was granted 'Cultural Heritage' status by the Riksantvikvaren, Norway's Directorate for Cultural Heritage, though with three further new ships on order it appeared that her Hurtigruten days were numbered. OVDS, however, made plans for her to operate shorter cruises working out of Bodø in summer and in winter to act as a relief vessel on the Hurtigruten. Replaced by the new *Finnmarken* on 2nd February 2002, she was sent for a thorough upgrade at the Kaarbø Verft Shipyard, Harstad, which included new fire safety systems in order that she could take over from the Antarctica bound *Nordnorge* that autumn. Whilst subject to all safety regulations, as a 'Cultural Heritage' ship the *Lofoten* was able to obtain some exemptions in order to avoid excessive major surgery to her interior. The ship took up Hurtigruten service again on 12th December 2002 and continued until 12th April 2003 when the *Nordnorge* returned from Antarctica.

At her 40th birthday celebration in March 2004, it was revealed that the *Lofoten* was estimated to have sailed 2,886,000 nautical miles, carried 1.25

The *Lofoten* viewed in 2011, southbound about to re-cross the Arctic Circle (John Bryant)

million passengers and made 75,296 calls at ports. In addition the ship's engine had run for 234,000 hours (26.7 years) and consumed 107,200 tonnes of diesel fuel! The *Lofoten*'s Hurtigruten departure from Bergen on 8th March became a celebratory event, with various choirs, orchestras and jazz bands joining the ship for parts of the voyage.

In 2005 the *Lofoten* made three 7 day cruises from Bergen in April, May and September, taking in Stavanger, Haugesund, the Hardangerfjorden, Flåm and the Stadlandet before returning south. In the summer peak the ship cruised further north up the Helgeland coast to Bodø, via Flåm, Ålesund, Molde, Brønnøysund, Torghatten, Alstahaug and Svartisen. Bodø then became the base for another series of weekly cruises in the Nordland and Lofoten areas.

For the summer of 2007 the *Lofoten* was based in Svalbard in conjunction with the Longyearbyen based Spitsbergen Travel Company, offering week long cruises under the marketing banner of *Spitsbergen Explorer*. Travellers would fly in and spend overnight at the Spitsbergen Hotel before joining the ship later that afternoon. The *Lofoten* would cruise around the islands that make up Svalbard; highlights would include visiting Ny-Ålesund, the Magdalenefjorden and the walrus colony at Moffen.

Since then with the sale of two of the 'mid generation' ships, the *Lofoten* has been permanently back in the Hurtigruten service, much loved by a loyal crew and a discerning clientele. Long may she continue!

In late 1962, immediately after the loss of their *Sanct Svithun*, Det Stavangerske Dampskibsselskab (DSD) was given permission to order a replacement. The new ship, to be named the *Kong Olav*, was constructed at the Bergens Mek Shipyard, Solheimsviken, Bergen, and launched a year later by Randi Gowart-Olsen on 15th November 1963. It was the first Hurtigruten ship to be built there since the *Midnatsol* of 1910. Although of the same basic design as the two consorts being built for VDS and ODS at Oslo, there is no doubt that this 16.5m kroner vessel was probably the finest looking of all the first generation postwar motorships for the Hurtigruten, beautifully set off by the well proportioned dummy funnel (in the distinctive Stavanger colours with its three red bands) aft of the bridge deck. The engine exhaust was discharged through the mainmast located aft. The *Kong Olav*

DSD's graceful *Kong Olav* (1964) is captured at Bergen in 1972 (Ivor Ireland/ Mike Bent Collection)

measured 2,604 gross tons and was 289.8 feet in length, with its holds having both refrigeration and deep-freeze facilities. The propulsion unit was a 7-cylinder Burmeister & Wain diesel generating 3,325 bhp, built under license by Akers. During her test runs the ship achieved 17.52 knots, more than adequate for a regular service of 14.5 to 15 knots. The ship was also the first Hurtigruten steamer to have a bow thrust (a 400 hp Liaaen unit), to aid manoeuvrability on and off the berths.

Passenger comforts were not forgotten as the ship boasted heaters on the saloon windows to prevent icing-up. The *Kong Olav* had a passenger certificate for 500 persons and cabins with a total of 222 berths in two classes. The internal design mirrored that of the *Lofoten*, with the first class lounge forward overlooking the bow.

The *Kong Olav* was handed over to DSD on 11th April 1964, and whilst berthed at its home port of Stavanger received a personal visit from Kong Olav of Norway himself, prior to setting out for her maiden Hurtigruten sailing from the Festningskaien, Bergen, on 11th May. The *Kong Olav* proved to be a very popular ship on the route and, as with the *Lofoten* and *Nordstjernen,* was involved in the Svalbard Express programmes which ran from 1968 until 1982, together with spring mini cruises to Aberdeen in the 1970s.

It came as a bit of a shock when DSD decided in March 1978 to sell the ship. Financial difficulties, together with the ship not being based around its home port, meant that the Hurtigruten operation was becoming less and less pertinent to the Rogaland region. As a result, on 11th April the *Kong Olav* was sold to Det Vesteraalens Dampskibsselskab for NOK 17.5 million

The powerful lines of the *Kong Olav* are shown to good efeect as she approaches Bergen in July 1985, note her VDS funnel livery (Brian Fisher Collection)

A third change of ownership in 1988 saw the *Kong Olav* sporting the OVDS funnel colours, pictured here near Ålesund (Aage Schjølberg)

(a million more than the ship had cost as new), and the dummy funnel repainted in the VDS blue, white and black livery. In the spring of 1986 the ship had a major modernization, with cabins upgraded and four new ones constructed in the former aft lounge area, the engine overhauled and the crane on the foredeck replaced.

Two years later, in January 1988, with the merger of the Vesteraalen and Ofotens companies to form Det Ofotens og Vesteraalens Dampskibselskap now completed, the *Kong Olav's* dummy funnel was repainted in the OVDS colours of red and white with a blue symbol on a yellow background.

By the mid 1990s with three further 'new generation' ships to be constructed at Ulsteinvik, the *Kong Olav's* time on the Hurtigruten was rapidly coming to an end. On 30th April 1997, after 33 years of excellent service, the ship docked in Bergen for the final time to be replaced by the new *Nordnorge*.

The ship was laid up at the Solheimsviken Shipyard, Bergen where it had been built, but was not to remain there long, being sold to a hotel group, the Andaman Club Co Ltd, Bangkok, Thailand. The ship was re-registered in San Lorenzo and the Honduras flag hoisted. On the morning of 2nd July 1997, with no name change, the ship sailed south for a new career. The plan was to use the ship on 2 and 3 day cruises for divers and tourists based on Phuket as well as act as a hotel and casino ship off the Similan Islands in the Andaman Sea on the west coast of Burma. However, the cabins and facilities on board proved to be inadequate for this purpose and needed to have air-conditioning installed. Observed in a floating dock in Bangkok in February 1998, the project, however, was hit by the Asian financial crisis of that year, which had major consequences for tourism. After docking, the *Kong Olav*

The *Kong Olav* is currently laid up off Ranong in the Southern Thailand Anchorage, as seen here in 2007. (Jan-Olav Storli)

was laid up in the Southern Thailand Anchorage off Ranong where she remains today. A number of knowledgeable people would like to bring the *Kong Olav* back to Norway but the chances of any future career appear minimal.

On 16th March 1962, ODS were given permission from the Samferdselsdepartement (Norwegian Ministry of Transport and Communications) to build a full-size Hurtigruten ship to replace their *Barøy* which had only been drafted onto the route as a result of the ongoing tonnage shortages. Ofotens (celebrating its golden jubilee) had originally intended for the new ship to be built by Trondhjems M/V, but when that shipyard was taken over by the Aker group in 1962, its construction was switched to the company's Oslo yard.

Costing 17m kroner, the ship was named *Nordnorge* and launched on 1st February 1964 by Randi Bratteli, wife of the then Minister for Transport. At 2,611 gross tons and 286.8 feet in length, the ship was marginally the largest member of the Hurtigruten fleet. Built to the same dimensions as her two consorts, her lounges were located on the promenade deck, with first class forward and second class aft together with a viewing lounge on the bridge deck. She had a passenger certificate for 500 persons and as a two class vessel had cabins for 57 first class berths and 180 second class berths, mainly on B deck. Her standard 7-cylinder Akers built Burmeister & Wain diesel engine of 3,325 bhp gave her a top speed of 17.55 knots.

She was handed over on 8th June 1964 and shortly afterwards sailed for Bergen to be ready for her first Hurtigruten voyage. Three days later, under the command of Captain H Waagønes, the new Hurtigruten flagship sailed from the Festningskaien, Bergen on her maiden voyage. On her southbound voyage she diverted to make a special call to her home port and headquarters of ODS, Narvik, which had not been served by the Hurtigruten since 1953.

A postcard view from the *Nordnorge* (1964) of Nordkapp. Hurtigruten ships no longer sail this way (David Parsons Collection)

A publicity photograph of the *Island Explorer* ex *Nordnorge*, sadly a short-lived venture

Some observers thought that she was even better looking than the *Kong Olav*, with her clean, classic lines, the balanced profile and the large, streamlined dummy funnel, set off by the yellow, red white and blue Ofotens livery. With the introduction of the *Nordnorge*, for the first time the Hurtigruten could now operate with 13 similar ships of the same standard capacity and 15 knot service speed, bringing both reliability and stability to the whole operation for almost the next two decades. It was not until the winter of 1982/3 with the new *Narvik* entering service there was any significant change. The *Nordnorge's* crew transferred to the new ship, whilst the crew from the now retired *Håkon Jarl* transferred to the *Nordnorge*.

In December 1985 as part of a NOK 4.5m upgrading of the ship the *Nordnorge* was sent to the Kaarbø Mek Shipyard at Harstad for her engine to be completely overhauled. As with her fleetmates, her interior was refurbished with many cabins rebuilt as en suite as well as new cabins being installed on the starboard side of the aft promenade deck saloon. Overall, however, the number of berths available was reduced to 207.

With the arrival of the new *Nordkapp*, the *Nordnorge* was laid up at Narvik from 1st April 1996. That August, the ship was sold to Templeman Inc of Panama, Liberian owned but having Norwegian interests. On 19th August 1996, the ship was formally handed over, renamed *Worldlink* and, sporting a plain yellow funnel, left for Greece. Sold on again to Universal Enterprises, Mali and renamed *Island Explorer*, the ship was revamped at Piraeus for service as a dive cruise vessel based around the Maldives. Furnishings and cabins were upgraded, with 56 de luxe cabins, air conditioning and a swimming pool. The outer deck was extended aft and the hull was painted white with a blue stripe. It looked as if her long term future was assured, but on 19th December 2005, whilst based at Ari Atoll, Kandholadhow, the decision was taken to sell her for scrap. In early January 2006, with a ride crew on board and under her own power, the ship departed the Maldives for Alang, India and demolition.

The *Nordnorge* at speed showing her well-balanced profile (David Parsons Postcard Collection)

The Svalbard Express

1968–1982

In the summer of 1951 regular sailings to Svalbard were revived after a gap of twelve years. The *Lyngen* from Troms Fylkes Dampskibsselskap (TFDS) continued to carry on from where she left off in 1939 and made three round trips that year. By the middle of the decade there were six departures from Tromsø each summer, the cruises connecting with the Hurtigruten service. With each trip designed to last eleven days, the actual day of departure varied in order to minimise turn-round time and maximise ship usage. Calls were made at Bjørnøya, Isfjord (where a tender was used to drop off supplies), Longyearbyen and Ny-Ålesund. If the weather was fair, the *Lyngen* had a sufficiently shallow draught to allow her to sail via the Forlandsundet between the two ports. From Ny-Ålesund she continued north to Magdalenefjorden but before returning south the steamer would sail as close as practicable to the edge of the polar ice pack around 80° N.

Both freight and mail traffic to Svalbard had increased, mainly from those working at the European Space Research Organisation's satellite-

Svalbard Express timetable (summer 1975)

NORTHBOUND		SOUTHBOUND
Saturday 11.00	Bergen	Thursday 07.15
Saturday 19.00	Måløy	Wednesday 23.45
Saturday 23.00	Ålesund	Wednesday 19.30
Saturday 23.30	Ålesund	Wednesday 19.00
	Kristiansund	Wednesday 15.00
Sunday 09.30	Trondheim	Wednesday 08.30
Sunday 13.00	Trondheim	Wednesday 06.00
Monday 09.00	Bodø	Tuesday 09.00
Monday 13.00	Bodø	Tuesday 07.45
Monday 17.30	Svolvær	Tuesday 03.15
Monday 20.45	Svolvær	Tuesday 00.30
Monday 23.00	Lødingen	Monday 22.00
Monday 23.30	Harstad	Monday 21.00
Tuesday 03.15	Finnsnes	Monday 18.00
Tuesday 06.00	Tromsø	Monday 15.00
Tuesday 08.00	Tromsø	Monday 10.00
Tuesday 16.00	Hammerfest	
Tuesday 17.00	Hammerfest	
Tuesday 20.00	Honningsvåg	
Wednesday 00.00	Honningsvåg	
Wednesday mid-pm	Bjørnøya	Sunday mid-am
Thursday early am	Isfjord Radio	Saturday pm
	Grønfjorden	Saturday pm
Thursday late am	Longyearbyen	Saturday early pm
Thursday late pm	Longyearbyen	Saturday mid-am
Friday late am	Polar Ice Pack	
Friday early pm	Magdalenefjorden	
Friday pm	Ny Ålesund	
Friday late pm	Ny Ålesund	
Saturday early am	Tempelfjorden	Saturday early am

Timetable north of Honningsvåg dependent on cargo requirements, weather and position of the edge of the ice pack.

tracking station at Ny-Ålesund and at the Norsk Polarinstitutt's base. Despite poor weather and adverse ice conditions the popularity of the Svalbard cruises grew, encouraging TFDS and Aftenposten (Norway's largest newspaper) to form in 1965 a joint venture company, Nordpolhotellet as a means of enticing visitors to spend longer on Svalbard. One of the old mining companies' buildings was rented and refurbished as a hotel, with a total of fourteen bedrooms. The hotel's staff would travel north on *Lyngen*'s first sailing of each summer, returning home on the last one. In 1965 there were eleven round trips with 796 passengers carried. The majority of guests were ornithologists, glaciologists, geologists, mountaineers, explorers and journalists. The summer of 1965 was noted for its warm weather and at Ny-Ålesund the temperature reached the comparatively dizzy heights of 18°C. The *Lyngen* managed to run aground at Ny-Ålesund on her second cruise, which had to be curtailed. The 1965 season was the *Lyngen*'s last and her final year for TFDS as she was sold to Alfred Jensen of Harstad, where she was rebuilt as a combined cargo and fishing boat, finally being scuttled off her home port on 2nd July 1987 at the grand old age of 66 years.

The following year, 1966, the service was maintained by the *Sørøy* and *Salten*, under charter to TFDS with nine round trips and 781 passengers carried. The hotel project was less successful and only used by around 60 guests, closing for good at the end of the season.

It was the Hurtigruten consortium as a whole which came to the rescue, being granted permission by the Samferdselsdepartement (Norwegian Ministry of Transport and Communications) to develop the Svalbard market for themselves. Each company would contribute its most recent ship (*Nordstjernen*, *Harald Jarl*, *Lofoten*, *Kong Olav* and *Nordnorge)* for fortnightly summer cruises from Bergen, returning thirteen days later and calling only at the major ports between there and Honningsvåg. The first sailing of this new venture was taken by the *Harald Jarl* and departed from Bergen on 8th June 1968. By 1970, no less than 11 weekly departures were on offer, made possible by bringing the southbound Hurtigruten departure from Trondheim forward by four hours from 16.00 to 12.00, resulting in a lunchtime arrival in Bergen the following day. Instead of lying over at Bergen for 26 hours the ship could then set off again late that evening. In addition, the daily Hurtigruten could be operated using eleven ships instead of twelve, thus making two available for summer cruises to Svalbard and elsewhere, as well as enabling winter overhauls of the Hurtigruten fleet to be carried out without the need to charter in relief ships.

The 'Svalbard Express', as it was now marketed, had a holiday cruise element about it, as vessels became one-class and fares were inclusive of all meals only varying according to the grade of cabin required, shades of today's Hurtigruten operation. From Honningsvåg the schedule had to be more flexible, depending on cargo requirements, weather, ice and the cruising ranges of the individual ships. On the way north, the ships would visit Trollfjord and later at Honningsvåg there was a coach trip to the Nordkapp plateau (calls at Skarsvåg had been discontinued).

The ships usually cruised eastwards from Longyearbyen up

Tempelfjorden, before a short deviation down Grønfjorden offered passengers a glimpse behind the Iron Curtain of the Russian mining town of Barentsburg. The itinerary allowed for time to be spent slowly cruising around in the glaciated bowl of Magdalenefjorden as well as penetrating the polar ice at well beyond 80° N.

Following the withdrawal of the *Erling Jarl* in 1980 the service became fortnightly only. A decision to reduce the fleet from twelve to eleven vessels from the winter of 1982/3 made the 'Svalbard Express' no longer viable. The last sailing was appropriately taken by the *Harald Jarl* which arrived back at Bergen on 28th August 1982.

The 'Svalbard Express' was not the only cruise market initiative during the 1970s as between 1976 and 1979 both the *Nordstjernen* and *Harald Jarl* undertook a number of excursions from Bergen and Trondheim to Lerwick and Aberdeen, for Norwegians to take advantage of the comparatively low cost of shopping in Britain. These trips, mostly in springtime, were extremely popular. The *Nordstjernen* is recorded as having undertaken no less than 16 of these North Sea crossings.

It was not the end for the Svalbard experience as we shall see later, though its revival was a long time coming.

The *Harald Jarl* on Svalbard Express duties, photographed at Longyearbyen in August 1974 (Mike Bent)

A Reality Check

The next five-year Hurtigruten contract began on 1st January 1963 and, anticipating the introduction of three new ships into service, a new timetable was devised based on a standard service speed of 15 knots. It was inaugurated on 16th September 1964 by the *Polarlys* with her 23.45 departure from Bergen. For the first time in its history the Hurtigruten was operated by a fleet of ships of almost standard size and standard performance characteristics, with a mere fifteen years between the oldest and most recent vessels. It appeared to be an almost perfect solution. Or was it? No more new builds were to appear for another 18 years.

In spite of the introduction of the new ships and the revised timetable, the overall performance of the Hurtigruten that year was not good. Freight levels were down and there was increasing competition from rail, air and bus services. Heavy expenditure was more than offsetting any increases in tariffs. The contract had to be extended on a year by year basis whilst the interminable negotiations faltered each time over future subsidisation levels.

In 1972 inflation was rampant. Freight rates were up by 12.5%, passenger tariffs up by 10% and diesel fuel up by no less than 95%, a consequence of the Yom Kippur war. In 1974, in order to save fuel and bring down costs, the summertime northbound Hurtigruten would run directly from Havøysund to Honningsvåg, rather than going via Skarsvåg and Nordkapp. The Hornvika stop had been dropped in 1962 after a number of health-related incidents befalling elderly passengers as they walked up the steep footpath to the top. The owner of the quay at Skarsvåg, which had replaced the call at Hornvika, was said to be quite glad since passengers were never given any time to visit his souvenir shop before they were whisked away by bus to Nordkapp! Since that time passengers have been bussed to Nordkapp from Honningsvåg, usually visiting a Sami encampment en route during the summer months.

There was better news at nearby Berlevåg, where the new Hurtigruten quay protected by two massive breakwater arms opened in late November 1974. Tenders were no longer needed to land passengers or cargo.

By the middle of the 1970s the on-going debate over the future of the Hurtigruten was gathering momentum. Should the Hurtigruten service be retained in its existing form? If not, what type of vessel should be employed on it?

The completion in 1962 of the Nordlandbanen linking Trondheim and Bodø was anticipated to have a marked influence on the future development of transport services along the stretch of coastline between the two ports, now only twelve hours apart by rail. In theory, travellers in a hurry would opt for rail rather than sea whilst express freight trains carrying fresh fish in refrigerated vans would draw some of this traffic away from the coastal ships. In reality, the Nordlandbanen failed to live up to expectations and in 1976 generated a deficit of 554 million kroner which had to be covered by the State. Even though freight rates and passenger fares were higher on the Hurtigruten for the same distances, in terms of real costs, transportation by sea remained cheaper than rail.

The establishment of domestic airline services during the interwar years was followed by a huge expansion post war. SAS inaugurated daily flights from Oslo to Bodø, as well as to Tromsø and Kirkenes. By the mid-1970s there were over thirty commercial airline companies in Norway dominated by SAS and Wideroe. Some of the flight schedules were more akin to a bus service, the Trondheim to Bodø service, for example, having intermediate stops at Sandnessjøen, Brønnøysund and Namsos. Fares were competitive with the Hurtigruten and certainly not excessive when compared with rail. The air services captured most of the business travellers who hitherto had used the coastal steamers and even light mail now went by air.

With improved roads, both local and long distance bus services developed rapidly, though here the local shipping companies were also the main operators. The transition of freight from load-on load-off shipping services to road hauliers was positively encouraged with roll-on roll-off ferry services being introduced on those fjord crossings which were too broad to be bridged. The result was a complete transformation of both public transport and road freight services, with far greater flexibility and drastically reduced journey times.

Dependence on local and coastal shipping services dwindled. Ship operation was also having to rapidly alter. In the late 1940s the Danish shipping company, Det Forenede Dampskibsselskab (DFDS), had introduced pallet loading using forklift trucks driven on and off vessels via doors in the sides of the ship's hull. Turn-round times in port were reduced, as were labour costs. Larger unit loads, beyond the capacities of pallets and fork-lift trucks, were lifted aboard by electrically powered cranes. Over the next two decades this new technology became almost universal, which put the current Hurtigruten ships at a distinct disadvantage. Indeed, from a cargo handling point of operation they were out of date from the day they were built.

Whilst car ferry services were now dominant across Europe, the Hurtigruten fleet was outmoded, only able to take a few cars or light vans which had to be craned on and placed wherever space permitted on exposed foredecks. Some of the fleet were now 25 years old and were beginning to show not just wear and tear but their overall standard of accommodation was well below what could be experienced elsewhere.

New ships therefore of similar size and design were perhaps not the right solution and a radical rethink was needed. The advent across Europe of fast craft (*hurtigbåt*) in the form of hydrofoils had already reached Norway when, in 1960, DSD introduced the *Vingtor* on an express service linking Bergen and Stavanger. This led to the eventual cessation of the Nattrute (night service) between the two cities and was one of the reasons why the Stavanger company sold their *Kong Olav* to VDS in 1978.

By the 1970s both Hardanger Sunnhordlandske (HSD) and Fylkesbaatane (now Fjord 1) had acquired both hydrofoils and catamarans for their longer local routes, totally changing travel between the western fjords and Bergen.

Fast craft between Tromsø and Harstad cut the journey time to 3 hours 30 minutes inclusive of several intermediate calls. Day return trips were now possible and as a result these boats gradually took over the passenger carrying rôle of the local steamers. To make matters worse, the 1977 figures showed that 22,700 passengers flew between Tromsø and Hammerfest while just 8,652 used the Hurtigruten. Was there really a future for the Hurtigruten?

In 1975 the question of how to replace the three 'Italia-Båtene' ships, now twenty five years old, was now in open debate, with the Hurtigruten companies envisaging a ship of around 3,000 gross tons (400 dwt) with berths for around 150 passengers and a service speed of 20 knots. A fleet of nine vessels of identical design and performance was being suggested, with a much-accelerated daily service. This option was turned down as being too costly, both initially and in the long term. Whilst in the short term benefits were clear to see (uniformity and compatibility), in the long term it would have created major issues, since all nine ships would eventually require replacement almost simultaneously.

By May 1976, the Storting (Norwegian Parliament) appeared to be resigned to abandoning the Hurtigruten south of Bodø and to providing a daily service from there to Kirkenes using just seven vessels. However, persistent lobbying convinced the Minister of Transport, Ragnar Christiansen, to change his mind. He announced that future transport policy would focus upon 'promoting those modes and routes which had the lowest social costs' (i.e. not on purely economic grounds). The Hurtigruten and other coastal shipping services were once again back in favour.

Hurtigruten timetable for Summer 1975

Northbound	Day	1	2	3	4	5	6	7
Bergen	1	23.00	23.00	23.00	23.00	23.00	23.00	23.00
Florø	2	05.30	05.30	05.30	05.30	05.30	05.30	05.30
Måløy	2	08.00	08.00	08.00	08.00	08.00	08.00	08.00
Torvik	2	11.15	11.15	11.15	11.15	11.15	11.15	11.15
Ålesund	2	12.15	12.15	12.15	12.15	12.15	12.15	12.15
Ålesund	2	14.15	14.15	14.15	14.15	14.15	14.15	14.15
Molde	2	17.30	17.30	17.30	17.30	17.30	17.30	17.30
Kristiansund	2	22.15	22.15	22.15	22.15	22.15	22.15	22.15
Trondheim	3	06.30	06.30	06.30	06.30	06.30	06.30	06.30
Trondheim	3	12.00	12.00	12.00	12.00	12.00	12.00	12.00
Rørvik	3	21.15	21.15	21.15	21.15	21.15	21.15	21.15
Brønnøysund	4	01.00	01.00	01.00	01.00	01.00	01.00	01.00
Sandnessjøen	4	04.30	04.30	04.30	04.30	04.30	04.30	04.30
Nesna	4	05.45				05.45		
Ørnes	4	09.15	09.15	09.15	09.15	09.15	09.15	09.15
Bodø	4	12.30	12.30	12.30	12.30	12.30	12.30	12.30
Bodø	4	15.00	15.00	15.00	15.00	15.00	15.00	15.00
Stamsund	4	19.30	19.30	19.30	19.30	19.30	19.30	19.30
Svolvær	4	21.00	21.00	21.00	21.00	21.00	21.00	21.00
Svolvær	4	22.00	22.00	22.00	22.00	22.00	22.00	22.00
Stokmarknes	5	01.00	01.00	01.00	01.00	01.00	01.00	01.00
Sortland	5	03.00	03.00	03.00	03.00	03.00	03.00	03.00
Risøyhamn	5	04.45	04.45	04.45	04.45	04.45	04.45	04.45
Harstad	5	07.00	07.00	07.00	07.00	07.00	07.00	07.00
Harstad	5	08.45	08.45	08.45	08.45	08.45	08.45	08.45
Finnsnes	5	12.15	12.15	12.15	12.15	12.15	12.15	12.15
Tromsø	5	15.00	15.00	15.00	15.00	15.00	15.00	15.00
Tromsø	5	18.00	18.00	18.00	18.00	18.00	18.00	18.00
Sjkervøy	5	22.00	22.00	22.00	22.00	22.00	22.00	22.00
Øksfjord	5	01.30	01.30	01.30	01.30	01.30	01.30	01.30
Hasvik	6							
Hammerfest	6	04.30	04.30	04.30	04.30	04.30	04.30	04.30
Hammerfest	6	05.15	05.15	05.15	05.15	05.15	05.15	05.15
Havøysund	6	08.00	08.00	08.00	08.00	08.00	08.00	08.00
Honningsvåg	6	14.00	14.00	14.00	14.00	14.00	14.00	14.00
Kjøllefjord	6	16.30	16.30	16.30	16.30	16.30	16.30	16.30
Mehamn	6	18.45			18.45		18.45	
Gamvik	6		19.00		19.00		19.00	
Berlevåg	6	21.15	21.00	21.15	21.00	21.15	21.00	21.15
Båtsfjord	6	23.45	23.45	23.45	23.45	23.45	23.45	23.45
Vardø	7	02.30	02.30	02.30	02.30	02.30	02.30	02.30
Vardø	7	03.00	03.00	03.00	03.00	03.00	03.00	03.00
Vadsø	7	07.00		07.00			07.00	
Kirkenes	7	08.50	06.30	08.50	06.30	06.30	08.50	06.30

Southbound	Day	1	2	3	4	5	6	7
Kirkenes	7	11.00	08.30	11.00	08.30	11.00	08.30	08.30
Vadsø	7		11.30			11.30	11.30	
Vardø	7	14.30		14.30	14.30	14.30	14.30	14.30
Vardø	7	15.30		15.30	15.30	15.30	15.30	15.30
Båtsfjord	7	19.00	19.00	19.00	19.00	19.00	19.00	19.00
Berlevåg	7	20.45	20.45	20.45	20.45	20.45	20.45	20.45
Gamvik	7		22.30			22.30		
Mehamn	7	23.30		23.30			23.30	
Kjøllefjord	8	02.00	02.00	02.00	02.00	02.00	02.00	02.00
Honningsvåg	8	05.45	05.45	05.45	05.45	05.45	05.45	05.45
Havøysund	8	08.00	08.00	08.00	08.00	08.00	08.00	08.00
Hammerfest	8	11.30	11.30	11.30	11.30	11.30	11.30	11.30
Hammerfest	8	12.45	12.45	12.45	12.45	12.45	12.45	12.45
Hasvik	8				15.15			
Øksfjord	8	16.00	16.00	16.00	17.00	16.00	16.00	16.00
Skjervøy	8	19.45	19.45	19.45	20.45	19.45	19.45	19.45
Tromsø	8	23.45	23.45	23.45	00.45	23.45	23.45	23.45
Tromsø	9	01.30	01.30	01.30	01.30	01.30	01.30	01.30
Finnsnes	9	04.45	04.45	04.45	04.45	04.45	04.45	04.45
Harstad	9	08.00	08.00	08.00	08.00	08.00	08.00	08.00
Harstad	9	09.00	09.00	09.00	09.00	09.00	09.00	09.00
Risøyhamn	9	11.45	11.45	11.45	11.45	11.45	11.45	11.45
Sortland	9	14.15	14.15	14.15	14.15	14.15	14.15	14.15
Stokmarknes	9	16.15	16.15	16.15	16.15	16.15	16.15	16.15
Svolvær	9	18.45	18.45	18.45	18.45	18.45	18.45	18.45
Svolvær	9	20.30	20.30	20.30	20.30	20.30	20.30	20.30
Stamsund	9	23.00	23.00	23.00	23.00	23.00	23.00	23.00
Bodø	10	03.00	03.00	03.00	03.00	03.00	03.00	03.00
Bodø	10	05.00	05.00	05.00	05.00	05.00	05.00	05.00
Ørnes	10	08.15	08.15	08.15	08.15	08.15	08.15	08.15
Nesna	10		12.00			12.00		
Molde	10							
Sandnessjøen	10	14.00	14.00	14.00	14.00	14.00	14.00	14.00
Brønnøysund	10	17.30	17.30	17.30	17.30	17.30	17.30	17.30
Rørvik	10	21.15	21.15	21.15	21.15	21.15	21.15	21.15
Trondheim	11	06.15	06.15	06.15	06.15	06.15	06.15	06.15
Trondheim	11	11.00	11.00	11.00	11.00	11.00	11.00	11.00
Kristiansund	11	17.30	17.30	17.30	17.30	17.30	17.30	17.30
Ålesund	11	21.15	21.15	21.15	21.15	21.15	21.15	21.15
Ålesund	12	23.45	23.45	23.45	23.45	23.45	23.45	23.45
Ålesund	12	00.15	00.15	00.15	00.15	00.15	00.15	00.15
Torvik	12	01.15	01.15	01.15	01.15	01.15	01.15	01.15
Måløy	12	04.30	04.30	04.30	04.30	04.30	04.30	04.30
Florø	12	06.45	06.45	06.45	06.45	06.45	06.45	06.45
Bergen	12	13.00	13.00	13.00	13.00	13.00	13.00	13.00

Towards the Next Generation

Two new proposals were put forward in 1978, one from the Samferdselsdepartement (Ministry of Transport) and the other from the Hurtigruten companies themselves. The latter's proposal was for a vessel of 3,000 gross tons (600 dwt), 360 feet in length, a service speed of 17.5 knots, a passenger certificate for 450 and berths for 200 persons.

The Ministry's proposal was for something around 30 feet shorter, a smaller deadweight capacity of 350 tonnes, a lower passenger certificate for 375 passengers and berths for just 85 persons.

The Ministry's vessel would be equipped with just a crane and a pallet lift for cargo handling, whilst the Hurtigruten companies' proposal would have also had a stern door, enabling her to accommodate all types of road vehicle. Clearly they were poles apart as to what they thought was needed.

From then on the debate focused on two issues - cabin capacity and ro-ro or lo-lo. The cabin argument was closely related to the Hurtigruten's rôle as a carrier of tourists and its worldwide marketing of the round trip from Bergen to Kirkenes as a package holiday.

Some felt it was not for the State to subsidise tourists, especially as during the winter months the additional cabin capacity provided would be underused. With fewer Norwegians now making use of the Hurtigruten for longer business journeys, the main demand, it was argued, would be for reclining seats on the lengthier overnight sectors.

On the other hand it was argued that tourism had a beneficial effect on Norway's balance of payments. Its job creation potential, especially in the far north, was considerable. In the long run the State would lose out if it refused to support travel by overseas visitors, as the Hurtigruten was a natural extension of the on-shore hotel and tourism industry of which the State was a keen sponsor.

The ro-ro/lo-lo debate was just as hard fought. The Ministry of Transport argued that ro-ro was unsuitable as very few of the 35 ports served by the ships were equipped with linkspans. The Hurtigruten companies envisaged linkspans only at larger ports, as elsewhere vehicles and other cargo could be craned ashore or driven on and off the ships through large doors in the sides of their hulls. On-board lifts would be able to cope with any variations in height between quay and vehicle deck.

By August 1979, there was general agreement that the starting point for the definitive design of the new ships should be based on the Hurtigruten companies' proposals. A working party was created under the leadership of Ragnar Kobro, administrative director for VDS. Four one class ships were envisaged, with passenger certificates for around 400 and berths for 150 persons. The estimated cost per ship of between NOK 80 and NOK 100 million escalated. The Gulf War caused oil prices to rapidly rise which fuelled general inflation, so that by November 1980 the cost per vessel had doubled to NOK 160 million. The decision was then made to only build three ships. The State would provide 76% of the total building costs as well as increase the operating subsidy for the new ships.

Sixteen Norwegian shipyards were invited to submit bids with the Ulstein Group based at Ulsteinvik, Kaarbo M/V of Harstad and Trondhjems M/V being awarded the contracts which they signed in early 1981 for one ship apiece.

One company facing problems was Det Stavangerske Dampskibsselskab, as since post war the value of the Hurtigruten to the Rogaland and Jæren districts, of which Stavanger was the hub, had been on the wane, largely due to the improved road and rail links with Oslo. The Stavanger to Bergen route was in the hands of the fast craft and DSD's main activities were now concentrated on local ferry and coastal cargo services. The *Kong Olav*'s operation had become a financial burden for little return. Early in 1978, the ship was sold to Det Vesteraalens Dampskibsselskab. On 16th April, resplendent in her changed funnel livery, the *Kong Olav* arrived at her new home port of Stokmarknes for celebrations, the name being retained by kind permission of Kong Olav himself.

The sale of the *Kong Olav* triggered off another takeover when Troms Fylkes Dampskibsselskap approached Det Bergenske Dampskibsselskab with a view to purchasing their four Hurtigruten ships. In a similar position to DSD, the Bergen company felt that their resources could be better utilised in

other areas of their business such as the North Sea oil industry, cruising and cargo operations. The sale and purchase were conducted in great secrecy before on 24th January 1979 the news was released. There was a storm of incredulity, where was the wisdom in the deal, paying NOK 32 million for four ships between 23 and 30 years old?

Over the next eight months BDS and TFDS worked together to run the four ships. On 30th August 1979 the *Nordlys* and *Polarlys* were officially handed over, followed by *Midnatsol* and *Nordstjernen* on 4th September. The jobs of the 250 or so crew members were all guaranteed.

During 1980, Det Nordenfjeldske Dampskibsselskab were also looking for a buyer for their *Håkon Jarl*. After negotiations with Saltens Dampskibsselskab fell through, Det Ofotens Dampskibsselskab purchased her for NOK 8 million on 17th January 1981. At the same time NFDS transferred its new Hurtigruten contract to ODS, whilst still continuing to operate the *Ragnvald Jarl* and the *Harald Jarl*.

The wheel had turned full circle as, for the first time since 1894, control of Hurtigruten operations was with the northern coastal companies. This new mix of Hurtigruten operators promised fresh ideas and a greater commitment to maintaining the service. ODS, VDS and TFDS were in a much more suitable position geographically to understand and cater for the transport needs of communities in the far north. It was a new era. No doubt Richard With would have had a smile on his face.

January 1st 1983 was a sad day in the history of the Hurtigruten as all on-board post offices were closed, and the transport of mail by sea continued only where no alternative existed. On most of the Hurtigruten ships the spaces formerly occupied by the mail rooms were converted into additional cabins, though on the *Nordnorge* a conference room was provided instead. However, in the 1990s the Coastal Express ships were once more allowed to fly the postal flag in recognition of the special status the Hurtigruten has in Norway.

The Mid Generation Ships

A TFDS postcard of the *Midnatsol* (1982) as originally built; note the open container deck at the stern
(David Parsons Collection)

On 22nd May 1982, Elisabeth Giæver, daughter of John Giæver, chairman of Troms Fylkes Dampskibsselskap, named and launched the company's new 'mid generation' ship *Midnatsol* at the Ulstein Hatlø Shipyard, Ulsteinvik. The ship was unlike anything seen before and at 4,131 gross tons (1,300 dwt) with an overall length of 108.55m (357 feet) was in effect twice the size of her predecessor with about three times the cargo capacity. The *Midnatsol* was a twin screw ship (a first for a Hurtigruten new build); powered by two 16 cylinder 4T Bergen M/V KVM diesels of 3,200 bhp, she had twin rudders and had two Brunvoll SPT-VP bow thrusters each developing 401 hp to aid manoeuvrability. Designed with a service speed of 17.5 knots, the diesels were adjusted so that she could operate efficiently at the lower 15 knot service speed demanded by the Hurtigruten timetable. Much use was made of floating floors and elastic mountings for both the main and auxiliary engines in order to reduce noise and vibration levels.

Later in her Hurtigruten career the ship was renamed *Midnatsol 1*, seen here laid up at Fiskerstrand Verft, near Ålesund, March 2005
(Aage Schjølberg)

In 2005 the *Midnatsol I* became the *Lyngen* and was to serve on the Hurtigruten for another two years. Seen here at Fiskerstrand Verft in May 2006 (Aage Schjølberg)

The new ship had a certificate for 410 passengers with 181 berths in 86 en suite cabins, the cruise price charged varying according to its grade. All cabins were situated in the forward part of the ship, spread over three decks. Two decks above, on E deck, there was a large panoramic observation lounge, whilst one deck below was a small dining room (which also doubled up as a conference room) together with other lounges. For the first time crew could enjoy a similar standard of accommodation to that provided for passengers.

All cargo space and cargo-handling equipment, including a 15 ton crane (18 metre reach), was to be found on the aft open deck which could take up to 22 standard TEU (20ft) containers and/or covered palletised loads. Inside, on B deck there was space for up to 40 vehicles. In theory another 40 cars could be accommodated aft on the exposed C deck but they would have to be crane loaded. The storage rooms for perishable goods were on A deck where there was also a large room (580 m³) for deep-frozen foods. There was no provision for stern loading, so cargo access to the ship was provided by large doors set on the port side. With no equivalent door on the starboard side this meant that berthing would always be on the port side. A new feature was the hydraulic gangway for passengers, making boarding and exiting the ship much more easy.

Extremely functional in design, the *Midnatsol* was hardly likely to win many plaudits. Her exhaust uptakes were concealed in a yellow painted box-like structure on the starboard side aft of the superstructure, giving the ship an

A 1990's edition of the TFDS Deck Plans for the *Midnatsol* (David Parsons Collection)

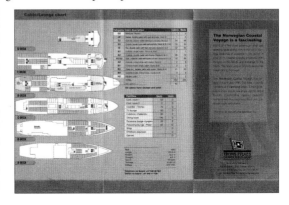

unbalanced look. The company colours, of black, white and red bands, were painted on the deckhousing at the base of her mast.

By 26th November the *Midnatsol* was ready for her delivery voyage to Bergen, where she was escorted by her predecessor, now renamed *Midnatsol II*. The contrast between the two could not have been more marked. Her maiden Hurtigruten voyage from Bergen was on Sunday 5th December 1982. The *Midnatsol II* was then laid up; her subsequent career is told elsewhere.

It was not long before the complaints came in, the new *Midnatsol* was just too small! The restaurant provision which had room for just 68 diners at one sitting received the greatest amount of adverse comment. On busy days in summer up to three sittings had to be provided. In an attempt to alleviate the problem during the autumn of 1983, the fixed bulkheads between the restaurants and adjacent lounges were replaced by moveable partitions to offer greater flexiblility.

It wasn't until the winter of 1987/8 that the accommodation issue could be properly addressed. The *Midnatsol* was sent to Motorenwerke, Bremerhaven, Germany, for a prefabricated passenger accommodation module to be fitted over the aft cargo deck. Two new funnel casings were constructed, one a dummy, which gave the ship a more balanced look. The restaurant was rebuilt with 68 new seats and in the new stern section there was a bar and lounge as well as new cabin accommodation with another 156 berths. Whilst this reduced her cargo capacity, the ship now measured 6,167 gross tons. The cost of this work was NOK 40 million. It wasn't until 14th March 1988 that the *Midnatsol* returned to service, sailing from the Freileneskaien, in Bergen. Whilst everyone agreed that the ship looked

Today the *Lyngen* (ex *Midnatsol*) operates as the expedition ship *National Geographic Explorer,* seen here departing Portsmouth in May 2012 (Andrew Cooke)

impressive, opinions were divided as to whether it was, visually, an improvement. A further major refurbishment to her lounges and cafeteria was carried out in October 1995.

The *Midnatsol* was a faithful servant and rarely strayed from the Hurtigruten route, though in October 2001 she undertook a temporary charter as a hotel ship based at Leith.

At the end of 2000 TFDS ordered a new ship to replace the 18 year old *Midnatsol,* still relatively young in terms of previous Hurtigruten longevity. On 13th January 2003 she was renamed *Midnatsol II* and three months later on 15th April the ship arrived at Bergen for what was thought to be her last time in service. Meeting up with her successor, again named *Midnatsol,* the contrasts were just as great as when she met the 1949 built *Midnatsol* in 1982. The *Midnatsol II* sailed north to lay up at Fiskerstrand Verft near Ålesund and was advertised for sale. She was joined there for the winter of 2003/4 by the *Nordstjernen.* Two years of inactivity followed until February 2005, when Croisieres Transboreale of Montreal explored the possibility of buying her for cruises around the Gulf of St. Lawrence area of Canada, but the deal fell through. In June 2005 came the surprising announcement that she would return to Hurtigruten service. On 7th July she was towed from Ålesund to the Fosen M/V Shipyard, Rissa near Trondheim, by the tug *Squalus.* Following a refit, the ship sailed to Lyngseidet where on 24th September she was renamed *Lyngen* after that region of northern Norway. The *Lyngen* returned to service the following day, standing in for the *Trollfjord* which had been chartered for a special cruise. With both the *Nordkapp* and *Nordnorge* away on Antarctic cruises from the end of September, the ship became the regular reserve ship.

Two more years of service followed and it wasn't until 10th October 2007 that the *Lyngen* arrived at Bergen for the final time in Hurtigruten service. Immediately sold to Lindblad Expedition for $8.6 million the ship was sent to the Götaverken Cityvarvet Shipyard, Gothenburg for conversion into an expedition ship. In January 2008 she sailed to Las Palmas for further work to be done. On 8th August that year, looking resplendent, she was renamed *National Geographic Explorer* and continues in her new role today.

A stern view of the *Narvik (1982)* at Trondheim, taken shortly before her new accommodation module was erected (Trondheim Havn)

An ODS postcard of the *Narvik* as new, showing her more functional profile (David Parsons Collection)

Early morning and southbound the reconfigured *Narvik* is seen off Måløy in May 2006 (John Bryant)

The second of the trio of new ships, the *Narvik*, 4,072 gross tons and 108.55m (357 ft), was launched at the Trondheim Mek Shipyard on 27th May 1982. With Captain Peder Pedersen in command (formerly of the *Nordnorge*) she made her delivery voyage north to Narvik, the headquarters of Det Ofotens Dampskibsselskab (ODS), arriving there on 16th December 1982. The *Narvik* was officially named by Anne-Marie Pleym, for many years the booking manager of ODS, prior to being formally handed over.

The following day, with most of her crew having been transferred from the *Nordnorge,* she took over *Håkon Jarl*'s southbound Hurtigruten sailing from Harstad. On 21st December the ship began her first full round trip from Bergen to Kirkenes. The *Narvik* was a powerful looking ship, with a red band along its black hull, which distinguished it from its sisters. Unlike the *Midnatsol*, she did not have an observation lounge on E deck and there were a number of other detail differences in her design. Her funnel was painted in the company colours rather than being left blank. Cabin capacity was as before (178 berths) and she had a certificate for 410 passengers on the coastal route, but for Svalbard and international services it was reduced to 240. Cargo capacity and arrangements were identical to the *Midnatsol*, as were her propulsion units and bow thrust units.

At the beginning of 1987 ODS acquired 68% of Det Vesteraalens Dampskibsselskab's shares and it was therefore not surprising that the two companies formally merged from 1st January 1988 to form Det Ofotens og Vesteraalens Dampskibsselskab AS (OVDS).

In the autumn of 1989, it was the turn of the *Narvik* to go to Germany to be rebuilt by Motorenwerke, Bremerhaven at a cost of 40 million kroner. A new passenger section was built on the aft deck with 140 new berths and a new lounge, increasing the cabin capacity to 312 and the passenger certificate to 580. A much needed panoramic lounge was installed, bringing her into line with the *Midnatsol*, the dining room also being enlarged.

On 16th April 1991, while crossing the Folla in a heavy sea with snow showers and poor visibility, the *Narvik* ran aground near Lysøsund developing an uncomfortable list. The local ferry, *Folla,* was nearby and was able to take the passengers off the stranded vessel. The *Narvik* was soon refloated and taken under tow for repairs at the Fiskerstrand Verft Shipyard, near Ålesund, lasting over a month at a cost of almost NOK 20 million.

The vessel had suffered considerable damage, especially on the port side underwater hull, the port rudder and propeller as well as some damage to the shaft gearing. Water leakage had also caused damage to cabins, corridors, cargo holds and electrical installations. On 29th May, the vessel left Fiskerstrand Verft as scheduled and was back in Hurtigruten service from 31st May.

Further refurbishment in 1995, this time at the Haugesund Mek Shipyard, brought improvements to the reception area, dining room and some of the cabins as well as providing for the growing conference market.

Although by the end of the 20th century the ship was no longer the largest on the Hurtigruten, the *Narvik* continued to perform reliably and had her own loyal following. On 22nd September 2001, the ship officially reopened the 5 km (3 miles) Risøyrenna Channel after four years of deepening work (some sources give this as the *Midnatsol*).

By late 2006, her time on Hurtigruten service was coming to an end. In October the ship was chartered to Norsk Hydro as an accommodation vessel for three weeks. Less than two months later, in the December, the *Narvik* was purchased for 62m kroner by the Young Christian Seafarers Association (Rogaland Videregående Sjøaspirantskole), Stavanger. Upon delivery (21st February 2007), the ship was renamed ms *Gann*, replacing the previous ship

Today, the Narvik is now the *Gann* (seen here at Svolvær), operated by the Rogaland Sjøaspirantskole, Stavanger as a training and cruise ship (Uwe Jakob)

of that name, the ex *Ragnvald Jarl* (sold on to Sørlandets Seilende Skoleskibs Institution for a similar role and renamed *Sjøkurs*). The *Gann* was in the news in late April 2010 when, in the wake of the disruption caused to flights from the erupting Eyjafjallajökull volcano in Iceland, she ferried stranded tourists from Stavanger to Newcastle. Today, the ship continues to attract young people from all over Norway to provide training for those wishing to become mariners as well as undertaking public summer cruises to Honningsvåg and Nordkapp.

VDS's new vessel was launched at the Kaarbø Mek Shipyard, Harstad on 18th September 1982 and was the last of the trio of 'mid generation' ships ordered by the Hurtigruten companies in 1980 to take to the water. Apart from her funnel livery, the *Vesterålen* was practically a twin sister of the *Narvik*. Delivered on 16th February 1983, she was formally named *Vesterålen* by Elsie Kobro at Stokmarknes. At Bodø on the following day, she met up with her predecessor, now renamed *Vesterålen II*, which was finally retired from service some two months later.

This new *Vesterålen* measured 4,131 gross tons (1,300 dwt) and had an overall length of 108.55m (357 feet). Her propulsion units and general specifications were identical to those of her sisters including the port side loading doors and hydraulic gangway for passengers.

Her first Hurtigruten departure from Bergen was on 20th March 1983; four weeks later she became the first Hurtigruten ship to use the new Breivika Quay facility at Tromsø (replacing the old Prostneset berth).

When this generation of new ships was designed, the accent was still on the crane loading of cargo, albeit in containers or pallets. However, it became clear early on that this was a mistake and at the expense of passenger capacity needs. In 1987, a contract was signed with Motorenwerke, Bremerhaven to rebuild the ship. Before this happened, on 1st January 1988 Det Ofotens Dampskibsselskab (ODS) merged with Det Vesteraalens Dampskibsselskab (VDS) to form Det Ofotens og Vesteraalens Dampskibsselskab (OVDS). The upshot was that the *Vesterålen* lost her attractive blue, white and black funnel livery together with the distinctive blue stripe along her hull.

Below: A postcard image of the *Vesterålen* (1983) as built; the VDS livery suited her (Uwe Jakob)

Below right: Late evening in the Land of the Midnight Sun, the *Vesterålen* in OVDS funnel livery approaches Berlevåg, May 2006 (John Bryant)

March and May 1988 saw a couple of engine problems which were remedied at her builder's shipyard, Kaarbøs M/V, Harstad. Finally, in October 1988, the *Vesterålen* was sent to the Motorenwerke Shipyard to have

In her current livery the *Vesterålen* is pictured approaching Tromsø, June 2010 (Uwe Jakob)

her new passenger accommodation module installed. Passenger capacity was increased by 140 berths, including a new panoramic lounge, with the work costing 45m kroner. Six weeks later, on 21st November 1988, the ship returned to Hurtigruten service. A further major upgrade and refurbishment was undertaken at the Haugesund Shipyard during January and February 1995.

In February 1998, the *Vesterålen* was chartered for a NATO exercise, taking a contingent of troops from Granvin in Hardangerfjorden to Narvik, hardly a cruise, although no doubt those on board enjoyed the trip. During that same year and into 1999, the *Vesterålen* became involved in a project with the Stavanger Research Institute, investigating climatic change and global warming. The ship carried a water temperature sensor, fitted at a depth of four metres on her hull which took measurements every five minutes, recording the precise location of each measurement through GPS.

March 2006 saw the merger of TFDS and OVDS to form Hurtigruten Group ASA and as a result the *Vesterålen's* funnels received another repaint into the company livery we see today. Whilst it may have seemed somewhat surprising that her two sister ships should be withdrawn and sold, rather than the older *Lofoten* and *Nordstjernen*, the *Vesterålen* has continued to perform reliably. In February 2008 she was sent to the Fredericia Shipyard in Denmark to have stabilisers fitted, a sure sign that she will remain in Hurtigruten service for some years to come.

The *Vesterålen* interiors are tastefully designed, from left to right; Restaurant, Fyret Panoramic Lounge, Cafeteria (Uwe Jakob)

Sailing away from Bodø, the
Vesterålen prepares to head
across Vestfjord towards
Stamsund in the Lofotens,
June 2008 (Uwe Jakob)

The New Generation

The introduction of the three 'mid generation' ships into service in 1982/83 marked the beginning of the end of the old order as far as the Hurtigruten companies were concerned. In that year Det Bergenske Dampskibsselskab (BDS) merged with the Sandefjord based Kosmos A/S. A year later, in October 1984, Det Nordenfjeldske Dampskibsselskab (NFDS) was purchased by Norcem, who in turn took Kosmos under their wing from April 1995. At the same time, large amounts of shares in Det Vesteraalens Dampskibsselskab (VDS) were being purchased by Ofotens Dampskibsselskab, so it was no surprise that on 1st January 1988 the two companies merged to form Det Ofotens og Vesteraalens Dampskibsselskab (OVDS). The latter company then sold the *Lofoten* to Finnmark Fylkesrederi (FFR) for 20 million kroner, bringing in another new company to the Hurtigruten table.

Below and opposite: A selection of brochure covers from the 1980s and 1990s; the 1987 brochure is of particular interest as it shows the *Midnatsol* (1982) in her original form off Torghatten (David Parsons Collection)

With Troms Fylkes Dampskibsselskap (TFDS), Det Stavangerske Dampskibsselskab (DSD) and Saltens Dampskibsselskap (SDS) joining forces in 1988 to found RoNoTro, the whole ball game changed when, in 1989, this new company acquired both BDS and NFDS from Kosmos. The Hurtigruten operation was now entirely in the hands of three companies based in northern Norway. 1990 was also the last year that the Hurtigruten served Alta and Gamvik (the most northerly port on the route), in future all sailings for the latter port would now call at Mehamn.

Continued dissatisfaction with the three 1982/83 ships, and in particular their passenger capacity, resulted in the 1988/89 rebuilding programme as detailed previously. The Hurtigruten companies had to finance the work themselves with no aid from the State. It was becoming clear that if the Hurtigruten were to survive then it would have to markedly expand its tourism rôle and to provide suitable facilities and experiences accordingly. Passenger numbers had fallen from 384,700 in 1978 to 277,000 by 1982. The rebuilding work arrested the

NORWEGIAN COASTAL VOYAGE
SEPTEMBER '85 – APRIL '86.
The World's Most Beautiful Voyage
HURTIGRUTEN
REDUCTIONS FOR SENIOR CITIZENS

decline but as we shall see, it was not until the arrival of the 'new generation' ships from 1993 that any real growth began to be experienced.

Entering the final ten years of the century, the 1950s built ships were in urgent need of replacement and a whole decade had passed since any new ships had been ordered. On June 13th that year, the Storting agreed that the Hurtigruten should receive State support of NOK 1.875 billion spread over twelve years. NOK 1.3 billion was to be used for new builds and the remainder as an operating subsidy. Skip Consulting A/S, Bergen, in consultation with the Hurtigruten companies, developed a specification for new ships which would have cruise liner standards of comfort and be larger and totally different to anything that had been built before. More than 20 shipyards were invited to tender, both in Norway and abroad.

Six proposals were shortlisted, with the German specialist cruise ship builders, Meyer Werft at Papenburg, being successful. Their design ideas included 212 outside cabins out of a total of 230 (92%). The actual building contract with options for two sister ships was awarded in March 1991 to Volkswerft GmbH, Stralsund, based in the former East Germany. Their bid of NOK 400 million per ship was NOK 100 million less than the lowest tender from any Norwegian shipyard.

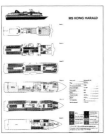

Deck Plan of *Kong Harald*

The beautiful Romsdal
Mountains provide the
backdrop as the *Kong Harald*
(1992), still in her TFDS funnel
livery, arrives at Molde in May
2006 (John Bryant)

The first of the 'new generation' of ships to be completed was the *Kong Harald* for Troms Fylkes Dampskibsselskap (TFDS), launched on 28th November 1992. The ship was handed over at Stralsund on 25th June 1993 and formally named by Hjordis Opseth, the wife of the then Transport Minister, Kjell Opseth. On 2nd July 1993, the vessel arrived at Trondheim to help celebrate the Hurtigruten's 100th anniversary. The *Kong Harald* immediately sailed to London for a promotional visit before beginning its maiden Hurtigruten voyage from Bergen on 6th July 1993. The new ship replaced the 1952 veteran *Polarlys* which went for layup at the Fiskerstrand Shipyard in Ålesund and was advertised for sale.

The *Kong Harald* was to set new standards both in terms of passenger comfort and interior design as well as that of expectation and ushered a new era in the Hurtigruten's history.

The *Kong Harald* measures 11,204 gross tons (902 dwt) and has a length of 121.8 metres. Loading and unloading is on the port side only, and is done by forklift truck through a large side portal which has a 5-ton pallet lift. The ship has 3 fridge/freezer units with a total volume of 880m^3 and a cargo deck capacity of 1,500m^3. The 600m^2 car deck can accommodate up to 45 cars. The *Kong Harald's* main engines are 2 six-cylinder four-stroke Krupp MaK DM 6 C M552 diesel engines each driving a propeller with a total output of 12,228 hp, giving a top speed of 20 knots. In addition, the ship has 2 Brunvoll bow thruster units, each with an output of 1,075 horsepower. The *Kong Harald* became the first Hurtigruten ship to be equipped with active-

stabilizer fins. Power supply is provided by two shaft generators of 2,875 kVA, 2 auxiliary engines at 1,500 kVA and an emergency generator of 265 kVA.

The *Kong Harald* pictured departing Rørvik in the late evening sunshine in June 2008, next stop Trondheim (Uwe Jakob)

Certified for 691 passengers in coastal service, the *Kong Harald* has 490 berths spread over 230 cabins of which 212 have outside views. A one class ship, her communal areas are spacious, with bars, a panoramic observation lounge, a cafeteria, a restaurant and conference rooms. Although named after the King of Norway other eminent Norwegians are honoured including the Fridtjof Nansen bar and the Roald Amundsen café. The main reception area is adjacent to the double width hydraulic passenger gangway.

In January 1995 the ship was sent to Bremerhaven for its guaranteed warranty docking and at the same time had a 1,200 hp azimuth thruster installed at the stern to further improve manoeuvrability.

On board the *Kong Harald*; below left, Café Roald Amundsen and below, Fridtjof Nansen Bar Lounge (Uwe Jakob)

A loss of power, believed to be as a result of air entering the pumps which feed sea water for cooling the engines, occurred on 21st April 2004 to the

A powerful picture of the
Kong Harald making light of
the conditions (Solfried Anita
Husøy/Hurtigruten ASA)

An early morning arrival at
Harstad for the OVDS liveried
Richard With in May 2006
(John Bryant)

Kong Harald, while northbound near Indre Kvarøy with 135 passengers on board. The vessel was only delayed for about an hour, before it could continue to Ørnes. The merger in 2006 between TFDS and OVDS to form Hurtigruten ASA meant a new funnel livery for the *Kong Harald*, but no change to her port of registry (Tromsø).

In all her time on the Hurtigruten the *Kong Harald* has been an extremely reliable ship and only rarely in the news, though 2011 was very much the exception to the rule. On 18th April, in a period of extremely low spring tides, the ship with 227 passengers on board touched the bottom whilst sailing the Lepsøyrevet en route from Ålesund to Molde. The ship suffered a 50 metre scratch and with holes in the two tanks on the starboard

side had to be taken out of service. Then over the Christmas period the storm force winds whipped up by Hurricane Dagmar forced the ship to seek shelter at Trondheim for four days until conditions had eased. The ship has many more years of service left and will be seen serving the route well after the end of the current contract in 2020.

The *Richard With* was the second of the Stralsund built trio and built for OVDS. The ship, appropriately, took the name of the route's founder and was intended as the Hurtigruten centenary vessel, though it was not handed over until 22nd November 1993. With the same dimensions as the *Kong Harald* (11,204 grt, 121.8m in length, space for up to 45 cars etc.), the ship followed in the wake of her fine predecessor built in 1909 and which served for 32 years before being sunk by military action in 1941.

The *Richard With* was named by Aashild Haugen on 19th December 1993 and was put into service the following day from Harstad, replacing the *Finnmarken* (1956). The latter vessel then returned to her home port of Stokmarknes for a protracted lay-up which lasted until 1999 when she became the main exhibit at the new Hurtigruten Museum.

The ship soon settled down to become extremely popular with both passengers and crew alike. Her facilities are identical to those of the *Kong Harald*, and so are not repeated here. Today, she now has two jacuzzis on Deck 6. Internally, much of the attractive art work on board was produced

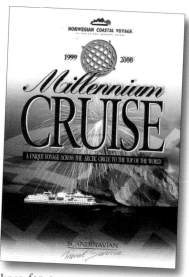

The centenary vessel, the *Richard With* (1993), approaches Tromsø in June 2008 (Uwe Jakob)

by three siblings from the Harr family based in Harstad, Eva, Jan and Karl Erik; the latter's 'Trollfjordslaget' (commemorating the 'Battle of Trollfjord' in 1890) on Deck 5 is quite stunning.

The ship has been used for a variety of charters over the years, generally in the off peak winter months. For example, during February/March 1997, together with the *Nordkapp,* it was used as a hotel ship in conjunction with the World Skiing Championships held in Trondheim. Later that year, in August 1997, the *Richard With* had the distinction of being the first Hurtigruten ship to sail into Geirangerfjord, thus setting the precedent which all northbound Coastal Express ships now follow as part of their summer timetable.

In February/March 1999 the ship was again chartered, this time by the Ministry of Defence as an accommodation vessel for the 'Battle Griffin' NATO exercise held in the Nord-Trøndelag region. Another charter followed in February/March 2002 when the *Richard With* was again used as a hotel

The ceiling of the Les Holtes Cafeteria on the *Richard With* (Backpack Foto/ Hurtigruten ASA)

All out war?! The *Richard With* has her water cannons in action as she passes the *Nordlys* (flying the Jolly Roger) off Berlevåg, June 2011 (John Bryant)

ship during the Junior Alpine Skiing World Championships in Narvik.

On 2nd December 2002, OVDS issued a press release stating that the company had, at the request of Nordnorge Sparebank (which had provided loans for the construction of *Richard With*), sold the ship to Kystruten KS, Fosnavåg, for NOK 375 million. The vessel was then leased back as a bare boat charter on a 15-year agreement with buy-back options after 10 and 15 years or a further additional five years on market terms. OVDS would be responsible and pay for the operation, insurance and all necessary on-going maintenance of the ship. The objective was not to dispose of the ship but to increase the company's available capital. In March 2006, OVDS and TFDS merged, eventually to become Hurtigruten ASA, and whilst the *Richard With's* house colours changed the ship retained its name and port of registry. In January 2009, it was agreed to defer the lease payments for a period of two years, with the deferred instalments to be repaid in full during 2012 and 2013, thereby reverting back to the original payment plan by August of the latter year.

In bad weather with high winds on the morning of 6th January 2009, the *Richard With* experienced great difficulty when trying to berth at Trondheim. The ship ran aground, resulting in damage to one of the propeller shafts as well as to the watertight stern gland, consequently taking

Dawn in May 2006 as the *Nordlys* (1994) in TFDS funnel livery pulls away from Måløy; she will arrive at Bergen later that afternoon (John Bryant)

One of the original deck signs
on board the *Nordlys*
(John Bryant)

on water which came into the engine room. As a precaution, the 153 passengers were taken off the ship via a fire tender ladder. Later in the day, the leakage from the starboard stern tube was stopped and the bilge pumps were able to empty the engine room of water. The ship was refloated and with the aid of a tug moored securely at Berth 1. Booms were placed around the ship in case of possible oil leaks. The *Richard With* was then sent to Bredo Werft at Bremen for repairs, not returning to Hurtigruten service until 5th April. The *Nordlys,* which had been temporarily laid up for the winter, was quickly reactivated and covered her roster.

Today, the *Richard With* remains a very popular and valuable ship in the Hurtigruten fleet.

The *Nordlys* (Northern Lights or Aurora Borealis) was the last of the trio of ships built by Volkswerft GmbH, Stralsund, Germany and was launched on 13th August 1993, being handed over to TFDS some seven months later on 16th March 1994. Costing 400m kroner, the ship is registered in Tromsø and has a passenger certificate for 691 (482 in international traffic) with a berth capacity for 490 persons, operating with a crew of 55 personnel. Internally, local Norwegian artists have created a distinct feel on board the ship; its art, décor and colours are all inspired by the Northern Lights, with wide use of fine textiles and attractive wood and brass fittings. Upon the handover, the *Nordlys* sailed directly to Copenhagen, Denmark for a promotional visit before doing the same at Hamburg, Germany.

Honningsvåg on a fine day is
a great place to take images
of the Hurtigruten ships; here
is the *Nordlys* in May 2011
(John Bryant)

The ship's dimensions and design are identical to those of both the *Kong Harald* and *Richard With*. In Oslo on 22nd March 1994, Kirsti Kolle Grondahl, the first female President of the Storting, formally named the ship, before it sailed to Stavanger and then across the North Sea to Newcastle upon Tyne and London, becoming the first Hurtigruten ship to berth at both the Tyne Bridge and Tower Bridge respectively. Returning to Bergen on 4th April, the *Nordlys* set out on her maiden Hurtigruten voyage that same evening, replacing the *Nordstjernen*.

Above: The distinctive funnel of the early 'new generation' ships (John Bryant)

Left: Kirkenes is 'journey's end' for some, the Nordlys preparing for her southbound run (John Bryant)

The *Nordlys*, with 107 passengers on board, had a minor problem on 19th February 2002: whilst southbound off the Helgeland coast near Nesna, water in the bunker tanks contaminated the fuel supply. The rescue services were alerted and a coastal patrol ship was dispatched. However, the fault was soon rectified and within an hour or so the *Nordlys* was able to resume her voyage.

A press release from TFDS, dated 30th April 2003, indicated that the company was planning to sell the *Nordlys* in order to raise capital. This was

On board the Nordlys; clockwise from top left, the Bridge, the Foyer, the Sirius Observation Lounge and the Arcade (Owe Jakob/John Bryant)

to be on the same basis as OVDS had done with the *Richard With,* i.e. on a lease back arrangement spread over 15 years with an option for an additional five years on market terms. Formally confirmed on 20th June, the ship was acquired for NOK 400 million by a consortium in which Kirberg of Bergen had a 50 % share and Den Norske Bank, 44 %. TFDS would undertake and pay for the operation, insurance and all necessary on-going maintenance of the ship. As an update, in February 2009, now under Hurtigruten ASA, it was agreed with Kirberg Shipping KS that charter fees would be deferred for two years, but would be added to the instalments due in 2012 and 2013, reverting to the original repayment plan in August 2013.

Christmas Eve 2003 should have been a night of expectant celebration on board the *Nordlys,* but the weather made for a far livelier occasion than passengers would have liked. Sailing southbound from Rørvik, the ship encountered very heavy seas through the Folla, so much so that she reached Trondheim some eight hours late (14.45) the following day. Waves of up to 15m in height were experienced making it very difficult to walk about on board.

Financial constraints meant that from 11th November 2008 the *Nordlys* was laid up at Åndalsnes, Romsdalsfjorden for the winter. However, she returned to service in January 2009 as a replacement for the *Richard With* which was damaged when attempting to berth at Trondheim on the 6th of that month.

Worse was to befall the *Nordlys* on 15th September 2011 as, whilst approaching Ålesund, a serious fire in the engine room killed both the Chief Engineer and a young Motorman Apprentice on his first voyage. Twelve others were hurt, two sustaining serious injuries. The ship managed to berth at Ålesund and all 207 passengers were taken off the ship, some of the 55 crew remaining on board to assist with firefighting operations. Owing to a loss of electrical power, the stabilizers, which were deployed at the time of the explosion, did not automatically retract as they should have done when the ship's momentum was below 6 knots. The starboard stabilizer hit the quayside and was forced back into the hull, allowing water

The *Nordkapp* (1996) is pictured at Trondheim in 2002 in her OVDS livery. Note the heightened funnel (Uwe Jakob)

to ingress. The ship tilted almost 22 degrees and there was some danger that it would capsize. A temporary concrete seal was eventually put in place and the vessel pumped free of water. The ship was then towed to Fiskerstrand Verft, near Ålesund, where the shipyard was later contracted to undertake the repairs. The *Nordlys* returned to Hurtigruten service on 28th March 2012, some 8 days later than scheduled, leaving southbound from Tromsø.

Whilst the official AIBN report on the incident made a number of recommendations, the sequence of events leading up to the fire is not entirely clear, though a later AIBN report (September 2012) indicated that fatigue cracks in fuel pipes were probably the cause. However, the ship's passengers and media were full of praise for the way in which both the crew and Hurtigruten ASA had handled a very difficult situation.

Such was the success of the first three 'new generation' ships, in 1994 TFDS and OVDS were both given permission to order another ship, the contract being awarded to the Kleven shipyards at Ulsteinvik, each vessel to cost around NOK 500 million. The *Nordkapp* was the first of two new ships to be built for OVDS and is a near sister to the *Polarlys* being built at the same time for TFDS; although of similar specifications (11,386 gross tons, 123.3 m in length, speed 18.5 knots, 691 passengers, 481 berths, and up to 45 cars etc.) there are differences, both externally and in terms of the propulsion unit chosen, the *Nordkapp*'s being two MaK 6M552C diesels.

Launched on 18th August 1995, the ship had its first sea trials on 19th January 1996. Two months later, on 23rd March, the ship's Godmother, Queen Sonia, performed the naming ceremony; reportedly she needed three attempts to get the champagne bottle to break. The ship was then formally handed over to OVDS. On the same day the *Polarlys* was similarly named at Ulsteinvik.

Heated bathroom floors, saunas and a fitness room were provided as standard for all ships of this class. Later upgradings would include four mini suites, two Jacuzzis and an internet café. Paintings by the renowned Harstad painter (whose work can also be seen on the *Richard With*), Karl Erik Harr, adorn the ship's communal areas with pictures of traditional Lofoten fishing boats (Lofotfisket) and other sailing motifs.

Just over a week later on 2nd April 1996, with Captain Edgar Solstad in command and 146 round trip passengers on board, the *Nordkapp* departed Bergen on her maiden Hurtigruten voyage. The ship replaced the *Nordnorge* (1964) which was sold later that year for cruises around the Maldives.

1996 was also the year that Finnmark Fylkesrederi (FFR) decided to

On board the *Nordkapp*; left to right Svalbard Salon, Fembøringen Bar, Polarsirkelen Panoramic Lounge (Uwe Jakob)

A stunning image of the
Richard With traversing the
beautiful Raftsundet
(Trym Ivar Bergsmo/
Hurtigruten ASA)

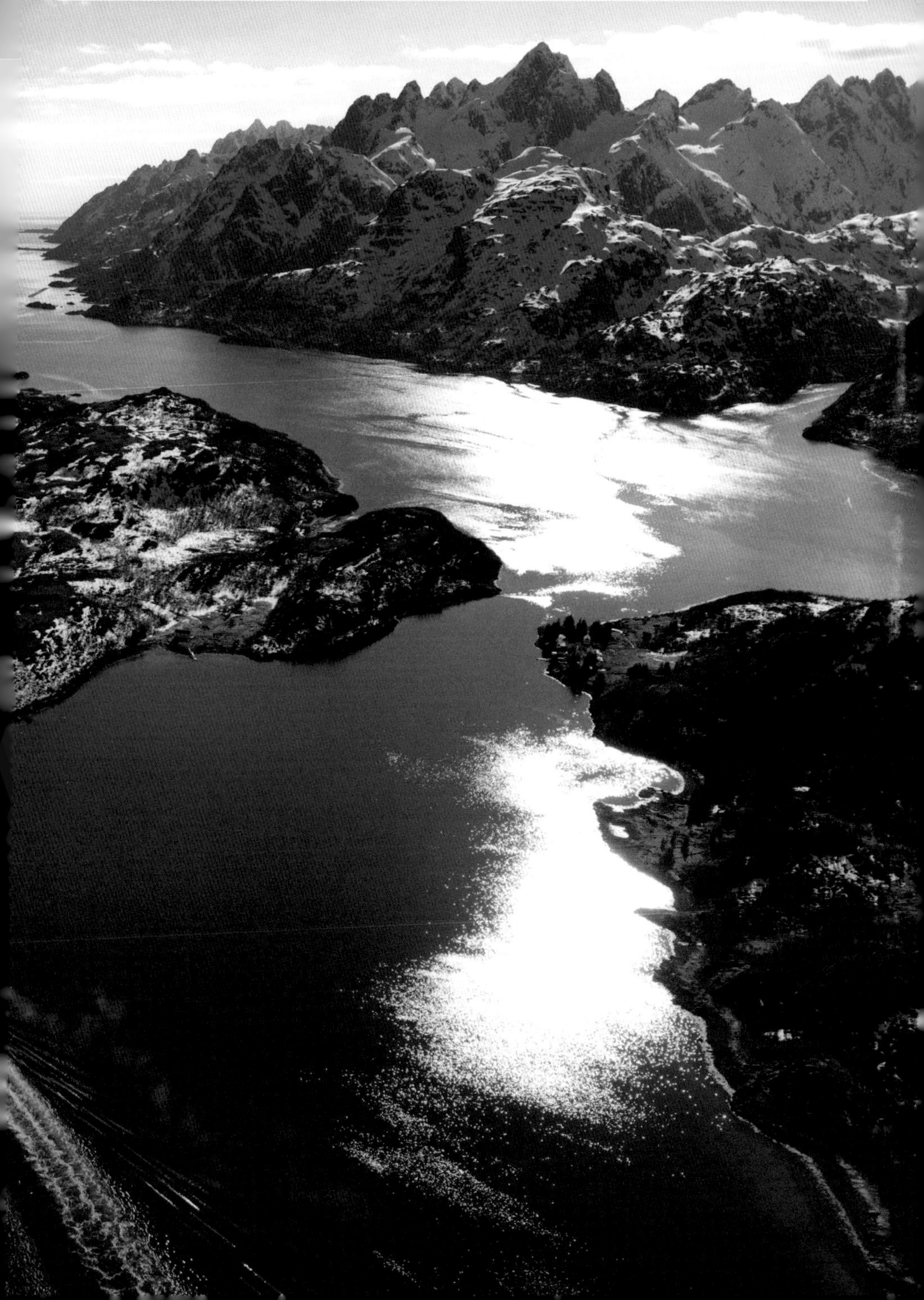

The *Nordkapp* glides past
Munkholmen as she prepares
to berth at Trondheim in June
2011 (John Bryant)

withdraw from Hurtigruten operations, and their *Lofoten* was sold back to OVDS.

The *Nordkapp* has frequently been used for charter work. In February and March 1997, for example, together with the *Richard With*, she acted as a hotel ship during the World Ski Championships being held at Trondheim.

On 29th November 2001 (some sources state 3rd December), the *Nordkapp* had a scare when she lost power whilst en route between Svolvær and Stamsund, off Henningsvær. A strong on-shore wind began to push her towards the coast of Ausvågøy and as a precaution passengers were ordered to boat stations. Fortunately, about two hours later, the ship's engineers managed to restore power, though by then she was getting rather close to the shore. The ship then sailed directly to Bodø.

The success of the *Nordnorge's* Antarctic voyages, begun in 2002, prompted OVDS to deploy the *Nordkapp* as well for the 2005/6 season. Prior to this, the ship was to offer an autumnal Baltic cruise departing from Oslo at 14.00 on 30th September 2005. Calls were scheduled for Rønne, Stockholm, Tallinn, St. Petersburg (with a 30 hour stopover to enable passengers to visit the Winter Palace and explore the city), Helsinki, Riga and Gdansk, returning to Oslo on 12th October. The cruise was repeated the following year. The *Nordkapp* continued to serve the Southern Hemisphere until the end of the 2006/7 season, with the *Nordstjernen* taking over her Hurtigruten schedule each winter. Meeting up in Antarctica with her newer sister ship, the *Nordnorge*, was always one of the highlights of the cruises.

On 30th January 2007, whilst off Deception Island, part of the South Shetland archipelago, on an Antarctic cruise, the *Nordkapp* ran aground, causing a 600mm gash in her hull. The incident made the news headlines

TFDS liveried *Polarlys* (1996) is
ready to leave Harstad in May
2006 on her journey south
(John Bryant)

on account of the possible environmental consequences. Whilst transferring light marine diesel fuel from the ruptured tank to an undamaged one it was estimated that some 500 to 750 litres escaped into the ocean.

The *Nordkapp* refloated herself and anchored in Whalers' Bay to await the arrival of *Nordnorge*, which was between eight and ten hours' sailing time distant. A transfer of the 294 passengers and eight of the crew of 76 took place the next morning and the *Nordnorge*, which already had 243 passengers and her own crew of 76, sailed for Ushuaia in Argentina, arriving just over 2 days later.

Although the damage to the *Nordkapp* was relatively limited and the vessel could have returned to Argentina, it was deemed prudent to make temporary repairs in situ, as well as accept the help of divers from a British naval vessel who made a thorough inspection of her hull.

With the arrival of the expedition ship, *Fram,* for the 2007/8 season, the *Nordkapp* has returned to full time service on the Coastal Express and has not visited Antarctica since.

Learning from the experiences gained from the Stralsund built *Kong Harald* and *Nordlys*, TFDS wanted their third new build of the 1990s 'new generation' class to have increased flexibility and in consequence greater earnings potential. A construction contract was signed with the Ulstein Verft Shipyard in Ulsteinvik on 14th July 1994. Three main areas were pinpointed for the new TFDS flagship: conference facilities to be increased in size and versatility, cargo areas redesigned so as to be some 30% larger, whilst down below, the engines and their management systems were to afford greater economy and flexibility.

Building commenced on 1st February 1995 and nine months later on 4th

Above left: The *Polarlys* is photographed at the southbound quay, Trondheim in June 2007. Note her funnel wings to improve the updraft for smoke emissions (Uwe Jakob)

Above: The way in which the windows are angled in the *Polarlys'* Panoramic Lounge probably offers the best outside views of any ship in the fleet (John Bryant)

Bottom left: The children's play area and below, the Art Deco work on board is quite stunning (John Bryant/Per Eide; Hurtigruten ASA)

November 1995 the hull was launched. Fitted out in less than five months, on 23rd March 1996 the ship was named *Polarlys* by the Governor of Svalbard, Ann-Kristin Olsen. She was the third Coastal Express ship to bear this name. On the same day at the Kvaerner Kleven Shipyard, Ulstenvik, the new OVDS ship *Nordkapp* was named by Queen Sonja of Norway.

Following this, the *Polarlys* set out on a short promotional cruise along Norway's west coast before sailing across the North Sea to visit both Shetland (Lerwick) and Orkney (Kirkwall). On 17th April, replacing the *Nordstjernen*, the ship under the command of Captain Arne R. Erntsen began her maiden voyage from Bergen. Originally, she was earmarked to replace the *Ragnvald Jarl,* but the latter had been sold the previous autumn.

The *Polarlys* measures 11,341 gross tons (1,150 dwt) and is 123.0m in length. As with all other ships of the 'new generation' class, loading and unloading is done using fork lift trucks through a large door on the port side. The main propulsion system differed from the *Nordkapp*'s consisting of four 9-cylinder Ulstein Bergen 4-stroke diesel engines connected in series in pairs on each propeller shaft; a BRM 9 in front and a KRG 9 to the rear. The engines are designed to run in various combinations depending on needs, providing better fuel economy. A unique feature of this is that the ship does not have auxiliary generators as both propulsion and electricity supply come from the power plant. At the stern the ship has a 1,200 hp azimuth thruster to aid manoeuvring. Used on its own in an emergency, it can generate a speed of up to 7 knots. At the bow are two 1,075 hp Brunvoll thruster units.

Certified for 737 passengers on the Coastal Express, the *Polarlys* has 479 berths distributed over 225 cabins, including six mini suites. The communal areas are spacious and include a bar, a panoramic observation lounge with large angled windows, a cafeteria, a restaurant and conference rooms. Her interior décor is outstanding, designed by architect Finn Falkum-Hansen.

The *Polarlys* has become known as 'a ship with a soul' or 'the elegant jewellery box' with her mixture of polished mahogany and brass, glasswork, paintings, marble carvings and sculptures.

One of the most reliable performers on the Hurtigruten, the *Polarlys* rarely figures in the news, though on 19th May 2005, whilst northbound at Havøysund with 336 passengers on board, a fire alarm went off. The police and fire brigade were summoned and the vessel evacuated, but no fire was discovered and half an hour later the ship was on her way to Honningsvåg.

In February 2008, bad weather truncated her voyage on 13th February, when ports beyond Hammerfest were deemed to be unusable owing to strong winds. The ship turned back off Havøysund and proceeded to Alta, lying over until she could resume her voyage southbound from Hammerfest some 36 hours later.

In the autumn of 2008, with Hurtigruten ASA temporarily facing large deficits, consideration was given to selling one of their ships, with the *Polarlys*, *Nordkapp* and *Nordnorge* seemingly on the short list. Fortunately, the situation improved and today all three ships continue to play an important part in the success of the Hurtigruten operation.

Permission was given to OVDS in late 1995 for an identical sister to the *Nordkapp* to be constructed by Kværner Kleven, Ulsteinvik, though the cost had risen slightly to NOK 511 million. The new *Nordnorge* was delivered to OVDS on 14th March 1997 and registered in Narvik. Her interior décor very much reflects an Art Nouveau and Art Deco influence and is graced by watercolours from the Lofoten artist Dagfinn Bakke as well as by Johanne Marie Hansen-Kone and Ellen Lenvik. On 20th March, the *Nordnorge* was formally named by Sissel Marie Rønbeck, the then Minister of Transport and Communications, having technically entered Hurtigruten service the previous day. Her arrival resulted in the retirement of the *Kong Olav*, which was later sold to the Andaman Club of Bangkok as a cruise ship.

As an historic footnote, whilst the name *Nordnorge* has been bestowed on four coastal ships, the *Nordnorge* of 1942 (ex *Visingø*, built 1883, bought by ODS in 1942 and rebuilt) never actually appeared on the Coastal Express, as during her delivery voyage from the shipyard at Sarpsborg on 24th March 1944 she was torpedoed off Stad by HMS *Satyr*.

The *Nordnorge* settled down to be a reliable performer on the route and in her early days was rarely in the news. However, this was to change in the winter of 2002/3, when the ship undertook a series of eight cruises from Argentina and Chile to the Antarctic, the *Lofoten* being scheduled to cover her on the Hurtigruten between November 2002 and March 2003. In that first season 1,700 passengers were carried, so the programme was repeated for the 2003/4 winter, with positioning cruises being advertised, enabling passengers to join for part or all of the voyage. The *Nordnorge* sailed from Bergen on 26th September 2003, calling at Ostend, Portsmouth, Lorient, La Rochelle, La Coruña, Lisbon, Cadiz, Tangier, Funchal and Las Palmas. For the winter of 2003/4 no less than 2,400 passengers were carried, with almost every cruise being fully booked.

The popularity of this venture led to OVDS announcing that the range of

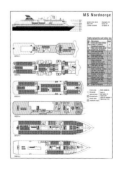

itineraries was to increase, to include the Falklands and South Georgia as well. The winter programme for 2004/5 included a new 18-day cruise itinerary from Ushuaia, embracing Antarctica, South Georgia and the Falklands, with visits to some of the old Norwegian fishing and whaling stations.

The *Nordnorge's* 45 day homeward positioning cruise in the spring of 2004 offered options from Lisbon, Bilbao, La Rochelle, Cherbourg, Amsterdam, Kiel Canal, Rønne and Copenhagen before reaching Bergen. In the following years other variations were on offer including a 43 day cruise between Hammerfest (the northernmost town in the world) and Ushuaia (the southernmost), a mere 9,915 nautical miles.

The northbound spring return in 2005 was extended into a Baltic cruise, with calls at Bremen (5th April 2005) then via the Kiel Canal to Copenhagen, Oslo, Gdansk, Visby, Riga, Klaipeda and Warnemünde before returning to Oslo, cruising in Lysefjorden, Stavanger and Bergen (19th April).

The winter of 2005/6 was the first involving both the *Nordnorge* and *Nordkapp* being based in the Southern Hemisphere. For the *Nordnorge* new ports of call were visited on her run south, including Sandefjord, Santander, Arrecife and Santa Cruz de Tenerife.

The *Nordnorge* was back in the news in 2007 when, firstly, on 30th January she came to the aid of her sister vessel, the *Nordkapp*, after she ran aground in the Antarctic and sustained a ruptured fuel tank. All 294 passengers were safely evacuated from the *Nordkapp* and were taken to Ushuaia, Argentina. The same year, but the following season, on 23rd November, the *Nordnorge* was involved in the rescue of all 100 passengers and 54 crew from the sinking expedition ship *Explorer*, after she had made underwater contact with an iceberg in the Antarctic.

The *Nordnorge* joined the new explorer ship *Fram* for the 2007/8 Antarctic season, running between Ushuaia and Punta Arenas. On departures from Ushuaia, she followed a route through the islands to the northern tip of Antarctica, returning northwards via Cabo de Hornos and

Puerto Williams, before traversing the Beagle Channel and eventually arriving at Punta Arenas. The Falklands and South Georgia cruises formed part of the *Nordnorge*'s positioning runs, southbound from Buenos Aires to Ushuaia, via the Falklands, before sailing via South Georgia, Grytviken, Strømsnes, Fortuna Bay, Drygalskifjorden and the northernmost extremities of Antarctica, thence to Ushuaia.

Having in April 2008 returned to her normal Coastal Express duties, at the end of the summer season on 9th September 2008 the *Nordnorge* sailed on a special charter cruise to the Orkney Islands. A bombshell was around the corner as on 21st October the ship was laid up at Åndalsnes. Fortunately, this was not for too long as she was then chartered to Aker Solutions ASA as an accommodation ship in the Adriatic for the offshore oil industry, departing Norway on 1st December. The original contract was extended from 5th April until 16th June and then further extended before being finally finishing on 13th August 2009. On 24th August 2009, the *Nordnorge* arrived at the Bredo Shipyard, Bremerhaven, for a major overhaul, including the refurbishment of the restaurant, and was made ready for Hurtigruten service once more. In April 2010, the ship returned to full time service on the route.

June 2011 saw the *Nordnorge* and her crew become national celebrities when the ship was used by Norwegian Television Company NRK for their 'Hurtigruten minutt for minutt' broadcast of the whole 134 hours of her Hurtigruten journey from Bergen to Kirkenes. Millions watched the broadcast and thousands of people came out to see her arrive and depart at each port. The broadcast can still be seen on the NRK website and a shortened 12 hour DVD version was also produced. It proved to be a great advertisement for Hurtigruten ASA.

The *Nordnorge* seemingly passes under the veils of the Seven Sisters as she cruises the Geirangerfjord in July 2008
(Lars Lund/Hurtigruten ASA)

No it's not the Antarctic or Svalbard but Alta in Northern Norway where the *Nordnorge* is now waiting to resume her schedule having been diverted after exceptionally stormy weather in March 2011 (Robert Waleczek/Hurtigruten ASA)

Above: A view of the Museum (John Bryant)

Below: Bust of the Hurtigruten's founder, Richard With (John Bryant)

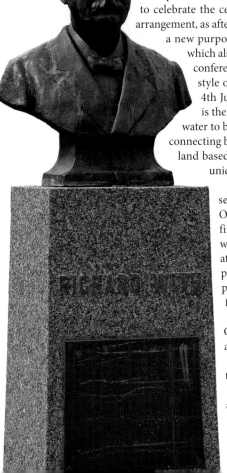

The Hurtigruten Museum

The Hurtigruten Museum is located in Stokmarknes, the home of the founding father of the Coastal Express, Richard With. Originally based in an administrative building belonging to Det Vesteraalens Dampskibsselskab (VDS), it was officially opened by the Minister of Transport and Communications, Kjell Opseth, on 2nd July 1993 in time to celebrate the centenary of the route. This was to be a short term arrangement, as after much hard work sufficient funding was secured for a new purpose built museum complex (the Hurtigrutemuseet) which also contains the 'Hurtigrutens Hus', a 42 bed hotel and conference centre. Strikingly designed with an interior in the style of a ship, the new museum was formally opened on 4th July 1999. The highlight of the permanent exhibition is the *Finnmarken* (1956), which has been lifted out of the water to become an integral part of the museum accessed by a connecting bridge. The *Finnmarken* is by far and away the largest land based museum exhibit in Norway, preserved in a totally unique environment.

The *Finnmarken* had been retired after 37 years of service in December 1993 when, in a bold move, OVDS donated the ship to the museum. Funding was finally secured in 1997/98 and in May 1999 the ship was sent under her own power to the Kaarbø shipyard at Harstad, where her hull was sandblasted and painted. On 16th June, the ship was lifted ashore and placed next to the new Hurtigruten Museum in time for its opening day.

The museum offers an historical tour of the Coastal Express, through exhibits, text and images aided by sound, colour and light from early ship design, whereby the master would have to stand at the helm outdoors all year round, to today's computer controlled world within the comforts of an enclosed bridge. Some of the original furnishings, fittings and rooms from the *Finnmarken* (1912) give a fascinating insight into how life was then, how the

mailroom operated, how cargo was loaded and unloaded, how navigation and sea safety have changed over the past 100 years. A slide show gives an insight into daily life along the coast throughout the four seasons and to the impact it has on local communities. The museum has been a great success and whilst most visitors are those who come directly from the Hurtigruten ship each day when it docks at Stokmarknes, interest levels in visiting the library to study Hurtigruten history are high amongst both school groups and the general public.

Top left: High and dry, the *Finnmarken* (1956) is an integral part of the museum, open to all visitors, and above, some of the fascinating interiors
(Clemens Franz/John Bryant)

The major issue for the museum is how to maintain the *Finnmarken* in the long term, as ships deteriorate from the top down. Because of progressive corrosion, the ship was quickly covered with a lightweight roof, initially as a winter measure, but now permanent. Whilst daily maintenance, sanding, painting and lubricating continues (the engine room is immaculate), the level of expenditure necessary to preserve the ship is not one that the museum is able to raise alone, so there is a need to find a solution which, as a major tourist attraction, needs to include further municipality, county and state aid.

In 2009 the architectural firm Narud Stokke Wiig drew up proposals to erect a glass structure over the whole of the ship, completely preserving it from the outside elements at a cost of around NOK 100 million. Both Nordland County Council and the Hadsel Municipality were willing to contribute NOK 20 million each, providing the Norwegian Government takes the rest of the bill. However, in 2010 no national funding was forthcoming and since then matters have become rather quiet.

What might be; a proposal to keep the ship safe from the outside elements (Narud Stokke Wiig architects)

Whatever happens, the whole concept is outstanding, innovative and worthy of a long term future.

The Millennium Class Ships

In 1999 Det Ofotens og Vesteraalens Dampskibsselskab (OVDS), still buoyed by the success of the 'new generation' ships, began to firm up plans for a new and enlarged version and, following agreement with the Ministry of Transport and Communications, signed another construction contract, this time worth NOK 750 million, with Kværner Kleven Verft, Ulsteinvik on 10th May 2000. OVDS had been pleased with the shipyard's performance with their two previous new builds, the *Nordkapp* and *Nordnorge*, so it was no surprise that they returned to the same shipyard. There were options for two further sister ships, but funding for these was allocated to TFDS. This new vessel would be a replacement for the *Lofoten*, the last of the 'traditional' ships still in regular service apart from the *Nordstjernen*. The design work was completed by 10th November 2000 and by 24th January 2001 the first modules for the keel were in situ. The modules came from several shipyards, Hjørungsvåg and Ulsteinvik in Norway as well as from Poland and Lithuania, with the cabin modules coming from Finland. Nine months later, on 15th September 2001, the new *Finnmarken* was launched and by 9th February 2002 she had begun her sea trials.

The *Finnmarken* is the third Coastal Express ship to bear this name, following on from those built in 1912 and 1956 for VDS of Stokmarknes . On 4th April 2002 at Ulsteinvik, the new OVDS flagship was formally named by Torhild Skogsholm, Minister of Transport and Communications.

Measuring 15,530 gross tons (945 dwt) and 138.5 metres in length the *Finnmarken* was, for a few weeks, the largest (and is still the longest) ship in the Coastal Express fleet with 40% more deck space than any other previous ship. Her main engines are two Wärtsilä 9L32 diesels developing 5,630 hp each, linked to two six-cylinder Wärtsilä W6L32 diesels of 3,780 hp each, with a total output of 18,820 hp. The propulsion system is designed so that it can run in five different modes, using both diesel-electric and conventional mechanical transmission, enabling one main engine to drive both propellers simultaneously. The *Finnmarken* has two 1,370 hp Brunvoll FU 80 LTC 2250 bow thrusters with, at the stern, a 1,650 hp Ulstein azimuth pod which can rotate 360°. Blohm & Voss active fin stabilisers are also installed amidships. Electrical power is produced by two 2,500 kVA shaft generators backed up by a Mitsubishi S6A3-mtpa diesel-powered emergency generator. The ship has three fridge/freezer rooms with a total volume of 790 m³. Loading and unloading is done in the usual way with a forklift truck through the large side doors on the port side, where there is also space for up to 50 cars.

Deck Plans of the *Finnmarken* as originally built

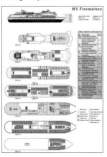

The *Finnmarken* in her OVDS livery, she was the first of the new 'Millennium' ships to come into service (Hurtigruten ASA)

The *Finnmarken* is certified for 1,000 passengers on the coastal route and has 628 berths spread over 285 cabins, which include 18 mini suites, and 14 large suites. All cabins boast heated bathroom floors, refrigerators, safes, telephones and televisions. The ship is tastefully decorated in the Art Nouveau style, with many local artists contributing drawings, watercolours, oil paintings, lithographs and sculpture. In addition to the panoramic observation lounge, bars, restaurant, cafeteria, shop and conference facilities, the ship also boasts, with recreational activities in mind, a fitness centre, an outdoor heated swimming pool, two jacuzzis, a solarium and a hairdressing salon.

In 2005, the *Finnmarken* was adapted to become an emergency hospital ship, the Norwegian Armed Forces being responsible for specifications, design and construction as well as covering the costs. With the ship having its own water plant, electricity and waste management systems, it means that she can be at sea for long periods of time. Given 10 days' notice, the ship would be fully operational, accommodating up to 200 casualties.

Two days after the naming ceremony, the *Finnmarken* embarked from Bergen on a two week promotional cruise taking in Orkney, the Hebrides, Isle of Man, Dublin, Southampton, Amsterdam, Hamburg, Copenhagen, Oslo and Stavanger. On 20th April 2002, she began her maiden Hurtigruten voyage from Bergen.

The ship had an unpleasant experience on the night of 13th November 2004 when, southbound from Ålesund in a storm, a huge breaker damaged

On board *Finnmarken*, top left clockwise; Swimming Pool, Bridge, Brotoppen Observation Lounge, Fløybaren Bar (John Bryant)

The *Finnmarken* arriving at Fremantle Western Australia in March 2010, prior to her Gorgon Oil and Gas Field Project charter (John Kent)

an emergency exit door on Deck 5 with water flooding down into Deck 2 where crew have their cabins. The ship's master took the decision, for the comfort of passengers and crew, to return to Ålesund as well as to get the door repaired. Repairs were quickly effected, the *Finnmarken* resuming her Hurtigruten service from Ålesund the following day, this time northbound.

On 6th October, 2009 Hurtigruten ASA announced that the *Finnmarken* had been chartered as an accommodation ship in connection with the development of the Gorgon Oil and Gas field off the coast of Western Australia. The contract was for 18 months, with options to extend, and worth around NOK 697 million to the company. In connection with the contract, Hurtigruten ASA created a subsidiary, Coastal Pty Ltd, to act as the contract partner. The ship was to be manned by key Hurtigruten deck and engineering officers, as well as by more local crew. Extensive upgrading work was carried out between November 2009 and March 2010 at the Westcom Shipyard, Ølensvåg, Western Norway, before the ship sailed via Cape Town to Fremantle for final preparations before the contract commenced on 30th April.

Sorely missed by both passengers and employees, it came as welcome news when it was announced in October 2011 that the contract would not be extended and that the ship would be returning to the Hurtigruten in 2012. After a major refit and refurbishment in Singapore, including her 10 year survey, the *Finnmarken* returned via the Cape of Good Hope to Bergen where on 16th February she began her first Hurtigruten voyage for over two years. The ship took up the *Nordlys'* roster until 22nd March after which she replaced the veteran *Nordstjernen*.

Back in the fold! The *Finnmarken* departing Berlevåg in May 2012 (Nick Widdows)

Hot on the heels of OVDS's announcement in May 2000 for a new ship, on 1st June TFDS signed a NOK 715 million construction contract with Fosen M/V, Rissa, near Trondheim for another Hurtigruten ship. In design, the ship was to be quite different from anything that had gone before and built very much with the wider cruise market in mind. On 22nd December, it was revealed that the vessel would be named *Trollfjord* after the famous narrow fjord off the Raftsundet in the Lofotens, visited daily in the summer months by the Coastal Express steamers.

Work started on the keel at Bruces Shipyard, Landskrona, Sweden on 18th April 2001, with the hull being lauched six months later on 10th October, whereupon it was towed to Rissa for completion. The ship was ready by 26th April 2002 for final trials after which it was handed over to TFDS on 13th May. The formal naming was performed by Kari Bremnes, a well known Norwegian singer/songwriter from Svolvaer in the Lofotens. This was some six weeks later than scheduled, which meant that an inaugural cruise programme had to be cancelled. The *Trollfjord's* maiden voyage under the command of Captain Tormod Karlsen began in Bergen on 18th May, replacing the *Nordstjernen*.

The *Trollfjord* was the now largest in the fleet and measured 16,140 gross tons (1,186 dwt) and 135.75m in length. The ship has a certificate for 822 passengers with 654 berths in 305 cabins of which 19 are suites and five have a balcony. Her crew of 74 share 53 cabins. Spread over nine decks, with a five deck atrium as its centrepiece, the ship has two conference rooms, restaurant, cafeteria, bars, shop and lounges including a twin level panoramic observation lounge. The décor on the *Trollfjord* is full of cool blues and contemporary images of icy landscapes and artwork, so is very much a winter ship. The ship also has on its top deck a small pool and an outside jacuzzi, with the water at a constant 37° C. This is quite an experience especially when the outside temperature is 20° C below zero; the advice is to protect all extremities and to wear a hat! Valuable paintings by

The *Trollfjord* (2002) in her TFDS funnel livery gently reverses towards the northbound berth at Trondheim, May 2006 (John Bryant)

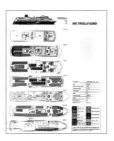

artist Kaare Espolin Johnson, previously displayed on board the 1964 built
Harald Jarl, now grace the *Trollfjord* and are to be seen on Deck 8. When
the *Harold Jarl* was put up for sale she was valued at NOK 10 million, whilst
the paintings were insured for NOK 15 million! In 2003, the ship won two
design accolades at the ShipPax Awards in the cruise ship category.

The *Trollfjord's* main engines are two 9-cylinder Wärtsilä 4-stroke
W9L32 diesels with an output of 8,280 kW, giving a service speed of 18
knots. Two Ulstein Aquamaster azimuth pods which can be rotated 360°,
eliminating the need for a rudder, are also fitted. Forward, there are three
1,200 kW Brunvoll FU-80-LTC-2250 bow thrust units. The *Trollfjord* has
three diesel-powered electrical generators and an emergency generator. Fuel
consumption on a round trip between Bergen and Kirkenes is about 200
tons. The ship's various tanks can hold up to 287 m³ (287,000 litres) of heavy
fuel oil, 60 m³ light diesel oil and 250 m³ of fresh water. The ship conforms
to all the latest environmental regulations, emits minimal CO_2 gases as well
as being quieter and near vibration free. Loading and unloading is done
using forklift trucks through a loading port on the port side, with flexible

Still at Trondheim, the
Trollfjord prepares for the next
leg of her journey to Rørvik
(John Bryant)

On board views, left to right;
Trollhall Panorama Lounge,
Espolin Johnson Room,
Atrium Lift (Uwe Jakob)

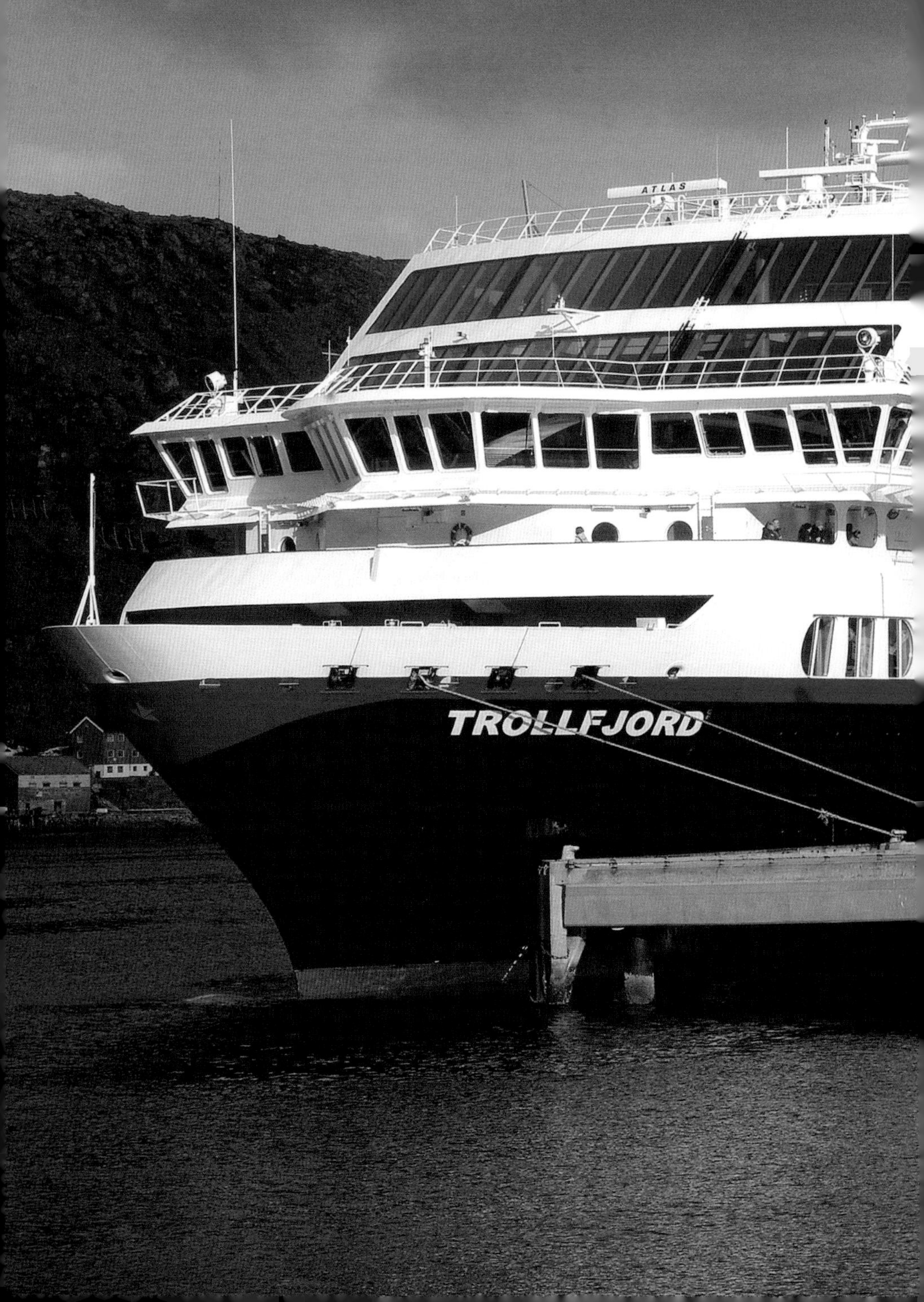
ATLAS
TROLLFJORD

The *Trollfjord* berthed at a
sunny Kjøllefjord in May 2012,
note the loading
arrangements (Nick Widdows)

height ramps to offset any differences between the quayside and the ship. The car deck has space for up to 45 passenger vehicles.

On 18th October 2002, the ship returned to the Fosen Shipyard for the installation of the third bow thrust unit together with alterations to her main switchboard, before returning to service twelve days later.

The *Trollfjord* has been a popular choice for charter work. In April 2004, TFDS in conjunction with Combitours offered an Easter cruise with the ship sailing on 2nd April from Bergen to Stavanger, Hamburg and Le Havre before returning via Amsterdam, arriving back in Norway some ten days later.

The Easter itinerary for 2005 involved a circumnavigation of Britain, departing on 20th March from Bergen then calling at Stavanger, Lerwick, Greenock, Douglas, Dublin, Portsmouth, Leith and Stavanger (again) before reaching Bergen on 1st April.

In the autumn of 2005, from 1st – 10th October, Det Norske Bokklubane (Norwegian Book Club Society) chartered the *Trollfjord* for a cruise between Oslo and Kirkenes, with calls at Fredrikstad, Kristiansand, Stavanger, Bergen, Geiranger, Ålesund, Molde, Trondheim, Reine, Svolvær, Trollfjord, Tromsø, Honningsvåg and Berlevåg. The ship then remained at Kirkenes until 15th October, before returning south on her normal Hurtigruten schedule.

A special cruise as a celebration of the life of Erik Bye (a well known Norwegian television personality, singer and journalist) with book readings, concerts and lectures was hosted by the *Trollfjord*, sailing as normal from Bergen on 23rd September 2005, but upon reaching Harstad the ship returned south calling at Trondheim, Bergen and Stavanger, before ending in Oslo on 30th September.

The merger between OVDS and TFDS in March 2006 to form the Hurtigruten Group (later renamed Hurtigruten ASA) meant that the *Trollfjord's* funnel received the new company colours with her port of registry (Tromsø) unchanged.

Later that year, on 5th November 2006 when southbound between Brønnøyund and Rørvik, the *Trollfjord* managed to entangle one of her screws in fishing nets and it took four hours to free it.

During early 2007 the *Trollfjord* was chartered as an exhibition/hotel ship for the Winter Festival Week in Narvik and later for the Northern Lights Festival in Tromsø. During March, this vessel made an anniversary voyage as part of the centenary celebrations for Kaare Espolin Johnson, the artist, some of whose works adorn the ship.

On 9th May 2007, the ship managed to touch the bottom in the Black Sound area of the Raftsundet. Upon reaching Svolvaer, divers found that three of the ship's tanks were punctured, but fortunately none of these contained oil fuel. A temporary seal was made and the ship sailed directly to the Bergen Mek Shipyard, Laksevåg for repairs. In 2011, during a period of extremely low tides, the ship again touched the bottom, this time in the Risøyrenna Channel. As a result, the Norwegian Coastal Agency will further dredge and deepen the channel during 2013.

Most recently in late December 2011, the *Trollfjord*, together with several other Hurtigruten ships, was caught up in storms generated by Hurricane

Dagmar which lashed the west coast over the Christmas and New Year period. With it unwise to sail, the *Trollfjord* remained at Trondheim for four days.

The news on 2nd January 2001 from TFDS that the company were to build a new *Midnatsol* (the fourth Coastal Express ship to be so named) indicated the likely demise of their 1982 'mid generation' ship after a relatively short life on the Hurtigruten. It was to be a repeat of the NOK 715 million *Trollfjord* contract with Fosen Mek at Rissa. Almost immediately after the hull of the *Trollfjord* had departed Bruces Shipyard, Landskrona, Sweden, on 17th October work began on the keel. By 26th April 2002 the hull was ready for launching and towed to Fosen's for completion.

Whilst the *Midnatsol* is a sister ship to the *Trollfjord*, with all the same dimensions, power plant, facilities, general accommodation etc., she differs in that she can also be used as a hospital ship in case of war, crisis or disaster. The Norwegian Navy contributed NOK 6.5 million towards the cost of her construction so that part of Deck 10 could be equipped as a full-scale hospital with beds for up to 200 patients, an intensive care centre and four operating theatres. The ship has her own water and electricity supply and waste management systems on board, which means that she can be at sea for long periods of time. The lifts are sufficiently large to take hospital beds and the vessel has a helideck. The car deck too can be converted into a field hospital with up to 70 doctors and nurses.

The *Midnatsol* has a passenger certificate for 1,000 passengers, 178 more than her sister ship, with 648 berths spread over 304 cabins, of which 15 are suites (some with a balcony) and seven are mini-suites. The restaurant is located aft on Deck 5 and can accommodate 335 guests at one sitting. Large

The *Midnatsol* (2003) on the day of her official naming at Hamburg, 22nd March 2003 (Uwe Jakob)

Midnatsol (2003) Deck Plan

glass expanses allow light to permeate throughout the ship, enhancing the décor's warm pastel yellows, oranges and russets which, together with complementary wood tones, evoke the aura of the midnight sun. The ship has, among other things, a library, cafeteria, bars and conference rooms with on Deck 9 a small heated pool and oudoor jacuzzi.

It was not until 14th March 2003 that the ship was formally handed over to TFDS. Two days later she sailed from Trondheim, calling at Ålesund, cruising both the Geirangerfjord and Sognefjorden before making her way down to Stavanger and on to Hamburg for her naming ceremony. At the mouth of the Elbe, she was met by *Nordstjernen* (which had been built at the Blohm and Voss Shipyard, Hamburg), and together they cruised up river to the German city. The official naming ceremony took place on 23rd March and was performed by Rut Brandt, former wife of Chancellor Willy Brandt, a gesture reflecting the importance of the German market to the Hurtigruten. After a gala dinner the *Midnatsol* sailed for Kiel via the Nord-Ostsee (Kiel) Canal and thence on to Copenhagen and Oslo. Two further promotional visits to the Shetlands followed, before on 15th April 2003, she was ready to make her maiden Hurtigruten voyage from Bergen. The old *Midnatsol* which had been renamed *Midnatsol II* was laid up at Fiskerstrand M/V near Ålesund and advertised for sale. Her subsequent career, including her return to the Hurtigruten service as the *Lyngen,* can be found elsewhere.

On the night of 13th/14th December 2003 the *Midnatsol* was southbound crossing the Stadhavet between Ålesund and Måløy in a gale when the main power supply failed. The anchors were deployed in an attempt to stop the drift, but had little effect. A tug was summoned but after efforts to get a towing hawser attached failed, all 102 passengers were ordered to the lifeboat stations. The situation was becoming critical, but only when 150 metres from the shore did one of the anchors finally take hold. Not long after, the engineers managed to restore power and the ship was able to resume sailing to Florø. The cause was a blocked inlet pipe to the engine's cooling system.

In August 2004 the NRK (Norwegian Broadcasting Corporation) began filming a 20 episode series entitled 'Coastal 365', depicting life on board the *Midnatsol*. Whilst only a total of ten hours of film were shown on television during the 20 episodes, some 500 to 600 hours of film were shot and afforded excellent publicity for the Hurtigruten route.

On 15th October 2004 the *Midnatsol* was chartered for the Drammen based TESS Industries Fashion Fair, sailing directly from Bergen to Oslo, spending three days there as a static exhibition ship for the trade fair. On the return journey to Bergen she visited Drammen, Arendal, Kristiansand, Egersund, Haugesund, Stord, Kristiansund, Trondheim, Ålesund and Ulsteinvik before finally returning to Bergen on 27th October.

In early 2006 the *Midnatsol* was again chartered, this time as a hotel ship, based at Savona, for the duration of the Turin Winter Olympics. On her outward cruise she sailed from Oslo on 27th January, calling at Hamburg, Rotterdam, Portsmouth, La Rochelle, Bilbao, Lisbon and Barcelona, arriving at Savona on 10th February. After the Winter Olympics the ship began a three

A busy scene at Rørvik in August 2011 as the *Midnatsol* loads its palletised cargo (Francy van Lieshout/ Hurtigruten ASA)

part return cruise on 27th February, via Naples, Catania, Valletta, La Goulette and Ajaccio to Nice. From Nice the second leg took in Livorno, Portoferraio, Cagliari, Maó and ended at Barcelona, then it was on to Palma de Mallorca, Alicante, Málaga, Gibraltar, Tangier, Lisbon, London (24th March) and home!

Very much viewed as the flagships of today's Hurtigruten ASA subsequently both the *Midnatsol* and *Trollfjord* have continued to be used on numerous trade charters and special cruises, often organised by Hurtigruten's agent in Germany, Norwegische Schiffahrt Agency (NSA). This reflects the popularity the Hurtigruten has in that country, which provides around half of the round trip passengers on the Coastal Express route.

The *Midnatsol* takes a sharp turn to port as it prepares to pass under Sortland Bridge in November 2010 (Trond G. Johnsen/Hurtigruten ASA)

FOOD FOR THOUGHT

Did you know that when a Hurtigruten ship embarks on the 12-day round trip from Bergen to Kirkenes and back, that apart from the breathtaking scenery en route, the culinary experience is a major part of the world's most beautiful voyage? A typical order list looks something like this:

Bread	800 loaves and 4,000 rolls	Fish	1,500 kg
Fruit	3,000 kg	Seafood	500 kg
Vegetables	3,000 kg	Soft Drinks	500 bottles (0.50 litres)
Eggs	500 kg	Coffee	250 kg
Cheese	300 kg	Tea	5,000 tea bags
Sausage	100 kg	Wine	400 bottles (0.75 litres)
Ham/Meat Balls	200 kg	Beer	2,000 litres
Meat	1,500 kg	Spirits	30 litres

Source: Hurtigruten ASA 2012

Fuel consumption on a round trip between Bergen and Kirkenes is about 200,000 litres (200 tonnes). The ships' various tanks can hold up to 287,000 litres of heavy fuel oil, 60,000 litres of light diesel oil and 250,000 litres of fresh water.

What could be better?
Christmas at Kirkenes,
December 2008 (Gunvald
Heitman/Hurtigruten ASA)

Towards Hurtigruten ASA

The 2001 and 2005 Agreements

The Hurtigruten has played an important role in the commercial life of Northern Norway for a long time, though its importance has changed as other transport means have been developed and constructed. However, it is still a top tourist attraction and as transporter of local residents and local goods is still highly valued at many destinations along the coast.

When the Hurtigruten was discussed in the Storting during the 1990s, there was a body of opinion which argued that after 2001 it should not be necessary to continue with subsidies. They suggested that a more market-oriented solution of splitting the route to smaller areas of operation gave more chance for the shipping companies to bear their own costs. The Storting as a whole were not convinced, believing that the value of the Hurtigruten to Norwegian society was central: as a transport infrastructure, as a driving force for tourism and as a driving force for regional development. The route is a homogeneous one encompassing cargo, passenger transport and cruise passengers with comprehensive facilities for all these needs and has spill-over effects on the commercial life of Nordland, Troms and Finnmark. Overall, the Storting believed that a totally free and market-oriented situation would change the structure of transport provision negatively for the communities along the coast, resulting in fewer calls and a more focused cruise activity.

The reality is that whilst the Hurtigruten cannot bear its own costs, the amount of subsidy given by the Norwegian Parliament (Storting) for each passenger is not excessive and sits in the middle when compared to that given for alternative transport facilities. The decision was for the Hurtigruten to continue and the support package would be there to subsidise passenger transport but not cargo or tourism.

If one looks at the freight element, northbound cargo to Tromsø and Finnmark consists mainly of consumer goods for households and industry. Southbound cargo consists mainly of fish, especially frozen fish. The cold store capacity of Hurtigruten is of major importance for the distribution of goods to the north and of frozen fish for outbound deliveries.

In Finnmark, Hammerfest is the biggest port but for the Hurtigruten has the least importance for cargo as there are alternatives. It is in such places as Kjøllefjord, Øksfjord , Mehamn and Berlevåg which are on the edge of the road networks that the Hurtigruten is crucial for survival with 70% – 90% of their goods transported by the Coastal Express. If the Hurtigruten disappeared, substantial structural changes to the transport of goods would occur in Northern Norway. When the Government buys transport services from Hurtigruten, it is contributing to the financing of its transport function and not to cruise activity, whilst at the same time recognising that the transport element is the base for the cruise service, which in turn provides mutual benefit for both local residents and tourists.

The 2001 agreement
In 2001, a new financial agreement was reached between the Ministry of Transport, OVDS and TFDS to enable them to continue to operate the Hurtigruten through to December 2004. The Storting also made it possible for them to buy new ships and as a result, by the time the *Midnatsol* was delivered in 2003, the fleet consisted of nine modern ships, built after 1993, and two modernised ships from the 1980s. In addition, the two Hurtigruten companies were also guaranteed a concession by the State for the Bergen-Kirkenes route until 2010.

The current Hurtigruten Timetable (Hurtigruten ASA)

RUTEPLAN - TIME SCHEDULE - FAHRPLAN

| NORDGÅENDE SOMMERRUTE | | | SYDGÅENDE SOMMERRRUTE | | |
HAVN	ANK.	AVG.	HAVN	ANK.	AVG.
Bergen		20:00	Kirkenes		12:45
Florø	02:00	02:15	Vardø	16:00	17:00
Måløy	04:15	04:30	Båtsfjord	19:45	20:30
Torvik	07:15	07:30	Berlevåg	22:15	22:30
Ålesund	08:45	09:30	Mehamn	01:00	01:15
*Geiranger	13:25	13:30	Kjøllefjord	03:15	03:30
Ålesund	18:00	18:45	Honningsvåg	05:45	06:15
Molde	21:30	22:00	Havøysund	08:15	08:30
Kristiansund	01:30	01:45	Hammerfest	11:15	12:45
Trondheim	08:15	12:00	Øksfjord	15.30	15:45
Rørvik	20:30	21:15	Skjervøy	19:15	19:45
Brønnøysund	00:45	01:00	Tromsø	23:45	01:30
Sandnessjøen	03:45	04:15	Finnsnes	04:15	04:45
Nesna	05:25	05:30	Harstad	08:00	08:30
Ørnes	09:15	09:30	Risøyhamn	10:45	11:00
Bodø	12:30	15:00	Sortland	12:30	13:00
Stamsund	19:00	19:30	Stokmarknes	14:15	15:15
Svolvær	21:00	22:00	Svolvær	18:30	20:00
Stokmarknes	00:45	01:00	Stamsund	21:40	22:00
Sortland	02:30	03:00	Bodø	01:45	04:00
Risøyhamn	04:15	04:30	Ørnes	07:00	07:15
Harstad	06:45	08:00	Nesna	11:00	11:15
Finnsnes	11:15	11:45	Sandnessjøen	12:30	13:30
Tromsø	14:30	18:30	Brønnøysund	16:15	17:00
Skjervøy	22:30	22:45	Rørvik	20:30	21:30
Øksfjord	02:00	02:15	Trondheim	06:30	10:00
Hammerfest	05:15	06:45	Kristiansund	16:30	17:00
Havøysund	09:30	09:45	Molde	20:45	21:30
Honningsvåg	11:45	15:15	Ålesund	00:00	00:45
Kjøllefjord	17:30	17:45	Torvik	02:00	02:15
Mehamn	19:45	20:00	Måløy	05:15	05:45
Berlevåg	22:30	22:45	Florø	07:45	08:15
Båtsfjord	00:30	01:00	Bergen	14:30	
Vardø	04:00	04:15			
Vadsø	07:30	08:00			
Kirkenes	09:45				

OBS: Alle tider er cirka tider, avhengig av vær og last.
All times are approximate, dependent on weather and freight.
Alle Zeiten sind ungefähr, abhängig vom Wetter und Fracht.89

The 2005 agreement
A new contract proposal from the Norwegian Ministry of Transport was presented to the shipping companies on 15th January 2004. This would involve the State providing funding of NOK 1.6 billion over the next eight years, together with an annual operating subsidy of NOK 200 million. Neither OVDS nor TFDS was happy about this, requesting instead NOK 230 million. There were also suggestions from other potential bidders that the service could be reduced to four days per week, and operated in two sections, Bergen to Tromsø, and Tromsø to Kirkenes. What price then for round trip passengers, with all change at Tromsø?! On 28th May 2004, the Norwegian Ministry of Transport formally announced the start of the tendering process. Not surprisingly, the only submission was a joint one from OVDS and TFDS. Discussions continued throughout the year with agreement reached on 5th November. The new contract would run from 2005 to 2012, with the companies receiving an annual subsidy of NOK 237 million (NOK 1.9 billion in total). The service would continue to be daily, in full, from Bergen to Kirkenes.

New Bergen Terminal

The building and opening of the new NOK 240 million Hurtigruten Terminal at Nøstebryggen, Bergen on 1st March 2005 allayed fears that the service south of Trondheim might one day be withdrawn. For nearly a century until the early 1980s the Coastal Express ships had berthed at the Festningskaien, in the Vågen at Bergen, before moving to the Frielenskaien Terminal, which was rather tucked away out of sight from the daily city centre landscape. The new Nøstebryggen terminal, with it 157m long quay and 280-space, multi-storey car park, is close to the city centre and opposite the attractive residential area of Nordnes where good views can be obtained of the ships arriving and departing.

Merger 2006!

In the meantime OVDS and TFDS were actively pursuing a merger of the two companies, the two boards of directors reaching agreement on 1st November 2005 and formally sanctioning it two weeks later. It was agreed that the workforce places should be shared between the two companies on a 50/50 basis, whilst any job losses resulting from the merger should also be shared 50/50. Shareholder approval was obtained on 19th December 2005, followed by the Monopolies and Mergers Board giving its consent on 21st February 2006. From 1st March that year, the Coastal Express would be operated by a single company, the Hurtigruten Group (subsequently renamed Hurtigruten ASA), with its head offices based in Narvik.

The 2006 fleet list showed no less than 14 Coastal Express ships, with one expedition ship on order, 17 fast ferries and 34 conventional ferries and the m/s *Jupiter*, formally of Fjord Line, then in use as an accommodation ship in Hammerfest but up for sale. In addition, the new Hurtigruten company had interests in travel agencies and hotels run by Via Travel, Combi Tours, Kystopplevelser AS and Spitsbergen Travel as well as in AS TIRB (regional bus company operating in Troms, Nordland and Finnmark) together with a 50% stake in Nor Lines, the coastal shipping company.

Subsequently, the fast ferry and conventional ferry operation was taken over on 5th January 2009 by the newly formed Torghatten Nord AS, responsible for scheduled local services in an area bordering Brønnøysund in the south and Finnmark in the north. Two of the fast craft were retained and chartered to Veolia Transport Nord AS. As a result the workforce reduced dramatically from 3,039 in 2008 to 1,971 in 2010.

Hurtigruten ASA was now in a position to focus purely on its core business areas, which are detailed later on.

The *Kong Harald* carefully negotiates the narrows of the Steinsundet as she sails on towards Bergen in Juky 2010 (Odd Haugsbakk/ Hurtigruten ASA)

The Expedition Ship

As far back as 2003, OVDS had been planning for a further new ship specifically intended for wintertime Hurtigruten service and for summertime cruising with the aim of further developing tourism around Greenland begun by OVDS in 1998 with their 'explorer programme'. A contract was signed on 9th September 2005 for the Fincantieri shipyard to build the 12,700 gross tons ship at a cost of NOK 530 million. Construction started in March 2006 with the keel laying ceremony taking place on 21st August 2006 at their Monfalcone shipyard, near Trieste, Italy. The *Fram* was floated out for the first time on 18th November 2006 and was ready for her sea trials in February 2007, Fincantieri delivering the ship to Hurtigruten ASA as scheduled on 23rd April 2007.

The *Fram* is named after Fridtjof Nansen's polar exploring ship, which was the first ship to explore the seas around both the North and South Poles. The name had to be approved by the management of the Fram Museum in Oslo, Norway, who also offered to contribute authentic expedition display pieces and information on the original *Fram*.

Registered in Narvik, the *Fram* has a reinforced hull for cruising arctic waters, is 114 metres in length, with a beam of 20.2 metres. Her MAK6M25 diesels (total output 7,920 kW) give the ship a maximum speed of 16 knots. She can carry up to 25 cars and 200 pallets of freight. Within its eight decks are 136 high quality cabins and 39 suites, with a total of 318 berths.

For coastal voyages she has a passenger certificate for 500 persons,

The *Fram* (2007) meets up with the *Nordnorge* in Paradise Bay, Antarctica in December 2008 (Mogens Neilsen/Hurtigruten ASA)

reduced to 400 for sailing in international waters. Facilities include an observation lounge, library, internet café, restaurant, bistro, sauna, jacuzzi, a fitness centre and two conference/lecture rooms with seating for up to 250 people. A specially designed tender deck makes passenger embarkation easy, ensuring that onshore expeditions are safe and comfortable.

The ship's interior very much reflects the culture and language of Greenland, with the public areas bearing Inuit words of symbolic meaning, for example: Qilak (sky or heaven) Lounge, Imaq (sea) Restaurant, Nunami (on land) Lobby. The furnishings feature extensive use of traditional Nordic materials of wool, leather and oak. Artworks from both Norwegian and Greenlandic artists are displayed throughout the ship.

A great view of the *Fram* set off by basking Weddell seals in the Antarctica summer sunshine in February 2009 (Tori Hogan/Hurtigruten ASA)

The *Fram's* delivery voyage was more in the way of a four part cruise. On 20th April 2007 she sailed from Venice for Barcelona, by way of Dubrovnik, Corfu, Naples, Livorno and Monte Carlo, arriving at the Spanish port 10 days later. The second leg from 30th April saw her visit Cádiz, Lisbon, La Coruña and Rouen, ending up at the Pool of London, having sailed through Tower Bridge. Finally on 12th May, her travels took her to Rotterdam, Hamburg and Copenhagen before arriving at Oslo on 18th May, where on the following day the ship's Godmother, Crown Princess Mette Marit, formally named the ship.

The fourth part of the cruise from Oslo was marketed as 'Sailing in the footsteps of the Vikings' and called at Bergen, Lerwick, Tórshavn and Heimaey before going on to Reykjavik. Her summer programme was to see her based around the west and southeast coasts of Greenland. Guests would fly to Kangerlussuaq, Greenland's major commercial airport, at the

Everyone is well catered for on board the *Fram*, clockwise from top left; Fitness centre, Nunami Lounge, Qilak Panorama Lounge, Mini Suite (Uwe Jakob/John Bryant)

The *Fram* under the shadow of London's Tower Bridge in April 2009 on one of her positioning cruises from the Southern Hemisphere (John Bryant)

The *Fram* in idyllic Antarctic surroundings February 2007 (Backpack Foto/ Hurtigruten ASA)

head of the 170 kilometre long Søndre Strømfjord, where they boarded the *Fram*, using her lifeboats as tenders. Calls were scheduled at Nuuk (Greenland's political and social capital), Qaqortoq (the largest community in southern Greenland), Uunartoq (with its thermal springs) and Tasiilaq (the largest settlement in eastern Greenland), before finally arriving at Reykjavik on day twelve. The itinerary was then reversed.

An alternative 15 day voyage involved the *Fram* sailing north from Kangerlussuaq and cruising via Sisimiut (Greenland's second largest town and major fishing port), Disko Bay, the former whaling station at Qeqertarsuaq and Uummannaq before reaching Qaanaaq (Thule) on day nine. On the return journey, visits were made to the Eqip Sermia Glacier and Evighedsfjord (with its 2,000m mountainous cliffs).

Having completed her final Greenland cruise of the season, the *Fram* sailed from Reykjavik on 18th September 2007 on a 67-day cruise, to Ushuaia, in Southern Chile. The inaugural Antarctic season offered departures from Ushuaia for an 800-kilometre, 35-hour crossing of Drake's Passage, before exploring the tip of the Antarctic Peninsula (including Deception Island, the South Shetlands, the Lemaire Channel, Wilhelmina Bay, Antarctic Sound and Brown Bluff) before retracing her voyage back to Ushuaia, arriving there on day ten. Subsequently, her itineraries have been modified and expanded to include Svalbard; the *Fram's* current 'Explorer Voyages' itineraries can be found further on in this book.

Early on in her career, on 29th December 2007, the *Fram*, with 300 passengers on board suffered an engine problem resulting in a brief loss of power near Brown's Bluff in the Antarctic. The ship drifted against a glacier face and suffered minor damage, with one lifeboat crushed and a railing bent. There were no reported injuries. Power was quickly restored and the *Fram* headed for King George Island where a fuller inspection was made.

Since then the *Fram* has settled down and has become an extremely well patronised ship, with high rates of occupancy particularly on her Antarctic cruises, varying her ports of call each year on her positioning voyages between the Arctic and Antarctic regions.

Mention should also be made of the *Polar Star*, a small cruise ship based at Longyearbyen, originally built in 1969 as the *Njord* by Wärtsilä of Finland for use as an icebreaker in the Baltic. In April 2000 she was bought by Karlsen Shipping Norge, renamed and rebuilt as a cruise ship for use in Arctic waters.

Spitsbergen Travel, a Hurtigruten ASA daughter company, chartered her in the absence of the *Nordstjernen* to complement the *Fram*'s sailings to Greenland and Iceland during the summer seasons.

The ship, which had an Ice Class IA* certificate, was 86.5m in length with a beam of 21.2m and a service speed of 11 knots. 105 berths were provided in 47 cabins, and in addition to a restaurant, bar, observation lounge and library, the *Polar Star* had six large zodiac boats designed for use as tenders. Week-long cruises operated by *Polar Star* were marketed under the *Spitsbergen Expedition* banner. Her itineraries were deliberately flexible, given the ice conditions which vary markedly from year to year.

Deck Plan for the *Fram*

Guests would fly in to Longyearbyen to join the ship, which then called at Barentsburg, Ny-Ålesund and Magdalenefjorden, sailing on to the walrus colony at Moffen and Nordaustlandet, before heading back south to Longyearbyen via the west coast.

This venture was not without its difficulties; the 2007 season had to be aborted because of major engine problems, whilst in 2011 with no less than 857 passengers booked on 11 voyages, the shipowners went into receivership just as the season was about to start. Whilst the company is back in business, the *Polar Star* has not been used by Hurtigruten since.

The *Polar Star* (1969) which was chartered for Svalbard Cruises from 2007 until 2011 (Hurtigruten ASA)

Explorer Voyages

The return of the *Finnmarken* to Hurtigruten service in the early spring of 2012 enabled the classic *Nordstjernen* (rich in character and exuding nostalgia) to make a final return to Svalbard for a series of fascinating summer voyages.

Two 'Spitsbergen Adventure Voyage' itineraries were offered, firstly positioning voyages which explored both the stunning Norwegian coastline and the rugged beauty of Spitsbergen and secondly the core product of 6 day 'Polar Encounters' voyages which focussed on Arctic landscapes, glaciers and bird cliffs, sailing if possible to reach 80°N.

Under the heading of 'Polar Bears, Islands and Fjords', the *Nordstjernen's* late May positioning voyage from Bergen cruised via Flåm, Geirangerfjord, Ålesund, Trondheim, Reine and Svolvaer (Lofotens), the bird cliffs at Bjarkøy and then on to Tromsø. From the 'Gateway to the Arctic', the ship headed for Honningsvåg (and Nordkapp) before sailing to Longyearbyen in Spitsbergen, with calls at Barentsburg and Ny-Ålesund (the world's northernmost year round community at 78°55'N, 11°56'E).

The 'Polar Encounters' voyages, throughout June, July and August, would begin in Longyearbyen. After an overnight stay at the Spitsbergen Hotel, guests would board the *Nordstjernen* to sail south to the Russian settlement of Barentsburg, cruise the Magdalenefjord before she turned northwards via Woodfjord and Liefdefjorden to Moffen Island (the land of the walrus) crossing the 80°N latitude, before retracing her path via Kongsfjord and Ny-

The *Nordstjernen* in the familiar surroundings of Spitsbergen in August 2008 (Trym Ivar Bergsmo/ Hurtigruten ASA)

Ålesund to Longyearbyen. As an alternative, some voyages offered cruises into Isfjord, the largest fjord system in Svalbard.

The *Nordstjernen*'s return cruise to Bergen in late August initially headed north to Magdalenefjord and Moffen Island before turning south for Honningsvåg, Tromsø, Trollfjord, Alstahaug (south of Sandnessjøen with its 12th century onion domed church and the Tjøtta International War Cemetery), Ålesund and the Geirangerfjord, before finally arriving at Bergen some twelve days later on 1st September.

The *Fram*'s Expedition Cruises each have four elements: Greenland, Spitsbergen, Antarctica and European. The ship, it seems, is always on the move.

Having started to venture north from Antarctica during late February and March, the *Fram* begins her customary 'Easter Voyages' with a cruise from Las Palmas in the Canary Islands to Lisbon via Agadir, Casablanca and Gibraltar. From Lisbon it is then a 10 day cruise to Hamburg via La Coruña, Bordeaux, the Channel Islands and Honfleur. Hamburg then becomes the starting point for 'Spring Adventure' around the Norwegian Fjords via Stavanger, Lysefjord, Hardangerfjord, Flåm, Sognefjord, Ålesund and the Geirangerfjord before the *Fram* retraces her path to Bergen.

In 2012, a 9 day 'Pearls of the Baltic' cruise followed via Oslo, Copenhagen, Helsinki, St Petersburg (a 30 hour stopover) and Tallinn with a final two day stay in Stockholm, whilst for 2013 the itinerary encompasses a two part circumnavigation of the British Isles, via the Shetlands and Orkneys, Leith (for Edinburgh), Newcastle and London, before continuing on to Portsmouth, Dublin, Douglas, Iona and around to Leith, finally ending at Hamburg.

In late May comes the penultimate part of the 'migration north' when she sails again via Leith, Aberdeen, the Orkneys and Shetlands, Faroe Islands and on to Reykjavik in Iceland. The final part is a 10 day 'Glaciers and Ice' cruise from there to the Southern Fjords of Greenland.

The *Fram* is captured in the beautiful surroundings of the Lemaire Channel, Antarctica in February 2011 (Tommy Simonsen/Hurtigruten ASA)

The *Fram* in the early autumn off Daneborg, Greenland, September 2010 (Bernhard Schaper/Hurtigruten ASA)

Throughout June the *Fram* takes on a quartet of 9 day 'Heart of Greenland' expeditions. With Kangerlussuaq on the west coast as the start and finish point, the *Fram* sailed first to Sisimiut, then onto Disko Bay and the two small towns of Uummannaq and Ukkusissat, before cruising past the five kilometre wide Equip Sermia Glacier, finally calling at the isolated settlement of Itelliq. Whilst the *Fram's* next expedition covered roughly the same territory, it was more of a positioning voyage, as the ship then turned south to call at Nuuk (capital of Greenland), cruising the fjord and glacier areas around Nassaq and the Prince Christian Sound before heading across the Denmark Strait to Reykjavik, the capital of Iceland.

In July, it is a return to Reykjavik en route for Spitsbergen, with a scheduled call at the rarely visited Jan Mayen Island on the way, before cruising in Longyearbyen, Ny-Ålesund and the Isfjorden triangle. This cruise is a precursor to a series of three 8 day 'Explorer Voyages' from mid July to mid August, which give an opportunity to study the west coastline of Spitsbergen, sailing southwards to Hornsund before turning north via Ny-Ålesund to reach Moffen Island and its walruses at 80°N. The last leg saw the ship traversing the polar bear domain of Liefdefjorden before arriving back at Longyearbyen, just to do it all again!

Three more 8 day cruises in late August under the 'In the Realm of the Polar Bear' banner are complete circumnavigations of Spitsbergen, the highlight being a visit to the bird cliffs of the North East Spitsbergen Nature Reserve with an attempt to reach 81°N and the islands of Sjuøyane, the closest European landmass to the North Pole, with seabirds and polar bears as its only inhabitants.

The *Fram's* high arctic voyages ended in early September when she set sail from Longyearbyen for Greenland, again via Ny-Ålesund and Moffen, as part of a 14/15 day exploration of the coastline which makes up the North East Greenland National Park. The ship spends six days steadily cruising southwards until reaching Scoresbysund, the most isolated town in the country. The final destination is Iceland with calls

GREENLAND

at Ísafjörður, Grundarfjörður and Reykjavik.

An 'Autumn Adventure' from Reykjavik to Bergen is scheduled for the latter part of September and marks the start of the *Fram's* migration south for the winter, with calls en route at Tórshavn, Lerwick, Kirkwall and Leith; for 2013, there is a more in depth cruise around Scotland's Western Isles. Departing again from Bergen, comes a 17 day cruise to Las Palmas in the Canary Islands, with calls at Hamburg, Rouen, Nantes, La Coruña and Casablanca amongst others, before the long 19 day trans-atlantic crossing from Las Palmas to Buenos Aires.

From Buenos Aires, *Fram* departs for Ushuaia on her first Antarctic expedition following in 'The Realm of the Great Explorers' voyage of the new season, with calls at the Falkland Islands, South Georgia, exploring the tip of the Antarctic Peninsula before sailing via Drake's Passage to Southern Chile. A number of 10 day 'Classic Expedition' voyages are on offer from late November until mid February, the *Fram* sailing via Drake's Passage to spend spend four days cruising around Deception Island, Paradise Bay, Neko Harbour (gentoo penguins), Wilhelmina Bay (whales) and the Lemaire Channel, before returning the same way to Ushuaia.

These cruises are broken up by 17/19 day circular 'Great Antarctic Expedition' voyages from the base port of Ushuaia to the Falkland Islands, South Georgia, South Orkney Islands, South Shetland Islands, Brown's Bluff and the Antarctic Sound before returning to Chile via Drake's Passage. Two 'Polar Circle/Weddell Sea Expedition' voyages follow, the *Fram* taking guests as far south as the Antarctic Circle and spending no less than 7 days exploring such places as Snow Hill Island, James Ross Island and Vega Island, Trinity Peninsula and the Prince Gustav Channel.

A final voyage of the season in late February is a repeat of 'The Realm of the Great Explorers' expedition but in reverse as the *Fram* returns to Buenos Aires. And so the cycle repeats itself all over again as the explorer ship migrates north for the next Arctic summer.

The thrill of riding on one of the *Fram's* Polar Cirkel Boats is captured here in the Lemaire Channel, Antarctica, January 2012 (Arnau Ferrer/ Hurtigruten ASA)

A spectacular run past the
Fram by one of her Polar
Cirkel Boats, Lemaire Channel,
Antarctica, January 2011
(Wilhelm Löhr/Hurtigruten
ASA)

Today's Scene

2013 Hurtigruten brochure

Since Richard With founded the service in 1893, Hurtigruten has given tourists unsurpassed travel experiences along one of the world's most beautiful coastlines. The company's unique position in Norway and abroad rests not only on scenic beauties but also as a transport artery for freight and passengers. Its community role was further reinforced in 2011 by the new and improved eight-year public procurement contract from the Government.

With 120 years of service behind it the Hurtigruten has seen in excess of 80 ships on the route. Initially taken from Norwegian domestic trade or foreign routes, facilities were quite basic, but eventually new ships were custom built to suit the ever changing needs of the service. Today's fleet of modern multi purpose vessels is designed with palletised loading, refrigerated compartments and hook ups, vehicle drive-on facilities and, of course, five star cruise liner standards.

Apart from providing a daily lifeline for the 34 communities served along the 1,352 nautical miles between Bergen and Kirkenes, Hurtigruten ships have always attracted a loyal following of round trip passengers. Many have achieved more than 20 such voyages, entitling themselves to a further trip 'on the house'. It is believed, but unconfirmed, that a Swede holds the unofficial record of 80 round trip voyages, all on the *Nordnorge* (II) which sailed between 1964 and 1996! Obviously more than a labour of love!

Today, Hurtigruten ASA recognises that it has a mission and a duty which extends beyond bringing tourists to its destinations. The ships play an important role along the Norwegian coast every single day and are an integral part of the coastal community from which it gains its livelihood. It is close to nature and the local culture and operates in some of the world's most vulnerable regions. Through close cooperation with more than 40 tourist providers, the company is able to offer its guests experiences which nobody else can match.

Passenger Numbers

Passenger numbers have varied over the years; from the mid 1950s until the early 1970s well over half a million people would travel annually on the Hurtigruten. The accompanying table shows that in the post war period there was an almost continuous increase in numbers right through until 1962, when it peaked at 569,579 passengers. During the 15 year period from 1949 until that date no less than 11 new ships had been constructed for service on the Hurtigruten and three more were to follow in 1964.

From that peak there was slow steady decline in numbers over the next decade with 509,933 passengers being carried in 1972, a drop of 10.47% overall. However, the next decade showed an accelleration in this decline so that by 1982 (the year in which the first 'mid generation' ships came into service) numbers were down to 277,249, representing a further fall of no less than 45.63%. Whilst, with the introduction of the 'mid generation' ships, passenger numbers stabilised over the next decade, in 1988 they were down to an all time post war low of 249,947, remaining well under the 300,000 mark until 1994.

The arrival of the six 'new generation' ships in the period 1993-97, with their totally new concept of travel, had an immediate impact with the 400,000 'barrier' being passed in 1997 so that by the time the three 'millenium' ships arrived in service in 2002/3 the figure was above the half million mark once more. Since then it has settled back to around the 450,000 mark. Despite difficult financial times around the world, current forecasts are for this number to increase by 5% so the half million mark might be attainable once more.

Hurtigruten Norwegian Coast

This is by far and away the most important part of the business as this sector accounts for 79% of passenger revenues and 62% of the total revenues for the whole company. Hurtigruten has reaped recognition for a long time as the world's most beautiful sea voyage, and has received many international awards as a cruise operator.

Operating all year round inevitably brings issues of how to deal with over capacity outside of the peak summer months. With strong marketing the so called 'winter code' was finally cracked by Hurtigruten with a 46% increase in travellers in the first three months of 2010 with its 'Hunting the Light' initiative, followed by a further 15% growth for the same quarter in 2011. The experience gained, is now being used to develop the other seasons, with, in 2012, the "Arctic Awakening" concept implemented throughout the fleet in an attempt to increase the number of passengers in March, April and May. Despite a very challenging year in operational terms, in 2011 capacity utilisation averaged 73.6 per cent for the full year, a rise of 4.5% over the previous year.

For 2013, after trials in late September 2012, the "Autumn Gold" experience may include

Hurtigruten Passenger Statistics 1938 to 2011 (Statistisk Sentralbyra)

Hurtigruten Passenger Statistics 1938 – 2011

Year	Passengers	Year	Passengers	Year	Passengers
1938	298 826	1966	540 919	1989	268 156
1939	292 573	1967	532 462	1990	276 145
		1968	529 632	1991	278 443
1946	376 563	1969	531 593	1992	268 516
1947	392 096	1970	522 324	1993	285 609
1948	386 408	1971	532 868	1994	362 727
1949	402 900	1972	509 933	1995	330 809
1950	406 188	1973	472 939	1996	369 138
1951	399 198	1974	474 267	1997	409 549
1952	434 475	1975	447 081	1998	441 040
1953	477 335	1976	447 810	1999	432 885
1954	507 503	1977	405 651	2000	421 208
1955	507 573	1978	400 207	2001	446 684
1956	525 387	1979	384 936	2002	546 977
1957	518 381	1980	370 082	2003	528 543
1958	503 043	1981	335 890	2004	510 554
1959	514 404	1982	277 249	2005	466 330
1960	546 374	1983	279 566	2006	479 297
1961	563 462	1984	274 550	2007	469 539
1962	569 579	1985	292 328	2008	460 102
1963	563 988	1986	283 652	2009	411 793
1964	552 752	1987	268 918	2010	449 395
1965	540 768	1988	249 947	2011	450 249

cruising to Urke, near Øye in Hjørundfjord, near Ålesund. The fjord is regarded by many as the "most beautiful in Norway" and is where tourism and cruising started in Norway, with both Kaiser Wilhelm II and British Royalty amongst the first to discover it.

The most important markets are in Germany, Norway, the UK, the USA, France and Sweden where the company has its own sales offices or representatives. Germany remains by far the largest foreign market, but recently there has been an increase in guests from the UK after the introduction of charter flights from Britain. A commitment is also being made to a centralised and stronger sales unit for the Nordic region in order to serve that market more effectively.

The courses and conferences element is also being strongly promoted towards the business market, public sector, groups and associations across Norway, with more two and three day 'short hop' packages being offered.

Port-to-port passengers still represent the bulk of travellers with Hurtigruten, close to 80% of the total numbers, accounting for 21% of the company's passenger revenues in 2011.

Hurtigruten carries substantial amounts of cargo along the Norwegian coast, and operates as an agent for Nor Lines AS. The latter is responsible for the marketing and sale of freight capacity on Hurtigruten vessels. Rising environmental awareness in the community means that growing numbers are choosing the Hurtigruten as a freight carrier, particularly with the large grocery chains on the section north of Tromsø. Hurtigruten carries freight over long distances and is often the only option open to the coastal population for the regular transport of fresh produce and products. In 2011, some 101,500 tonnes of freight were carried reducing the burden on the road network by the equivalent of about 10,000 lorries per year.

The main strategic aim is to increase autumn, winter and spring sales while safeguarding summer occupancy, promoting that experiences to be found along the coast are no less as great in the autumn, winter and spring as in the summer.

In close collaboration with the travel trade and Government agencies Hurtigruten has increased the number of direct air routes from abroad to coastal destinations in Norway in order to make all Hurtigruten's products along the Norwegian coast more accessible, particularly outside the summer peak. The 71 charter flights operated in 2011 (13 from the UK and 58 from Germany) increased to 117 in 2012.

Explorer Products/MS Fram
In comparison with its core business along the Norwegian coast, and whilst their explorer products are a fairly new area for Hurtigruten, the company is already a world leader in this market. The business is concentrated on three geographical areas: Spitsbergen, Greenland and the Antarctic together with the *Fram's* autumn and spring positional voyages around Europe, now well established.

The *Fram* began operating in May 2007 to Greenland in the summer and the Antarctic for the winter season. Since then the Greenland season has been shortened to the benefit of Spitsbergen, including circumnavigations of Svalbard. Greenland cruises are now concentrated more on the west coast, with the focus on Disko Bay.

For many, Antarctica is the most inaccessible of destinations but with the *Fram* travellers can experience it at close hand from November to March. Most voyages start from and finish at Ushuaia in Argentina. The biggest markets for Antarctic cruises have so far been Germany and the USA, and the proportion of US guests has shown the largest increase over the past couple of years.

The European cruises are becoming firmly established, designed to make the transfer between the Northern and Southern Hemispheres more profitable. These cruises pay special attention to important cultural history sites along the European coastline and are of varying duration between Las Palmas and Reykjavik, aimed at differing Hurtigruten markets. Some experiences, including cave excursions, cross-country skiing and expedition cruises are mainly geared towards the corporate sector and operated in conjunction with Ing G Paulsen AS, a trading company (which supplies snowmobiles, equipment and outdoor clothes) and Spitsbergen Travel who provide facilities for meetings, courses, conferences and experience trips.

Spitsbergen

The company's operations are run through Spitsbergen Travel AS, with subsidiaries in Longyearbyen, Svalbard's oldest tour operator which originally organised trips to the mainland for coal miners. Hurtigruten is the clear market leader in Svalbard; its experience cruises in polar waters are aimed towards an active, broad and affluent international public with a generally wider spread of ages than is typical for the traditional Hurtigruten voyages.

Charter

With the *Finnmarken* having returned to the Hurtigruten, it is unlikely that long term charter opportunities will be as readily available in the short/medium term at least until new or alternative tonnage arrives. However, the terms of the new contract do allow for short charters, mainly geared at the corporate sector.

Other Business

Hurtigruten ASA has had substantial activities in the freight and bus transport sectors with a 71.3% interest in AS TIRB, which operates buses through its Cominor AS subsidiary, involving some 300 buses and just over 400 permanent employees. The loss of the tenders in the Tromsø area will reduce this operation. The company's two remaining fast craft (*Fjordkongen* and *Fjorddronningen*) were up for sale in 2012.

Organisation and Employees

As has been noted, Hurtigruten ASA has its own sales offices in the UK, Germany and France and is also represented in Sweden, Denmark, Finland and the USA. The Tallinn reservation centre has now become part of the Hurtigruten Group. In addition, the company is the majority shareholder in Spitsbergen Travel AS and Cominor AS.

The company employed the equivalent of 1,919 full time employees in 2011. Maritime personnel form the largest part of the workforce. Employee breakdown was as follows:

	FTE
Hurtigruten ASA - Maritime Personnel	1 238
Hurtigruten Pluss AS - Norway/the Nordic region	138
Continental Europe incl. Germany & France	69
Hurtigruten Ltd - UK/USA/Rest of World	27
Spitsbergen	117
Bus Transport	430

FTE = full time equivalent/work years

Each ship has two crews and, depending on the class of ship, between 54 and 74 crew are normally employed, working on a 22 days on and 22 days off basis. This is very much appreciated by those with families. Senior bridge crew tend to work six hours on and six hours off duty, but with 24-hour availability; others may work an 8 hour/4 hour on and off cycle. Living on board for 22 days requires a good standard of living and many crew have their own individual cabins. The quality of the accommodation, recreational facilities provided and food is excellent; the latter may be due to the fact that the restaurant also serves as a training ground for practitioners from different restaurant schools.

Hurtigruten crews are very close knit and the corporate ethos is quite marked throughout all the fleet. The company is proactive in its desire to strengthen the organisation through purposeful activity, both with its management programme as well as with the development of expertise and talent.

Hurtigruten currently has 163 apprentices in training on its ships, represented in all parts of the shipboard operation, hotel, engine room and deck. The apprentice programme has been and remains an important recruitment channel for the company whose goal is to work even more effectively with these trainees so that it can speedily recruit the next generation of able and committed employees

An Apprentice's Tale

Carina Hansen, who lives in Stamsund in Lofoten, was one of those selected for an apprenticeship with the Hurtigruten. She is also an accomplished photographer and runs an unofficial modern day Hurtigruten enthusiasts' website. She writes:

'All my life the twice daily arrival and departure of the Hurtigruten at the pier at Stamsund just a few miles from our house has been part of our everyday life. When I was 13 I started to develop a special interest in working on the Hurtigruten and quickly decided to pursue a career on board. I now have two wonderful years as an apprentice on board to look back on.

I started my education in the nearby town of Leknes and after finishing a year's course on Electrical Studies followed by another year's course on Maritime Studies in Bodø, I became an able-bodied seaman on the Hurtigruten. For the first few months of the apprenticeship I worked on the *Nordkapp*, before I was

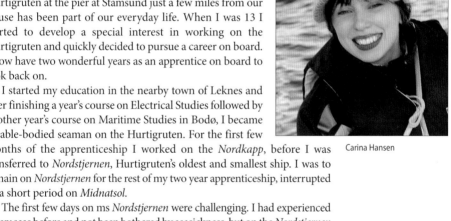

Carina Hansen

transferred to *Nordstjernen*, Hurtigruten's oldest and smallest ship. I was to remain on *Nordstjernen* for the rest of my two year apprenticeship, interrupted by a short period on *Midnatsol*.

The first few days on ms *Nordstjernen* were challenging. I had experienced heavy seas before and not been bothered by seasickness, but on the *Nordstjernen* the movement of the ship was very noticeable and completely different compared to the newer ships with their stabilizers so for the first 3 days on board, I was rather seasick. I gradually became used to the movements of the ship and luckily cured my seasickness and started to like the boat very much.

Being a small boat, with smaller numbers of crew I soon got to know them

The *Nordstjernen* in Svalbard, taken by Carina Hansen whilst as an apprentice on board the ship (Carina Hansen)

well, with 22 days on board followed by 22 days at home the ship and crew became like a family and my second home. The difference in the crew accommodation between *Nordstjernen* and the newer ships was huge, with so much less space, my cabin having only a bed and wash basin. The crew mess too was small, but despite this life on board was much easier and nicer especially when we all ate together around the 2 tables instead of spreading ourselves around as on the larger ships.

My job as an apprentice meant primarily to participate in the mooring of the ship, loading and discharging, the maintenance of almost everything from chairs in the lounges to flushing the deck with fresh water each morning. Most of the crew worked on shifts for 6 hours at a time, giving a total of 12 hours working time each day. For me as an apprentice for the first year the working day started at 8 a.m. and lasted until 6 p.m. whilst in the second year I worked 6-hour shifts along with the rest of the crew. The first year gave me the evenings off, which was a great opportunity to socialize when not on duty, but when I worked on shift my off-time was mostly used to catch up on some sleep!

Being over 50 years old everything on the *Nordstjernen* functioned in the old way. The mooring lines were set by hand or by using a capstan and the cargo was loaded on board by crane, to be stowed in the cargo hold with a hand jack. With just one propeller, the anchor was, as part of normal procedure, frequently used to aid docking and undocking, functioning as a more modern ship's bow thruster.

The working environment on board was good, which is one of the most important factors on a workplace, but the landscape and the ever-changing views from the workplace made life on board more exciting. During the two years I also sailed on cruises outside the Norwegian coast to the Baltic Sea, to Germany and to Svalbard. On the cruises, the workdays and procedures were almost the same as on the Norwegian coast, except on Svalbard where we often used our polar circle boats as tenders to take tourists ashore or close to the glaciers. My apprenticeship came to an end after the *Nordstjernen* had been cruising for well over a month around Svalbard and so my time on the Hurtigruten had to be over for the present.

I went back to college and now have my theoretical certificate as a second mate/navigator and need a further six months as an apprentice at sea in order to gain the full certificate. For me, a career path on the Hurtigruten is definitely where I am aiming to be."

Nordstjernen departing Stamsund on her last Coastal Express Voyage in March 2012 (Carina Hansen)

The 2012 Agreement

(PUBLIC PROCUREMENT CONTRACT)

In 2010, with the 2005 agreement nearing the end of its course, the Transport Ministry invited tenders for a new contract. The importance of continuing both the freight and passenger transport service represented by the Hurtigruten ships was the background to the public procurement contract with the Government. Bids could cover three options:
- daily sailings or
- five days a week in the winter and seven in the summer or
- five days a week year-round.

The requirements for vessel size were reduced by 20 per cent from the previous contract, to 320 passengers and 120 berths.

With no other bid received, Hurtigruten ASA were awarded and signed the new contract with the Ministry in April 2011. Running from 1st January 2012 to 2019, this agreement ensures daily departures from all 34 existing ports of call throughout the year with the Government having an option to extend the contract for one year after it expires. The contract is worth a total of NOK 5,120 million (in 2011 values) or NOK 640 million per annum. The eleven ships on the route are scheduled to make no less than 25,000 port calls every year.

It would not have been possible to secure the new contract from the Government without a strong commitment by politicians along the whole coast. A key element in these talks was adjustments in the event of lost sailings. It was agreed that service variations caused by bad weather will not lead to deductions from the remuneration and that whilst lost sailings owing to technical factors will give rise to such deductions, they would not provide a basis for default penalties. The company also has the opportunity to take ships out of service for up to 22 days per year for festivals and the like without deductions from the remuneration.

Financial

The very nature of the industry means that extraordinary factors and incidents can have a marked impact on the financial viability of the company. For example, 2011 was an extreme year, as a pre tax profit of NOK 22 million in 2010 became a pre tax loss of 153 million in the following year. Of this at least NOK 100 million was the result of cancellations owing to extreme weather and other incidents, including the fire on the *Nordlys*. The Norwegian coast was buffeted in November and December by storms Berit, Cato and Dagmar, with winds verging on hurricane strength, leading to a record number of cancellations; as many in the last five weeks of the year as these would normally be in a whole 12-month period. In addition came two groundings with the *Kong Harald* in Lepsøyrevet and *Trollfjord* in Risøyhamn adversely affecting business. Fuel costs also rose by NOK 55 million in 2011 as a result of price increases. On each classic round voyage a ship can use up to 200 tonnes (200,000 litres) of heavy diesel oil, a major expense.

On the plus side, capacity utilisation has never been higher at 73.5% and booking figures for 2012 showed as at 29th February, that the volume, roughly half of the total expected, was up by 5.7% cent over the previous year.

The Hurtigruten received a great publicity boost in June when Norwegian Broadcasting Corporation (NRK) dedicated its second-largest TV channel to 134 hours of live transmission of the *Nordnorge's* voyage from Bergen to Kirkenes. The weather was almost perfect, nobody had ever done anything similar before and it is unlikely to be repeated. NRK2, which normally attracts four per cent of Norwegian viewers, became the country's biggest TV channel with a 36 per cent share.

Hurtigruten have also indicated that there may be one or two new builds during the life of this contract, presumably replacing the *Lofoten* and *Vesterålen*, now 48 and 29 years old respectively. It will be interesting to see what form the new designs will take. Whilst Hurtigruten ships tend to have great longevity, by the next procurement contract from 2020 the new generation and millennium ships will range between 17 and 27 years old. Hurtigruten will not want to be in a position where everything needs to be replaced at once as was the case with the 1950s and 1960s vessels, as progress can quickly make everything appear obsolete in a challenging market.

The company believe that there is a good basis for growth and for favourable progress in the time to come. The Hurtigruten is a fantastic product and great credit goes to all who make it so.

Lang kan Hurtigruten seil!
Long may the Hurtigruten sail!

The *Richard With* glides along the Raftsundet in August 2006 (Carina Hansen)

Postscript

TUNNEL VISION or FUTURISTIC?

One exciting idea which might affect future Hurtigruten operation is the possible construction of the Stad Tunnel, which has been well publicised on board the Hurtigruten fleet. Whether it will materialise is uncertain.

The west coast of Norway, particularly to the north of Bergen, is well known as an exposed area where seas can be quite rough, making navigation difficult and passages dangerous. In 2007, the Kystverket (Norwegian Coastal Administration, NCA) began to evaluate proposals for a ship tunnel (the Stad Skipstunnel), which would bypass the Stad Peninsula in Selje, Norway. The aim was to provide a more protected passage as well as minimize journey times as frequently ships have to seek shelter and wait for the weather conditions to improve.

It is not a new idea as the first proposal for such a tunnel was raised in an article in *Nordre Bergenhus Amtstidende* in 1874. Shortly afterwards, an alternative and cheaper option of a railway tunnel was proposed across the peninsula, which would have allowed boats to be raised onto wagons and to be hauled across.

The Kystverket have proposed two tunnel paths, a shorter tunnel of 1,800m from the narrowest and innermost place of the peninsula, from Eide in Moldefjorden and under the Mannseidet to Kjødepollen, or for a slightly longer tunnel from Skårbø to Fløde. Early publicity indicated that up to 90% of all ship traffic would go through the Stad Skipstunnel and that it would become a major tourist attraction, especially as the Hurtigruten ships would traverse it twice daily. The tunnel would be 36m wide, of which the shipping

Maps showing the location of the proposed Stad Tunnel situated north of Måløy (NCA)

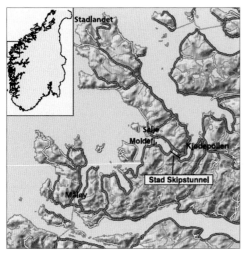
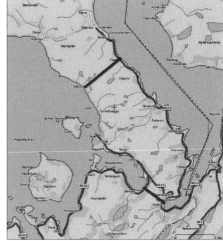

The *Fram* amongst the
penguins of Antarctica in
February 2009 (Anton
Oudshoorn/Hurtigruten ASA)

lane would be 26.5m wide and 12m deep, making it large enough for
the Coastal Express vessels to use. The cost was estimated at NOK 1.7 billion
with a construction time of 7 years.

Whilst the initial report concluded that such a tunnel would be economically
viable, the Kystverket asked for a new assessment from Det Norske
Veritas (DNV) and the Institute for Research in Economics and Business
Administration (SNF). They came to a different view, concluding that a tunnel
would not be economic as both the saved waiting costs and saved accident costs
were relatively minimal to the overall construction costs and questioned whether
the economic benefit to the local community would be sufficient.

In February 2011 a conference held at the Ålesund University College
appeared to put the project back on the map as environmentalists, scientists,
academics and politicians became once more involved in questioning the
current conclusions from the NCA. Further quality assurance work has now
been undertaken and its report was submitted at the end of March 2012 to the
Ministry of Fisheries and Coastal Affairs. The three major storms which hit
the west coast of Norway during 2011 gave further weight to the argument for
such a tunnel. If permission is given then building could go ahead as early as
2013/4. In the end the decision is likely to be one of political will rather than
on purely economic
grounds.

Now where have
we heard that one
before?

Impressions of how the Stad
Tunnel might look (NCA)

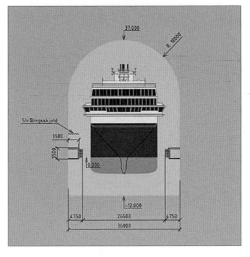

Appendix (margin text)

Vesteraalen (I) - VDS

Call Sign:	JTGS/LFFX
Built:	1891 - Akers Mek, Oslo
Hurtigruten Service:	1893 - 1941
Gross Tons:	623
Dimensions:	165.8' x 27.1' x 20.2' (50.5m x 8.3m x 6.1m)
Passengers:	204
Machinery:	500 ihp triple expansion steam engine
Speed:	10 knots

Torpedoed and sunk by Russian Submarine SHCH-402 off Nusvåg, near Øksfjord, 17th October 1941.

Lofoten (I) - VDS

Call Sign:	LKGP/LDTP
Built:	1884 - Akers Mek, Oslo
Hurtigruten Service:	1893-1903 (relief)
Gross Tons:	425
Dimensions:	141.2' x 23.6' x 10.9' (42.1m x 7.0m x 3.0m)
Passengers:	200
Machinery:	50 hp Akers 2 cyl compound
Speed:	10 knots

On Hurtigruten in relief capacity, otherwise on VDS kombinerte services. Destroyed by fire in August 1912.

Sirius - BDS

Call Sign:	JVTL/LEUS
Built:	1885 - Flensburger Schiffbau
Hurtigruten Service:	1894 - 5
Gross Tons:	877
Dimensions:	191.5' x 28.8' x 20.1' (58.3m x 8.7m x 6.1m)
Passengers:	277
Machinery:	750 ihp Flensburger 2 cyl compound steam
Speed:	11 knots

On Hurtigruten for one year and subsequently possible relief. Rebuilt in 1927 as a cargo vessel. Bombed and sunk on 18th May 1940 by German aircraft off Dyrøy, near Hammerfest.

Olaf Kyrre - NFDS

Call Sign:	JSPW
Built:	1886 - Martens, Olsen & Co., Laksevåg, Bergen
Hurtigruten Service:	1895 - 1903
Gross Tons:	963
Dimensions:	195.8' x 29.2' x 20.7' (59.7m x 8.9m x 6.3m)
Passengers:	200
Machinery:	840 bhp, Martens, Olsen triple expansion
Speed:	11 knots

Stranded on rocks 10th July 1909 whilst crossing Hustadvika, near Molde subsequently sinking.

Appendix

Erling Jarl (I) - NFDS

Call Sign:	JSNP/LDUK
Built:	1895 - Trondhjems Mek, Trondheim
Hurtigruten Service:	1895 - 1943
Gross Tons:	737 (1909)
Dimensions:	189.6' x 27.0' x 15.1'(57.8m x 8.2m x 4.6m)
Passengers:	200
Machinery:	835 ihp TMV triple expansion
Speed:	12 knots

First purpose built ship for Hurtigruten. Sank and salvaged Brønnøysund 1941. Sold to Erling Sannes, renamed *Bødø* and chartered to ODS. Scrapped at Sandnessjøen 1960.

Jupiter (I) - BDS

Call Sign:	JPDL
Built:	1856 - Caird & Co, Greenock, Scotland
Hurtigruten Service:	1895 - 1896
Gross Tons:	625 (1886)
Dimensions:	180.5'x 26.2'x 20.1'(55.0m x 8.0m x 6.1m)
Passengers:	234
Machinery:	114 nom hp Bergens M/V 2 cyl compound
Speed:	10 knots

Possible relief service post 1896. Grounded and sank 4th December 1912, Fensfjorden, near Bergen

Orion - BDS

Call Sign:	JQLF
Built:	1874 - H Murray and Co., Port Glasgow
Hurtigruten Service:	1896 - 1903
Gross Tons:	681
Dimensions:	10.5' x 26.2' x 20.9' (55.0m x 8.0 m x 6.4m)
Passengers:	234
Machinery:	760 ihp triple expansion (1902)
Speed:	11 knots

Constructive loss following a fire off Båtsfjord, 12th December 1903. Engine and boilers salvaged, reused in d/s *Lyra* (1905).

Sigurd Jarl (I) - NFDS

Call Sign:	JSHC/LEUN
Built:	1894 - Akers Mek, Oslo
Hurtigruten Service:	1897 - 1940
Gross Tons:	884
Dimensions:	208.3' x 29.1' x 15.2' (63.5m x 8.9m x 4.6m)
Passengers:	292
Machinery:	963 ihp Akers M/V triple expansion
Speed:	12.5 knots

Bombed and sank Vågseterbukta, near Molde on 23rd April 1940. Raised November 1942, beyond economic repair.

Kong Halfdan - NFDS

Call Sign:	JSPD
Built:	1874 - W Lindberg's Warf & Werkstads, Stockholm
Hurtigruten Service:	1898 - 1908
Gross Tons:	547
Dimensions:	171.1' x 24.9' x 18.8' (52.1m x 7.6m x 5.7m)
Passengers:	170
Machinery:	400 ihp 2 cyl Lindberg compound engine
Speed:	11 knots

Hurtigruten relief capacity 1917/18. Stranded and sank off Ruselv when northbound from Tromsø on 19th January 1918.

Capella - BDS

Call Sign:	JVNT/LDBQ
Built:	1885 - Martens, Olsen & Co., Laksevåg, Bergen
Hurtigruten Service:	1898 - 1910
Gross Tons:	873
Dimensions:	191.9' x 28.8' x 20.3' (58.5m x 8.8m x 6.2m)
Passengers:	140
Machinery:	800 ihp 2 cyl Martens & Olsen compound engine
Speed:	11.5 knots

Rebuilt 1915/16 as cargo vessel for Oslo/Finnmark route. In 1950 as *Hillevåg*, off Greenland, suffered propeller damage, towed back to Norway. Scrapped in Belgium, January 1952.

Røst - VDS

Call Sign:	JTDV/LETE
Built:	1898 - Trondhjems Mek, Trondheim
Hurtigruten Service:	1899 – 1920 (relief only)
Gross Tons:	290
Dimensions:	131.6' x 21.0' x 9.8' (40.1m x 6.4m x 3.0m)
Passengers:	81
Machinery:	390 ihp triple expansion
Speed:	12 knots

Normally on local Lofoten/Vesterålen services, sporadic Hurtigruten relief 1916 to 1920. May 1952 working at site of *Tirpitz*, sank with 100 tonnes of munitions on board. Raised and scrapped.

Haakon Adalstein - NFDS

Call Sign:	JSMD/LDKH
Built:	1873 - C Mitchell, Newcastle- upon- Tyne
Hurtigruten Service:	1899 - 1936
Gross Tons:	703 (1910)
Dimensions:	188.5ft x 26.1ft x 15.7ft (57.7m x 8.0m x 5.1m)
Passengers:	200
Machinery:	750 ihp NE Marine two cyl compound
Speed:	10 knots

Cargo only 1936. Hurtigruten service between Tromsø and Kirkenes, 1945. In 1946 sold to Ole T. Flakk, Kristiansund, renamed *Goma*. Sank 10th September 1947, off Halland (Sweden) with 271 horses on board.

Appendix

Appendix

Astræa - BDS

Call Sign:	JPLC
Built:	1900 - Akers Mek, Oslo
Hurtigruten Service:	1900 - 1910
Gross Tons:	765
Dimensions:	193' x 28.2' x 20.3' (58.8m x 8.6m x 6.2m)
Passengers:	220
Machinery:	1,400 ihp Akers triple expansion
Speed:	14.25 knots

Grounded on 5th January 1910, near Stabben Lighthouse, Florø, sinking in shallow water. Condemned and scrapped. Some machinery reused in 1921 built BDS ship *Mercur*.

Andenæs - VDS

Call Sign:	MBLF/LCLI
Built:	1903 - Fredrikstad Mek, Fredrikstad
Hurtigruten Service:	1903 - 1932
Gross Tons:	813
Dimensions:	186.1' x 28.6' x 18.4' (56.7m x 8.7m x 5 .6m)
Passengers:	200
Machinery:	550 ihp FMV triple expansion
Speed:	12 knots

Mainly in relief capacity, otherwise on 'kombinerte' routes and cruising. On 20th May 1938, at Stavanger, rammed by BDS steamer *Leda*, and sinking. Scrapped immediately.

Lyra (I) - BDS

Call Sign:	MCDJ
Built:	1905 - Bergens Mek, Bergen
Hurtigruten Service:	1905 - 1913
Gross Tons:	784
Dimensions:	185.7' x 28.2' x 20.8' (56.6m x 8.6m x 6.3m)
Passengers:	230
Machinery:	750 ihp BMV triple expansion
Speed:	11.5 knots

Sold December 1913 to Vapeur Ottomane, Istanbul, renamed *Biga*. Torpedoed and sunk on 10th July 1916 by British submarine E-7, near Mudanya in Marmara Sea.

Haakon Jarl (I) - NFDS

Call Sign:	JSPG
Built:	1879 – Lindholmens Verksted, Gothenburg
Hurtigruten Service:	1905 - 1924
Gross Tons:	873
Dimensions:	197.3.' x 27.1' x 21.5' (60.1m x 8.3m x 6.5m)
Passengers:	200
Machinery:	Akers Mek 760 hp 2 cyl triple expansion (1906)
Speed:	11 knots

On 17th June 1924 collided in fog with *Kong Harald* off Landegøde, north of Bodø, sank with loss of 17 lives.

Richard With (I) - VDS

Call Sign:	MFQT/LERM
Built:	1909 – Trondhjems Mek, Trondheim
Hurtigruten Service:	1909 - 1941
Gross Tons:	905
Dimensions:	205.0' x 28.9' x 16.0' (62.5m x 8.8m x 4.9m)
Passengers:	300
Machinery:	1,150 ihp TMV triple expansion
Speed:	12 knots

Torpedoed and sunk by HMS *Tigris* off Rolvsøya, north of Hammerfest with much loss of life on 13th September 1941.

Hera - BDS

Call Sign:	JPBG
Built:	1899 – Earles Shipbuilders, Hull
Hurtigruten Service:	1910 - 1930
Gross Tons:	1,097
Dimensions:	215.1' x 30.4' x 22.2' (65.7m x 9.3m x 4.5m)
Passengers:	350
Machinery:	1,200 ihp triple expansion
Sspeed:	13 knots

Southbound to Hammerfest on 17th/18th March 1931, grounded at Havøygavlen in heavy seas and adverse currents. Declared a total loss.

Midnatsol (I) - BDS

Call Sign:	MGBT/LELR
Built:	1910 - Bergens Mek, Bergen
Hurtigruten Service:	1910 - 1950
Gross Tons:	978
Dimensions:	202.7' x 31.3' x 19.7' (61.8m x 9.5m x 6.0m)
Passengers:	300
Machinery:	1,508 ihp triple expansion
Speed:	13 knots

In March 1949 renamed *Sylvia*. She finished service on 10th October 1950 and was immediately sold for scrapping by SA Elba at Antwerp.

Polarlys (I) - BDS

Call Sign:	MHFV/LEPY
Built:	1912 - Burmeister & Wain, Copenhagen
Hurtigruten Service:	1912 - 1952
Gross Tons:	1,070
Dimensions:	208.3' x 31.5' x 19.7' (63.5m x 9.6m x 6.0m)
Passengers:	300
Machinery:	1,473 ihp B&W triple expansion
Speed:	13 knots

Renamed *Sylvia* in April 1952 and in October laid up at Bergen. Bought by Royal Norwegian Navy as 'mother ship' to MTB fleet. Renamed KNM *Valkyrie*, serving until 1963, when withdrawn and scrapped.

Appendix

Appendix

Finmarken (I) - VDS

Call Sign:	MHRD/LDVK
Built:	1912 - Trondhjems Mek, Trondheim
Hurtigruten Service:	1912 - 1957
Gross Tons:	1,119
Dimensions:	214.2' x 31.8' x 15.4' (69.0m x 9.7m x 4.7m)
Passengers:	350
Machinery:	1,550 ihp TMV triple expansion
Speed:	14.5 knots

Renamed *Vågan* 1956. Sold to Sjøguttskole Rogaland, Stavanger, 1957, renamed *Gann* as youth training ship. September 1960, scrapped Netherlands. Some interior furnishings and rooms form part of Hurtigruten Museum, Stokmarknes.

Olaf Trygvesøn - NFDS

Call Sign:	JSNQ
Built:	1876 - J. Wigham Richardson & Co, Newcastle
Hurtigruten Service:	1916 – 1921 (relief)
Gross Tons:	663 (1902)
Dimensions:	175.8' x 25.2' x 12.9' (53.6m x 7.7m x 3.9m)
Passengers:	199
Machinery:	470 ihp triple expansion
Speed:	10 knots

After 1921 mostly on Norwegian coast freight services until spring of 1934, sold to Anda Brothers, Stavanger for scrapping.

Neptun - BDS

Call Sign:	JVGR
Built:	1890 – John C. Tecklenborg, Geestemünde
Hurtigruten Service:	1919 - 1921
Gross Tons:	1,113 (1904)
Dimensions:	198.4' x 30.1' x 20.3' (60.5m x 9.2m x 6.2m)
Passengers:	399
Machinery:	1,040 hp Pauksch triple expansion
Speed:	12 knots

Withdrawn from Hurtigruten 1921, returned to the Hamburg/Finnmark route. Scrapped at Stavanger April 1926.

Kong Haakon - DSD

Call Sign:	LEGU
Built:	1904 - Schömer & Jensen, Tönning, Germany
Hurtigruten Service:	1919 - 1952
Gross Tons:	874
Dimensions:	196.0' x 28.7' x 21.1' (59.7m x 8.7m x 6.4m)
Passengers:	300
Machinery:	1,200 ihp Schömer & Jensen triple expansion
Speed:	13.2 knots

In 1952 withdrawn from Coastal Express, laid up at Stavanger. In January 1953 scrapped by Eisen & Metall AG Hamburg,

Tordenskjold - NFDS

Call Sign:	MCQT/LFCH
Built:	1906 - Trondhjems Mek, Trondheim
Hurtigruten Service:	1920/1946 - 1950 (relief)
Gross Tons:	921
Dimensions:	196.1' x 29.7' x 21.7' (59.7m x 9.0m x 6.6m)
Passengers:	200
Machinery:	800 ihp TMV triple expansion
Speed:	12 knots

Withdrawn 1950, sold to Ostende Remorquage Letzer S/A, Antwerp as excursion boat *Wenduyne*. Scrapped, Bruges, June 1954.

Haakon VII - NFDS

Call Sign:	MDGT
Built:	1907 - Trondhjems Mek, Trondheim
Hurtigruten Service:	1922 - 1929
Gross Tons:	1,347
Dimensions:	250.3' x 33.2' x 21.6' (76.3m x 10.1m x 6.6m)
Passengers:	532
Machinery:	1,712 ihp TMV triple expansion
Speed:	14.5 knots

On 6th October 1929 hit rocks off Melshølmen, south of Florø. Nine passengers and nine crew lost. Scrapped Stavanger March 1930.

Kong Harald (I) - NFDS

Call Sign:	JSQN/LEGV
Built:	1890 - John C. Tecklenborg, Geestemünde
Hurtigruten Service:	1924 - 1950
Gross Tons:	953
Dimensions:	198.2' x 30.2' x 20.3' (60.4m x 9.2m x 6.2m)
Passengers:	286
Machinery:	834 ihp Pauksch triple expansion
Speed:	12 knots

Sold February 1951 to Ostende Remorquage Letzer S/A, Antwerp, renamed *Westende* for summer excursions. Scrapped Bruges 1954, aged 64 years.

Dronning Maud – NFDS

Call Sign:	LFDS/LDTR
Built:	1925 - Fredrikstad Mek, Fredrikstad
Hurtigruten Service:	1925 - 1940
Gross Tons:	1,505
Dimensions:	235.9' x 37.7' x 13.8' (71.9m x 11.5m x 4.2m)
Passengers:	400
Machinery:	2,000 ihp FMV triple expansion
Speed:	17 knots

On 1st May 1940, as designated hospital ship, attacked by 3 German aircraft, Foldvik, north of Tromsø. 18 people killed and 31 wounded. Ship left to burn and sink.

Appendix

Appendix

Sanct Svithun (I) - DSD

Call Sign:	LDTS
Built:	1927 - International Shipbuilding Co., Danzig
Hurtigruten Service:	1927 - 1943
Gross Tons:	1,376
Dimensions:	235.8' x 35.1' x 21.3'(71.7m x 10.7m x 6.5m)
Passengers:	400
Machinery:	1,650 ihp Lenz double compound
Speed:	14 knots

Bombed by RAF on 30th September 1943 crossing Stadlandet. Managed to run aground on Købbeholmen, Ervik, 57 lives lost. The ship's bell can be seen in the local church.

Mosken - VDS

Call Sign:	LDQP/LEMF
Built:	1924 - Trosvik Mek, Brevik
Hurtigruten Service:	1927 - 1932
Gross Tons:	410
Dimensions:	140.4' x 23.0' x 16.1' (42.8m x 7.0m x 4.9m)
Passengers:	200
Machinery:	78 nhp TMV triple expansion
Speed:	10 knots

Sold 1957 to Sivert Bakke, Bergen, resold 1960 to Britt Wadner, renamed *Cheetah II Gambia* as North Sea pirate radio ship. Last known as hotel/restaurant ship, Bathurst (Banjul), Gambia. Believed scuttled following fire.

Mira - DSD

Call Sign:	JVHN/LELV
Built:	1891 - A & J Inglis, Glasgow
Hurtigruten Service:	1928 - 1937
Gross Tons:	1,112 (1907)
Dimensions:	221.7' x 30.1' x 21.3' (67.6m x 9.2m x 6.5m)
Passengers:	396
Machinery:	1,450 ihp Inglis triple expansion
Speed:	12 knots

In reserve 1937, in Hurtigruten service 1941 but sunk 4th March 1941 off Brettesnes (Lofotens) by *HMS Bedouin*.

Kong Gudrød - NFDS

Call Sign:	MGFB/LEGT
Built:	1910 - Trondhjems Mek, Trondheim
Hurtigruten Service:	1929 - 1936
Gross Tons:	1,091
Dimensions:	226.9' x 30.8' x 21.7' (68.9m x 9.4m x 6.6m)
Passengers:	242
Machinery:	800 ihp TMV triple expansion
Speed:	12.5 knots

Sold January 1936 to Pärnu Laeva AS, renamed *Estonia* for Tallinn to Stockholm route. Several owners 1949 – 1967, sold to Greece, as *Efthycia* (later *Phaedra* 1970). Unclear after this, either Phillipines (1977), in possible service 1990s; or Greece until 1993.

Mercur - BDS

Call Sign:	HDGB/LFXA
Built:	1883 - Motala Mek, Gothenburg
Hurtigruten Service:	1930 - 1932 (relief)
Gross Tons:	989
Dimensions:	207.0' x 29.7' x 21.5' (63.1m x 9.0m x 6.6m)
Passengers:	270
Machinery:	1,040 ihp Motala triple expansion
Speed:	11.5 knots

Withdrawn January 1939, sold to Einar Cook, Bergen, resold to Kristiania-Portland Cementfabrikk, Oslo, renamed *Else*. Bought 1951 by Johan Nilsen, Fredrikstad, sold February 1952 to Belgian interests.

Irma - DSD

Call Sign:	MCHD/LDTP
Built:	1905 - Sir Raylton Dixon & Co., Middlesbrough
Hurtigruten Service:	1931 - 1944
Gross Tons:	1,322
Dimensions:	244.0' x 32.8' x 21.1' (74.4m x 9.9m x 6.4m)
Passengers:	144
Machinery:	1,500 ihp Dickson triple expansion
Speed:	13.5 knots

Torpedoed 13th February 1944 by Norwegian crewed MTBs whilst crossing Hustadvika between Molde and Trondheim. 25 survivors, 61 lost their lives.

Prinsesse Ragnhild - NFDS

Call Sign:	LDKN/LEQG
Built:	1931 - Fredrikstad Mek, Fredrikstad
Hurtigruten Service:	1931 - 1940
Gross Tons:	1,590
Dimensions:	251.6' x 37.6' x 21.0' (76.7m x 11.5m x 6.4m)
Passengers:	400
Machinery:	2,500 ihp FMV double-compound 'steam motor'
Speed:	16.5 knots

Torpedoed and sunk by British submarine HMS *Taku* on 23rd October 1940, off Landegøde, near Bodø. Over 300 lost their lives, 156 persons rescued.

Lofoten (II) - VDS

Call Sign:	LKGO/LDTQ
Built:	1932 - Fredrikstad Mek, Fredrikstad
Hurtigruten Service:	1932 - 1964
Gross Tons:	1,571
Dimensions:	248.6' x 38.1' x 14.4' (75.8m x 11.6m x 4.4m)
Passengers:	400
Machinery:	2,200 ihp FMV triple expansion
Speed:	17.25 knots

Renamed *Vågan* 1963, last service May 1964. Sold to Cyprus Sea Cruises, renamed *Kypros*. On 10th November 1966 fire broke out, ship beached, no casualties. Scrapped at Haifa.

Nordnorge (I) - ODS

Call Sign:	LDHR/LENR
Built:	1924 - Trondhjems Mek, Trondheim
Hurtigruten Service:	1936 - 1940
Gross Tons:	991 (1936)
Dimensions:	213.3' x 29.7' x 19.6' (64.9m x 9.0m x 4.8m)
Passengers:	270
Machinery:	1,010 ihp TMV triple expansion
Speed:	13 knots

Sunk on 10th May 1940 by British destroyers at Hemnesberget, near Mo i Rana.

Barøy (I) - ODS

Call Sign:	LCMO
Built:	1929 - Trondhjems Mek, Trondheim
Hurtigruten Service:	1936 - 1941
Gross Tons:	424
Dimensions:	152.9' x 24.0' x 10.9' (46.6m x 7.3m x 3.3m)
Passengers:	200
Machinery:	560 ihp TMV triple expansion
Speed:	12 knots

On 13th September 1941, off Nordland coast torpedoed and sunk by British aircraft operating from HMS *Victorious*.

Prins Olav - NFDS

Call Sign:	LESQ/LCVM
Built:	1908 - A & J Inglis, Glasgow
Hurtigruten Service:	1937 - 1940
Gross Tons:	2,147 (1937)
Dimensions:	248.3' x 40.1' x 15.4' (86.5m x 12.2m x 4.7m)
Passengers:	450
Machinery:	3,500 ihp FMV double compound
Speed:	17 knots

June 1940 attacked and eventually sunk by enemy bombers in company of *Ariadne*, some 80 miles west of Lofotens whilst trying to escape to Britain.

Nordstjernen (I) - BDS

Call Sign:	LJNB
Built:	1937 - Fredrikstad Mek, Fredrikstad
Hurtigruten Service:	1937 - 1954
Gross Tons:	1,919
Dimensions:	263.5' x 38.8' x 13.7' (80.2m x 11.8m x 4.2m)
Passengers:	590
Machinery:	2,545 ihp FMV double compound 'steam motor'
Speed:	16 knots

On 20th September 1954, in Raftsundet, struck rocks, ship sinking in 160 feet of water. Five people lost their lives.

Ariadne - BDS

Call Sign:	JHTP/LDNI
Built:	1930 - Nylands Verksted, Oslo
Hurtigruten Service:	1939 - 1940
Gross Tons:	2, 029
Dimensions:	271.3' x 38.2' x 19.4' (82.7m x 11.6m x 5.9m)
Passengers:	300
Machinery:	2,140 ihp Nylands triple expansion
Speed:	14.5 knots

On 8th June 1940 attacked, eventually sinking, by enemy bombers in company of *Prins Olav* some 80 miles west of Lofotens whilst trying to escape to Britain.

Hadsel – VDS

Call Sign:	LKNQ
Built:	1940 - Moss Værft & Dokk, Moss
Hurtigruten Service:	1941 - 1950
Gross Tons:	406
Dimensions:	145.2' x 25.1' x 15.4' (44.2m x 7.6m x 4.7m)
Passengers:	150
Machinery:	540 bhp 6-cylinder 4T DM MAN diesel
Speed:	12 knots

Struck rocks on 29th January 1958 off Nakkmean, Lofotens; no casualties. The ship then slid off rocks and sank within three minutes.

Nova - BDS

Call Sign:	LFGP/LCUK
Built:	1925 - Ateliers et Chantiers de la Seine-Maritime du Trait, France
Hurtigruten Service:	1939 - 1940
Gross Tons:	1,382
Dimensions:	231.4' X 34.1' x 21.7' (70.5m x 10.4m x 6.6m)
Passengers:	250
Machinery:	900 ihp Worms & Cie triple expansion
Speed:	10.5 knots

On Hurtigruten for winter of 1939/40. In June 1940 escaped to Britain to join Nortraship fleet. December 1949 stranded off Jæren, near Stavanger, declared constructive total loss.

Ryfylke - DSD

Call Sign:	LESX
Built:	1917 - København Flydedok og Skibsverft, Copenhagen
Hurtigruten Service:	1940 - 1941
Gross Tons:	1,113
Dimensions:	220.4' x 32.8' x 17.4' (67.1m x 10.0m x 5.3m)
Passengers:	250
Machinery:	1,100 ihp København Flydedok triple expansion engine
Speed:	13.5 knots

Leased November 1940 to NFDS for Hurtigruten service. On 5th February 1941, off Stad, sunk by British submarine, HMS *Sealion*, with cannon fire. No casualties.

Appendix

Appendix

Dronningen – HDS

Call Sign:	LDGY
Built:	1894 - Fevigs Jernskibsbyggeri , Arendal
Hurtigruten Service:	1945 - 1946 (charter from HDS)
Gross Tons:	661
Dimensions:	186.6' x 26.9' x 2.1' (56.9m x 8.2m x 6.1m)
Passengers:	250
Machinery:	750 ihp BMV triple expansion
Speed:	12 knots

HDS - Det Helgelandske Dampskibsselskab. Sold to Ole T. Flakk, Kristiansund, January 1948, resold to Haralambos Typaldos, Piraeus, as *Ionion*. Laid up in 1962, possibly not scrapped until 1985.

Christiania – DSD

Call Sign:	LDCQ
Built:	1898 - Helsingørs Jernskibs og Maskinbyggeri, Helsingør
Hurtigruten Service:	1944 - 1948
Gross Tons:	646
Dimensions:	180.5' x 27.3' x 20.1' (55.0m x 8.3m x 6.1m)
Passengers:	250
Machinery:	800 ihp Helsingørs Jernskibs triple expansion
Speed:	13 knots

On Hurtigruten 1945 - 48 as relief. Laid up August 1952, sold for scrapping in November at Michael Brecker & Co., Granton, Scotland.

Ragnvald Jarl (I) - NFDS

Call Sign:	LKNC
Built:	1930 - Burmeister & Wain, Copenhagen
Hurtigruten Service:	1942 - 1956
Gross Tons:	1,789 (1942)
Dimensions:	244.7' x 38.1' x 18.5' (77.6m x 11.6m x 5.6m)
Passengers:	540
Machinery:	1,600 bhp B & W six-cylinder 4-stroke diesel
Speed:	14 knots

February 1956, renamed *Harald Jarl*. Sold to Lübeck Linie GmbH, renamed *Nordland* for Baltic cruises. In 1970 sold to Karelia Lines O/Y, Helsinki renamed *Suvetar*. In April 1974 scrapped at Bilbao.

Sigurd Jarl (II) - NFDS

Call Sign:	LKSZ
Built:	1942 - Fredrikstad Mek, Fredrikstad
Hurtigruten Service:	1942 - 1960
Gross Tons:	2,335
Dimensions:	289.6' x 43.2' x 14.2' (88.2m x 13.1m x 4.3m)
Passengers:	650
Machinery:	1,800 ihp FMV double compound 'steam motor'
Speed:	14 knots

Withdrawn June 1960, sold to the People's Republic of China as *Xin Hua*. Transferred to the China Ocean Shipping Company 1974, possible sighting Dalian Xiangang region 1990.

Skjerstad - NDS

Call Sign:	LKOX
Built:	1925 - Schiffswerft von Henry Koch, Lübeck
Hurtigruten Service:	1945 - 1958
Gross Tons:	762
Dimensions:	202.5' x 29.4' x 12.7' (61.7m x 9.0m x 3.9m)
Passengers:	250
Machinery:	817 ihp Lübecker Maschinenbau Gesellschaft triple expansion
Speed:	12 knots

Sold September 1959 to Holiday Lines of Panama, renamed *Holiday*. Laid up 1965, owners bankrupt. Towed to Cape Haiti for use as hotel/entertainments centre. By 1982 disappeared from Lloyds Register.

Lyra (II) - BDS

Call Sign:	LCSU
Built:	1912 - Vulcan Werke, Stettin, Germany
Hurtigruten Service:	1945 - 1953 (relief)
Gross Tons:	1,508
Dimensions:	241.5' x 34.4' x 15.4' (73.6m x 10.5m x 4.7m)
Passengers:	175
Machinery:	1,180 ihp, Vulcan triple expansion engine
Speed:	11.5 knots

February 1954 sold to Sivert Bakke, renamed *Nora*. Resold to Adel Abdul-Wahib, of Beirut, as *Lyra*, as pilgrim ship linking Lebanon, Egypt and Jeddah (for Mecca). July 1958 ran aground in Red Sea and sank.

Lyngen (I) - TFDS

Call Sign:	LEJX
Built:	1931 - Trondhjems Mek, Trondheim
Hurtigruten Service:	1945 - 1949
Gross Tons:	489
Dimensions:	161.3' x 25.9' x 16.4' (49.1m x 7.9m x 5.0m)
Passengers:	150
Machinery:	618 ihp TMV triple expansion
Speed:	12.5 knots

Sold 1966 to Alfred Jensen, Harstad, renamed *Alfred Jensen*, rebuilt as purse seiner, re-engined (1,000 bhp Munktel diesel). Active until 1984, scuttled off Harstad 2nd July 1987.

Saltdal - NDS

Call Sign:	LDGY
Built:	1884 - Motala Verkstad, Norrköping, Sweden
Hurtigruten Service:	1946 - 1950
Gross Tons:	581
Dimensions:	165.4' x 25.6' x 13.5' (50.4m x 7.8m x 4.1m)
Passengers:	150
Machinery:	480 ihp Berg Sunds Mek, Stockholm triple expansion (1904)
Speed:	10.5 knots

Purchased by NDS 1945, rebuilt 1948 including oil firing. Sold 1957 to Høvding, Sandnessjøen, renamed *Meisfjord* as a mother ship for diving operations. Scrapped July 1976.

Appendix

Appendix

Oslo - NFDS

Call Sign:	LHPN
Built:	1929 - Nylands Verksted, Oslo
Hurtigruten Service:	1948
Gross Tons:	881
Dimensions:	188.0' x 31.5' x 20.3' (57.3m x 9.6m x 6.2m)
Passengers:	600
Machinery:	1,350 ihp Lenz double-compound
Speed:	14.5 knots

Sold 1959 to Epirotiki Steamship Navigation Co, renamed *Aegeus* for services out of Piraeus. Resold 1961 to Ionian Steamship Company, later renamed *Kefaelinia*. Caught fire during refit 1968 near Piraeus and scrapped.

Ottar Jarl - NFDS

Call Sign:	LMBB
Built:	1929 - Lake Washington Shipyard, Houghton, USA
Hurtigruten Service:	1947 - 1948
Gross Tons:	1,262
Dimensions:	186.0' x 35.1' x 19.7' (56.7m x 10.7m x 6.0m)
Passengers:	75
Machinery:	1,120 bhp 2 x Washington Iron Works 8-cylinder 4T EV DM diesels
Speed:	11 knots

Hurtigruten December 1947 - February 1948. Sold October 1955 to Refrigerated Shipping Co.. Puerto Limón (Costa Rica), renamed *Titika*. Grounded off Keflavik, Iceland on delivery voyage, scrapped Netherlands.

Erling Jarl (II) - NFDS

Call Sign:	LHKC
Built:	1949 - Cantieri Riuniti de Ancona, Ancona
Hurtigruten Service:	1949 - 1980
Gross Tons:	2,098
Dimensions:	268.8' x 41.0' x 14.2' (81.9m x 12.5m x 4.3m)
Passengers:	575
Machinery:	2,500 bhp 8-cylinder 2T EV DM Fiat diesel
Speed:	15 knots

Sold October 1981 to Oslo Carriers of Høvik, renamed *Balder Earl*; ship laid up Grimstad, Bergen, scrapped at Belgian shipbreakers January 1985.

Midnatsol (II) - BDS

Call Sign:	LNYL
Built:	1949 - Cantieri Riuniti de Ancona, Ancona
Hurtigruten Service:	1949 - 1982
Gross Tons:	2,098
Dimensions:	267.6' x 41.0' x 14.2' (81.6m x 12.5m x 4.3m)
Passengers:	575
Machinery:	2,500 bhp 8-cylinder 2T EV DM Fiat diesel
Speed:	15 knots

Purchased January 1983 by Drangsholt, Forsberg, Flekkefjord, for use as hotel ship renamed *Midnatsol Norge*. Sold on 1984 to Coast Hotels for same at Oslo. February 1987, during refit at Sarpsborg Mek, ship capsized. Condemned and scrapped in Belgium.

Vesterålen (II) - VDS

Call Sign:	LHUQ
Built:	1950 - Cantieri Riuniti de Ancona, Ancona
Hurtigruten Service:	1950 - 1983
Gross Tons:	2,098
Dimensions:	268.0' x 41.0' x 14.2' (81.9m x 12.5m x 4.3m)
Passengers:	575
Machinery:	2,500 bhp 8-cylinder 2T EV DM Fiat diesel
Speed:	17.75 knots (trials)

1983 as *Rålen* sold to Northern Shipping AS, Oslo and then Fekete & Co. AS, Tønsberg, renamed *Annexet*. In 1986 at Drammen as asylum seeker/refugee centre. In 1990, renamed *Nordstjernen af Sundsvall*. Resold 1991 to Etoile Marine of Cyprus, tow ended at Rotterdam. Sold October 1995 to Spanish breakers.

Sanct Svithun (II) - DSD

Call Sign:	LKGQ
Built:	1950 - Cantieri Riuniti de Ancona, Ancona
Hurtigruten Service:	1950 - 1962
Gross Tons:	2,098
Dimensions:	267.7' x 41.0' x 14.2' (81.6m x 12.5m x 4.3m)
Passengers:	575
Machinery:	2,500 bhp 8-cylinder 2T EV DM Fiat diesel
Speed:	17 knots

Veered off course en route to Rørvik, hit rocks and sank near Nordøyan, Folla, on 21st October 1962 with loss of 42 lives.

Alta – FFR

Call Sign:	LACH
Built:	1950 - Trosvik Verstad, Brevik
Hurtigruten Service:	1950 - 1958
Gross Tons:	685
Dimensions:	167.0' x 27.9' x 11.3' (50.8m x 8.5m x 3.5m)
Passengers:	175
Machinery:	850 ihp 5-cylinder Atlas Polar diesel
Speed:	12 knots

Sold 1967 as *Tui Lau* to Maritime Co-Operative Shipping Ltd, Suva, Fiji. On 25th October 1968 grounded on a reef and sank about 120 miles from home port.

Sørøy – FFR

Call Sign:	LEHX
Built:	1949 - Trosvik Verstad, Brevik
Hurtigruten Service:	1950 - 1964
Gross Tons:	686
Dimensions:	167.0' x 27.9' x 11.3' (50.8m x 8.5m x 3.5m)
Passengers:	175
Machinery:	850 ihp 5-cylinder Atlas Polar diesel
Speed:	12 knots

Sold 1965 as training ship, renamed *Skule*, at Trondheim, later 1981 transferred to Østfold Fylkeskommune as *Østfold*. In 1991 renamed *Glommen*, sold 2003 as private residence near Stavanger. Resold 2004 to Reef Line/Zambesi Shipping of Dubai, renamed *RTS Sindbad*, based at Port Rashid, Dubai. Still in service.

Appendix

Appendix

Nordlys (I) - BDS

Call Sign:	LAHB
Built:	1951 - Aalborg Verft, Aalborg
Hurtigruten Service:	1951 - 1983
Gross Tons:	2,162
Dimensions:	262.2 x 40.1' x 14.8' (80.0m x 12.2m x 4.5m)
Passengers:	469
Machinery:	2 ,950 bhp 8-cylinder 2T B&W DM diesel
Speed:	15.5 knots

1983 purchased as accommodation vessel for Alexander L. Kielland Oil Platform project. In April 1988 undergoing rebuild at Sarpsborg Mek, caught fire and condemned. Under tow to Bilbao grounded off Farsund later sinking 100 km northwest of Texel.

Håkon Jarl (II) - NFDS

Call Sign:	LAKV
Built:	1952 - Aalborg Verft, Aalborg
Hurtigruten Service:	1952 - 1982
Gross Tons:	2,173
Dimensions:	265.1' x 40.1' x 14.8' (80.8m x 12.2m x 4.5m)
Passengers:	600
Machinery:	2 x 1,520 bhp 8-cylinder Atlas Polar diesels
Speed:	16 knots

Bought by Fekete & Co. AS, Tønsberg, 1983, renamed Håkon Gamle. Resold as restaurant/hotel ship, Pipervika, Oslo, owners bankrupt 1988. Late 1991 reopened as hotel ship, Bonaparte Dock, Antwerp, as Christian V. Marketed later as 'Diamond Princess'; in 2012 derelict.

Polarlys (II) - BDS

Call Sign:	LAMO
Built:	1952 - Aalborg Verft, Aalborg
Hurtigruten Service:	1952 - 1993
Gross Tons:	2,163
Dimensions:	262.5 x 40.1' x 14.8' (80.1m x 12.2m x 4.5m)
Passengers:	450
Machinery:	2,950 bhp 8-cylinder 2T B&W DM 850-VF-90 diesel
Speed:	15.5 knots

In April 1994, sold to Mercy Ships, Lindale, Texas, rebuilt as medical centre, renamed as Carribbean Mercy serving Carribbean Basin, Central and South America. June 2005 laid up; seen 2012 at Christobel, Panama, now a derelict hulk.

Barøy(II)- ODS

Call Sign:	LAKW
Built:	1952 - Trondhjems Mek, Trondheim
Hurtigruten Service:	1952 - 1964
Gross Tons:	860 (1956)
Dimensions:	208.0' x 27.9' x 11.5' (63.3m x 8.5m x 3.5m)
Passengers:	250
Machinery:	1,190 bhp 6-cylinder Atlas Polar diesel.
Speed:	14 knots

Sold 1963 to Birger Svendsen, Fredrikstad for ferry services across Skagerrak. 1966 purchased by Government of the Gilbert and Ellice Islands, Pacific Ocean as a training ship, renamed *Teraka*. After mechanical problems condemned and scuttled, Tawara, in 1973.

Salten - NFDS

Call Sign:	LCQT
Built:	1953 - Trosvik Mek, Brevik
Hurtigruten Service:	1953 - 1964
Gross Tons:	677
Dimensions:	173.9' x 28.2' x 18.7' (53.0m x 8.6m x 5.7m)
Passengers:	180
Machinery:	870 bhp 6-cylinder Atlas diesel
Speed:	13.5 knots

In 1967, bought as training ship based at Grimstad, renamed *Sjøkurs*. In 1973, moved to Kristiansand. 1995 sold to the Ryfylke Steamship Company, Stavanger renamed *Gamle Salten*. In 2008, purchased by Saltens A/S Bodø, still in active service.

Jupiter (II) - BDS

Call Sign:	MSTR/LEBA
Built:	1915 - Lindholmens Verkstad, Gothenburg
Hurtigruten Service:	1953 - 1955
Gross Tons:	2,511
Dimensions:	305.1' x 41.7' x 18.8' (102.9m x 12.6m x 5.7m)
Passengers:	300
Machinery:	309 nom hp Lindholmen triple expansion engine
Speed:	15.5 knots

September 1955 sold to Epirotiki Steamship Navigation Co. Ltd, Piraeus, Greece for rebuilding as cruise ship *Hermes*. 1960, at Piraeus destroyed by fire.

Meteor - BDS

Call Sign:	LARG
Built:	1955 - Aalborg Verft, Aalborg
Hurtigruten Service:	1955 - 1970 (relief after 1956)
Gross Tons:	2,856
Dimensions:	282.3' x 44.9' x 20.0' (86.0m x 13.7m x 6.1m)
Passengers:	200
Machinery:	5,000 bhp 9-cylinder 2T DM B&W diesel
Speed:	18 knots

May 1971, Vancouver after Alaskan cruise, caught fire, 32 crew lost their lives. Sold to Epirotiki, Greece renamed *Neptune* for cruises in Aegean and Mediterranean. Scrapped 2002 at Aliaga, Turkey.

Ingøy- FFR

Call Sign:	LAHC
Built:	1950 - Drammens Slip and Verksted, Drammen
Hurtigruten Service:	1955 - 1956
Gross Tons:	435
Dimensions:	144.4' x 25.6' x 10.7' (44.0m x 7.8m x 3.3m)
Passengers:	150
Machinery:	600 bhp Nohab diesel
Speed:	12 knots

In 1971 sold to Gardline Shipping, Lowestoft, renamed *Researcher*. Resold 1974 to Sidney Sea Search, Cayman Islands. Bought 1983 by South Carolina Wildlife & Marine Rescue Department and scuttled to form an artificial reef.

Appendix

Appendix

Nordstjernen (II) – BDS/TFDS/HRG

Call Sign:	LATU
Built:	1956 - Blohm & Voss, Hamburg
Hurtigruten Service:	1956 - present day
Gross Tons:	2,194
Dimensions:	265.0' x 41.5' x 20.2' (80.7m x 12.6m x 6.1m)
Passengers:	400
Machinery:	3,000 bhp 6-cylinder 2T B&W DM diesel
Speed:	17.26 knots

2012 scheduled to be the *Nordstjernen*'s swansong, last voyage on Hurtigruten ended Bergen 22nd March. Temporarily laid up at Fiskerstrand Shipyard, Ålesund, before summer season of cruises to Svalbard. Sold in November 2012.

Finnmarken (II) – VDS/OVDS

Call Sign:	LAUV
Built:	1956 - Blohm & Voss, Hamburg
Hurtigruten Service:	1956 - 1993
Gross Tons:	2,189
Dimensions:	266.6' x 41.5' x 16.0' (81.3m x 12.6m x 4.9m)
Passengers:	425
Machinery:	3,600 bhp 10-cylinder G 10 52/74 MAN diesel
Speed:	16.6 knots

December 1993 laid up and donated to Hurtigruten Museum. June 1999 having been sandblasted and repainted, lifted out of water to become largest land based museum exhibit in Norway.

Ragnvald Jarl (II) – NFDS/TFDS

Call Sign:	LAVN
Built:	1956 - Blohm & Voss, Hamburg
Hurtigruten Service:	1956 - 1996
Gross Tons:	2,196
Dimensions:	266.4' x 41.3' x 16.0' (81.2m x 12.6m x 4.9m)
Passengers:	399
Machinery:	2,960 bhp 10-cylinder 2T EV DM MAN diesel
Speed:	17 knots

Sold January 1996 to Rogaland Sjøaspirantskole, Stavanger, renamed *Gann* for use as training and cruise ship, Replaced in March 2007 by *Narvik*, sold to Sørlandets Seilende Skoleskibs Institution, renamed *Sjøkurs*.

Harald Jarl – NFDS/TFDS

Call Sign:	LAMQ
Built:	1960 - Trondhjems Mek, Trondheim
Hurtigruten Service:	1960 - 2001
Gross Tons:	2,568
Dimensions:	286.7' x 43.6' x 15.0' (87.4m x 13.3m x 4.6m)
Passengers:	600
Machinery:	3,450 bhp, 5-cylinder 2T EV B&W diesel
Speed:	18 knots

Sold 2002, to Elegant Cruises Inc, renamed *Andrea*. Refurbished as 4-star cruise ship, for 106 passengers. Mainly used around the Adriatic. April 2012, sold to Russian cruise company, for further service as *Serenissima* under Premier Cruises banner.

Kronprinsesse Märtha - DSD

Call Sign:	LHJC/LEHP
Built:	1929 - International Shipbuilding and Engineering, Danzig
Hurtigruten Service:	1962 - 1964
Gross Tons:	996 (1956)
Dimensions:	182.2' x 31.2' x 19.9' (55.4m x 9.5m x 6.0m)
Passengers:	275
Machinery:	1,200 bhp 16-cylinder General Motors 2-stroke diesel
Speed:	13 knots

Withdrawn 1974, renamed *Koster* as an accommodation ship. Sold March 1979, to Sport Rover Shipping, as mother ship for diving operations. In April 2000, became restaurant/hotel ship, 'LogInn Hotel m/s Kronprinsesse Märtha', Stockholm.

Lofoten (III) – VDS/OVDS/FFR/HRG

Call Sign:	LIXN
Built:	1964 - Akers Mek, Oslo
Hurtigruten Service:	1964 - present day
Gross Tons:	2,597
Dimensions:	286.8' x 43.6' x 22.0' (87.4m x 13.2m x 6.7m)
Passengers:	400
Machinery:	3,325 bhp, 7-cylinder DM 742 VT 2BF-90 B&W diesel
Speed:	17.5 knots

In service 2013

Kong Olav – DSD/VDS/OVDS

Call Sign:	LJRW
Built:	1964 - Bergens Mek, Bergen
Hurtigruten Service:	1964 - 1997
Gross Tons:	2,604
Dimensions:	286.8' x 43.6' x 22.0' (87.4m x 13.2m x 6.7m)
Passengers:	510
Machinery:	3,325 bhp 7-cylinder 2T B&W DM diesel
Speed:	17.5 knots

Last Hurtigruten sailing 30 April 1997. Sold to Andaman Club of Bangkok, Thailand, for cruising, retaining original name. Currently laid up in Ranong, in the Southern Thailand Anchorage.

Nordnorge (II) – ODS/OVDS

Call Sign:	LKCG
Built:	1964 - Akers Mek, Oslo
Hurtigruten Service:	1964 - 1996
Gross Tons:	2,611
Dimensions:	286.8' x 43.6' x 22.0' (87.4m x 13.2m x 6.7m)
Passengers:	500
Machinery:	3,325 bhp 7-cylinder DM 742 VT 2 BF-90 B&W diesel
Speed:	16.5 knots

Sold 1996 to Templeman Inc., Panama, renamed *Worldlink*. Resold to Universal Enterprises, Mali, as *Island Explorer*, revamped at Piraeus as dive cruise vessel based around Maldives. In 2006, ship scrapped at Alang, India.

Appendix

Appendix

Midnatsol (III)/Lyngen (II) – TFDS/HRG

Call Sign: LLMH
Built: 1982 - Ulstein Hatlø Shipyard, Ulsteinvik
Hurtigruten Service: 1982 - 2007
Gross Tons: 4,131 (6,167 as from1988)
Dimensions: 108.6m x 16.5m x 4.7m
Passengers: 516
Machinery: 2 x 3,200 bhp 16-cylinder 4T Bergen Diesel KVM-16
Speed: 17.5 knots
Withdrawn 1983 but reactivated 2005 as *Lyngen* on Hurtigruten. 2007 sold to Lindblad
Expedition for conversion into explorer ship, renamed *National Geographic Explorer*.

Narvik – ODS/OVDS/HRG

Call Sign: LLNV
Built: 1982 - Aker Trøndelag (Trondhjems Mek), Trondheim
Hurtigruten Service: 1982 - 2007
Gross Tons: 4,072 (6,257 as from 1989)
Dimensions: 108.6m x 16.5m x 4.7m
Passengers: 516
Machinery: 2 x 3,200 bhp 16-cylinder 4T Bergen Diesel KVM-16
Speed: 17.5 knots
December 2006 purchased by Rogaland Videregående Sjøaspirantskole (Young Christian
Seafarers Association) for use as training and summer cruise ship and renamed *Gann*.

Vesterålen (III) – VDS/OVDS/HRG

Call Sign: LLZY
Built: 1983 - Kaarbøs Mek, Harstad
Hurtigruten Service: 1983 - present day
Gross Tons: 4,131 (6,261 as from 1989)
Dimensions: 108.6m x 16.5m x 4.7m
Passengers: 516
Machinery: 2 x 3,200 bhp 16-cylinder 4T Bergen Diesel KVM-16
Speed: 17.5 knots
In service 2013

Kong Harald (II) – TFDS/HRG

Call Sign: LGIY
Built: 1993 - Volkswerft, Stralsund, Germany
Hurtigruten Service: 1993 - present day
Gross Tons: 11,204
Dimensions: 121.8m x 19.2m x 4.7m
Passengers: 622
Machinery: 2 x 6,120 bhp 6-cylinder 4T Krupp MaK DM 6 M552 C diesels,
Speed: 19 knots
In service 2013

Richard With (II) – OVDS/HRG

Call Sign:	LGWH
Built:	1993 - Volkswerft, Stralsund, Germany
Hurtigruten Service:	1993 - present day
Gross Tons:	11,204
Dimensions:	121.8m x 19.2m x 4.7m
Passengers:	623
Machinery:	2 x 6,120 bhp 6-cylinder 4T Krupp MaK DM 6 M552 C diesels,
Speed:	19 knots

In service 2013

Nordlys (II) – TFDS/HRG

Call Sign:	LHCW
Built:	1994 - Volkswerft, Stralsund, Germany
Hurtigruten Service:	1993 - present day
Gross Tons:	11,204
Dimensions:	121.8m x 19.2m x 4.7m
Passengers:	622
Machinery:	2 x 6,120 bhp 6-cylinder 4T Krupp MaK DM 6 M552 C diesels,
Speed:	19 knots

In service 2013

Nordkapp – OVDS/HRG

Call Sign:	JWPE3
Built:	1996 - Kværner Kleven, Ulsteinvik
Hurtigruten Service:	1996 - present day
Gross Tons:	11,386
Dimensions:	123.3m x 19.5m x 4.7m
Passengers:	622
Machinery:	2 x 6,120 bhp Krupp MaK DM 6M 552C diesels
Speed:	18 knots

In service 2013

Polarlys (III) – TFDS/HRG

Call Sign:	LYHG
Built:	1996 - Ulstein Verft, Ulsteinvik
Hurtigruten Service:	1996 - present day
Gross Tons:	11,341
Dimensions:	123.0m x 19.5m x 7.2m
Passengers:	619
Machinery:	10, 800 bhp - 2 x Bergen BRM 9 diesels + 2 x Bergen KRG 9 diesels
Speed:	18 knots

In service 2013

Appendix

Nordnorge (III) – OVDS/HRG
Call Sign:	JWPC3
Built:	1997 - Kværner Kleven, Ulsteinvik
Hurtigruten Service:	1997 - present day
Gross Tons:	11,384
Dimensions:	123.3m x 19.5m x 4.7m
Passengers:	623
Machinery:	2 x 6,120 bhp Krupp MaK DM 6M 552C diesels
Speed:	18 knots

In service 2013

Finnmarken (III) – OVDS/HRG
Call Sign:	LLRY
Built:	2002 - Kværner Kleven, Ulsteinvik
Hurtigruten Service:	2002 - present day
Gross Tons:	15,530
Dimensions:	138.5m x 21.5m x 5.0m
Passengers:	1,000
Machinery:	18,820bhp–2x4T DM Wärtsilä W 9L 32 + 2 x Wärtsilä W6L 32 diesels
Speed:	18 knots

In service 2013

Trollfjord – TFDS/HRG
Call Sign:	LLVT
Built:	2002 - Fosen Mek, Rissa, near Trondheim
Hurtigruten Service:	2002 - present day
Gross Tons:	16, 140
Dimensions:	135.8m x 21.5m x 5.1m
Passengers:	822
Machinery:	2 x 5,630 bhp 9-cylinder 4T DM W 9L 32 Wärtsilä diesels
Speed:	18 knots

In service 2013

Midnatsol (IV) – TFDS/HRG
Call Sign:	LMDH
Built:	2003 - Fosen Mek, Rissa, near Trondheim
Hurtigruten Service:	2003 - present day
Gross Tons:	16,151
Dimensions:	135.8m x 21.5m x 5.1m
Passengers:	1,000
Machinery:	2 x 5,630 bhp 9-cylinder 4T DM W 9L 32 Wärtsilä diesels
Speed:	18 knots

In service 2013

Fram - HRG

Call Sign:	LADA7
Built:	2007 - Fincantieri,Trieste
Hurtigruten Service:	2007 - present day
Gross Tons:	11,647
Dimensions:	114.0m x 20.2m x 5.1m
Passengers:	400
Machinery:	7,920 kW -2 x MAK6M25 diesels
Speed:	16 knots

In service 2013

VDS	Det Vesteraalens Dampskibsselskab AS	1893 - 1987
BDS	Det Bergenske Dampskibsselskab AS	1894 - 1979
NFDS	Det Nordenfjeldske Dampskibsselskab AS	1895 - 1989
ODS	Ofotens Dampskibsselskab AS	1936 - 1987
DSD	Det Stavangerske Dampskibsselskab AS	1919 - 1979
NDS	Det Nordlandske Dampskipsselskap AS	1945 - 1958
TFDS	Troms Fylkes Dampskibsselskap AS	1979 - 2006
OVDS	Ofotens og Vesteraalens Dampskibsselskab AS	1987 - 2006
FFR	Finnmark Fylkesrederi og Rutelskap	1988 - 1996
HRG	Hurtigruten ASA	2006 –

Appendix

The *Nordlys* is seen berthed at Tromsø in May 2011, the 'Gateway to the Arctic' (John Bryant)

Farewell *Nordstjernen*, faithful
servant! Seen here departing
Bodø
(Uwe Jakob)

A flurry of activity in 1964
following the arrival of the
Nordlys (1951). Contrast this
with the picture on page 47,
taken just fourteen years
previously
(Bård Kolltveit Collection)

AUTHOR'S NOTES

With so many excellent pictorial books about the Hurtigruten, a detailed history of the service, the companies involved, the ships that have served on the route etc., is harder to find. In more recent times there have been 'Coastal-sea route to the north' by Dag Bakka Jr.; Seagull Publishing (various eds 1982–2009) and most recently in 2011 'Livslinje og Eventyrreise' (Lifeline and Adventure Travel); Bodoni Forlag – all in Norwegian and Mike Bent's labour of love 'Coastal Express – the ferry to the top of the world'; Conway Maritime Press (1987) and the subsequent e:book 'Bergen to Kirkenes Hurtigrute'; Lulu (2007).

The intention of this book is to sit in the 'gap' by pulling the threads together and is in no way intended to be a definitive work and I have deliberately not tried to give details of every ship to ply the Hurtigruten, as some served only for short periods as relief cover. These ships almost always came from vessels owned by the Coastal Express companies serving on their other routes.

What name to use?

In Norwegian it is 'hurtigrute'; in German it is 'Die Hurtigrute', whilst in French it is l'Express Côtier'. In English it is 'Hurtigruten' which is also today's brand name. I've used both 'Hurtigruten' and 'Coastal Express' as they seem to be interchangeable and also in an attempt not to be too repetitive.

Linear measurement of ships is given as originally recorded generally in feet. This appears to be the case until the 1980s when the metric Si units became the norm. Where possible I have used overall length, though you will note that with earlier vessels a ship's length was often recorded as registered length which is less and no doubt used as a means to minimise port dues.

Where there has been more than one ship bearing the same name in actual Hurtigruten service, the second and subsequent ships have the suffix (II), (III) or (IV) after the name.

Currency – the speciedaler was in use until in 1875 when replaced by the krone (kroner is plural). In 1978, under the International Standards Organisation agreement (ISO 4217) for all monetary and banking purposes it is now written as NOK.

Author's Notes

The *Trollfjord* arriving at
Bergen at the end of another
voyage in May 2012
(Andrew Cooke)

The *Midnatsol* arriving at
picturesque Skjervøy in June
2010; note the snow still on
the surrounding mountains
(Uwe Jakob)

ACKNOWLEDGEMENTS

I am grateful to Miles Cowsill and John Hendy of Ferry Publications, together with their colleagues at Lily Publications, for giving me the opportunity to tell this story as the Hurtigruten reaches its 120th birthday in 2013. Mike Bent, who now lives in the Asturias in Spain (with whom I had the pleasure of meeting in the summer of 2012), has been a fantastic help; his generosity in allowing me to make use of not only his writings, but also of his line drawings and photographs, has been invaluable.

The internet has opened up a whole new world of resources and there are a number of splendid enthusiast websites devoted to the modern Hurtigruten which attract a large number of followers. Much care has been taken to identify both photographers and sources, though this has not always been possible to verify. The Hurtigrutemuseet site contains invaluable information as well as links to other sources. Carina Hansen and Jan-Olav Storli who run such websites have been a great source in ensuring the realisation of this book. Equally important has been the support that Ragnar Norum, Communications Director at Hurtigruten ASA has given to this project including the use of their Image Library and to Alastair Brent (Hurtigruten UK) in providing the profiles of the current fleet. Uwe Jakob, too, has also been very generous in providing many of the images of the modern Hurtigruten.

I would like also to thank the following for their assistance with photographs and images for this book: Bjørn Andersen, Mike Bent, Bob Blowers, Andrew Cooke, Miles Cowsill, Brian Fisher, Erik Hagger, Henk Jungerius, Bryan Kennedy, John Kent, Bård Kolltveit (former curator, Norwegian Maritime Museum), Folke Österman, David and Dorothy Parsons, Bruce Peter, Aage Schjølberg, Neil Watkin and Nick Widdows.

John Hendy both proof read and edited the original manuscript and made helpful observations throughout. Marilyn Gardner has done an excellent job with the maps (these are copyright of Lily Publications Ltd.) and Ian Smith must be thanked for his hard work and skills in the design of this book.

Finally, I must thank my wife, Cathy, for the support she has given during the writing of this book.

Acknowledgements

Bibliography

BIBLIOGRAPHY

Selected Books/Periodicals

Bakka Jr, Dag	Skipene Som Bandt Kysten Sammen (1893 – 1890) various editions AS Bergens Tidende/J W Eide
Bakka Jr, Dag	Livslinje og Eventyrreise - Historien om Hurtigruta - Bodoni Forlag, Bergen 2011
Bent, Mike*	Coastal Express - The Ferry to the Top of the World – Conway, London 1987
Bent, Mike*	The Bergen to Kirkenes Hurtigrute - Lulu (e:book) 2007
Bergen Line	Sing Songs – Bergen Line 1975
Danielsen, Rolf & Vedeld, Olav	Det Nordenfjeldske Dampskibsselskab (1857-1957) Trondheim 1957
Eliassen, Per	Hurtigruten – To Foto AS Harstad 2004
Eliassen, Per	Hurtigruten Panorama – To PhotoAS Harstad 2008
Espolin Johnson, Pal	Norway's Coastal Voyage – Cappelen 2000
Hurtigruten	Annual Financial Reports 2006 - 2011
Liland, Berit	Hurtigruten – 11 day Voyage – Forgalet 67N 2008
Nilsson, Per Åke	Norwegian Coastal Express Paper No 27 – Nexø, Denmark 2005
Möbius, Michael & Ster, Annette	Hurtigruten (Norwegian Coastal Voyage) Dumont 2009
Storrusten Erling	The World's Most Beautiful Voyage – Hurtigruten ASA Bergen 2009
Welle-Strand, Erling	12 days on the Norwegian Coastal Steamer – J W Eide Bergen 1956
Welle-Strand, Erling	2 500 miles on the Norwegian Coastal Steamer - J W Eide Bergen 1968

European Ferry Scene & Cruise Ship Review – No 31 Winter 1996/7
European Ferry Scene & Cruise Ship Review – No 76 Spring 2008
European Ferry Scene & CruiseShip Review – No 81 Summer 2009
Scandinavian Travel Service) Norwegian Coastal Voyage) various brochures - David Parsons Collection 1987 - 2012 Hurtigruten ASA)

* nb Mike Bent's work can also be accessed at:-
http://sites.google.com/site/mmikebententerprises/contents

Websites

Some Useful Websites

www.aftenposten.no - Oslo based, Norway's biggest selling evening paper
www.aibn.no - Accident Investigations Board for Norway
www.arkivverket.no - Norwegian National Archives
www.bergenfjords.com - Brief Hurtigruten history.
www.bt.no - Bergens Tidende (newspaper)
www.cybercruises.com - General Information on Hurtigruten
www.dagbladet.no - Oslo based national newspaper
www.digitaltmuseum.no - Digital Images from most National Museums
www.fiskerstrand.no - Shipyard near Ålesund
www.fotoweb.no - To Foto of Harstad (large photo archive)
www.hist.uib.no - University of Bergen
www.hurtigruten.com - Hurtigruten ASA website
www.hurtigrutemuseet.no - Hurtigruten Museum website
www.marmuseum.no - Norwegian Maritime Museum
www.nis-nor.no - Norwegian Ships Register
www.norphoto.com - Photos around Norway incl. Hurtigruten
www.norskfolkemuseum.no - Norwegian Museum of Cultural History (Oslo)
www.nrk.no - Norwegian Television news site
www.samferdselsfoto.no - Transport photo site
www.sverresborg.no - Sverresbørg Trondelag Folk Museum (Trondheim)
www.ssb.no - Statisisk Sentralbyra – Norway's Office for Statistics
www.timetableimages.com - Useful maritime section
www.vrakdykking.com - Wreck diving on sunken WW2 vesssels around Norway
www.visitvesteralen.com - Tourism in area incl. Hurtigruten
www.warsailors.com - Histories from WW1 and WW2
www.wikipedia.org - The fount of all knowledge!

Selected Enthusiasts' Websites

www.captainsvoyage.com - Jan-Olav Storli's excellent Hurtigruten forum (in English)
www.hurtigforum.de - German Hurtigruten forum
www.hurtigruta.info - Informative Hurtigruten website run by Kai Leithe
www.hurtigrutenschiffe.de - A private photographic Hurtigruten website (German)
www.hurtigruten-web.com - Carina Hansen's superb modern day Hurtigruten website
www.hurtiwiki.de - Karsten Schröter's and Joachim Botsch's expansive German forum
www.norwegische-postschiffe.de – A first class Hurtigruten website (German)
www.simplonpc.co.uk - Ian Boyle's detailed Ferry Postcard website
www.skipsmagasinet.no - Per Rydheim's own attractive Hurtigruten website

The *Polarlys* cruising the
beautiful Geirangerfjord in
July 2011 (Hilmar Peschel/
Hurtigruten ASA)

The *Nordkapp* has just sailed
under the bridge at Finnsnes,
which links Senja with the
mainland, bound for Tromsø,
June 2010 (Uwe Jakob)

Index

The businesslike *Richard With* approaches Berlevåg in June 2011 (John Bryant)